**THE MAN WHO
DREW TOMORROW**

THE MAN WHO DREW TOMORROW

ALASTAIR CROMPTON

additional material
ALAN VINCE

Who Dares Publishing

'Dan was the man I always wanted to be, Digby, his batman, was the man I saw myself as'
Frank Hampson

'May your dreams come as true as mine did, that magic year of 1950.'
Frank Hampson, on the first of his great years.

'Although I often wished he would, Dan Dare refuses to lie down and die. But that's just what I intend to do now.'
Frank Hampson, 1981.

Text Copyright © Alastair Crompton 1985

Dan Dare — Pilot of the Future, The Road of Courage and all reproductions from Eagle magazine © IPC Magazines Ltd. 1985

All Rights Reserved. No part of this publication may be reproduced, stored in a retrieval system, or transmitted, in any form or by any means electronic, mechanical, photocopying, recording, or otherwise without the prior permission of the Copyright owner.

Phototypeset, Printed and Bound in Great Britain by Burgess & Sons (Abingdon) Ltd. for the Publisher, Who Dares Publishing, 3 Durrant Road, Bournemouth, Dorset BH2 6NE.

Designed by Cherriwyn Magill
Assisted by Anne Colwell and Nick Donovan

ISBN 0 948487 01 1 TPB
0 948487 00 3 HARDCOVER

First printing 1985

ACKNOWLEDGEMENTS

I should like to express my thanks to all the following, without whose help and guidance it would not have been possible to complete this book. To Marcus Morris, editor of the original Eagle, later Deputy Chairman of the National Magazine Company, now retired. To Harry Montgomery of the Holding Library for the Thompson Newspaper Group in Manchester. To Royston Jones, Acting Principal of the Southport College of Art. To Raymond Geering, art tutor to Frank Hampson at Southport College. To Denis Earle, Circulation Manager of the Daily Mail. To Leonard Matthews, one-time head of the Mirror Group's juvenile publications, now Managing Director of Martspress Ltd. To Denis Gifford, comic historian and archivist, founder of the Association of Comic Enthusiasts. To Wolf Mankowitz, Professor of Theatre Arts at the University of New Mexico. To Frank S. Pepper, creator of Captain Condor, Jet-Ace Logan, Rockfist Rogan, Roy of the Rovers and one time script-writer on Dan Dare. To Cedric Greenwood of the Southport Visiter. To John Sanders, Managing Director of the International Publishing Corporation's Youth Group. To David Hunt, Editor of the current Eagle. To Greta Edwards, Jocelyn Pattinson, Donald Harley, Keith Watson and the late Eric Eden, artists in the original Dan Dare studio. To N. F. D. Pault, for his thoughts on the law of copyright. To Charles Gunther, joint-editor of 'Eagler' and life-long Dan Dare enthusiast.

I should like to pay special tribute to Alan Vince who helped to provide much of the artwork for this book and who has been a mine of invaluable information throughout its preparation. Commercial artist and long time friend of Frank Hampson, Alan provided me with important leads and information and checked the book in manuscript for factual data, dates, names and places.

INTRODUCTION

On Friday, April 14th, 1950, a million schoolboys lay awake in bed with the same question on their minds. 'Will the Kingfisher reach Venus?' The Kingfisher was a spaceship, launched that morning in a new comic strip to try and discover whether Venus could grow enough food to sustain a starving Earth. The comic was Eagle, and the strip was one the boys will never forget: Dan Dare, Pilot of the Future.

This is the story of Frank Hampson, the man who created Eagle, and in particular, the two pages that sold it every week, Dan Dare. Not that the idea of introducing a new paper for boys was his; for that we have to thank Marcus Morris, the first editor and later Deputy Chairman of the National Magazine Company. But it's one thing to think something should be done; quite another to set to and do it.

In the beginning, these two men worked closely together. But once the new paper was flying, Morris cared for it in his office in London, Hampson from his studio in Epsom, and meetings between them grew few and far between. But Morris had the trust and understanding simply to let Hampson get on with it, and perhaps that was genius enough.

The print run for the first issue was almost one million copies and the readership rarely fell below 750,000 for the first ten years of Eagle's brief life. Then, in 1959, Morris left the paper to join National Magazine, and two years later Hampson left too, for what was to become fourteen years virtually in the wilderness.

In 1975, at The Eleventh Salon of Comics, Animation and Illustration, which is held bi-annually at Lucca in Tuscany, Hampson finally received the recognition he deserved. Judges from the USA, USSR, Italy, France and Yugoslavia, the strongholds of the strip cartoon, named him the '*prestigioso maestro*' and gave him the award as the best writer and artist of strip cartoons since the end of World War II. Many would go further, and say he created the best strip cartoons the world has seen.

If you were one of the schoolboys who hurried to the newsagents in those early years and followed Dan's adventures to Venus, Mercury, Saturn, then out into galaxies light years from home; if you marvelled at the floating city of the Treens and the enlightened, creative lifestyle of the Therons; if you listened while Dan battled against the Mekon on Radio Luxemburg, or ever owned a Dan Dare pistol, space suit, jig-saw or diary; if you pored over Hampson's imaginative and minutely detailed pictures and wondered how such work was ever done, this is your story.

PREFACE

This book is born of three parents and they are, in order, gratitude, fixation and indignation. The book is also a kind of self-exorcism, written to try and clear my system of the sludge of ideas that have been around too long. I don't know if the exorcism has worked. I hope it has but if it hasn't, so much the worse for me. The advantage to the reader is that he will be able to complete his picture of Frank Hampson of whom he has known (but not in depth), since boyhood. Eagle was launched a month after I turned fifteen and for six weeks my school playground was flecked with the scarlet from its masthead, yet I disdained even to glance at it. Older boys may be ensnared but I would not be seen as the kind of youth who still read comics.

Until one mid-morning a classmate brought over his copy, asked me what I thought of it and I took it from him with a snooty eye. Conversion was instant. I nipped out of the playground at once to the nearby newsagents and pored over my Eagle the whole of that evening. Nor could I wait for next week's issue but scraped together a shilling and sixpence and sent anxiously for all six back-numbers. I enclosed nothing for package and postage, but Hulton sent the comics anyway, keen enough, I suppose, to win another new reader.

I kept my Eagles mint and unfolded, taking them out often to go over them again. I marvelled at the inventions which crammed the strip and was disappointed on those weeks when Hampson didn't sign his work. He told me later he signed only pages with which he was particularly pleased and just once in the nine years he spent drawing did he sign pages one *and* two. Soon reading Dan Dare was not enough, I had to draw him too; my method was to buy card and carbon from the local art-shop and with a hard, sharp pencil trace over the original. I found it better to watercolour the resulting image before beginning work with my Indian ink, since this left the black undimmed and solid and I was surprised to learn (years later), that in Hampson's studio they often had to go over the black parts twice, for the same reason. Even with this blatant cheating I couldn't achieve half Hampson's effect, too ignorant of printing processes to know artwork could be (and frequently was) drawn larger than it was published. Nor did I understand the effect photogravure printing had on watercolours, making them much softer in the comic than in the original.

I did this drawing upstairs while downstairs my parents sat astonished at the dedication with which I was swotting for 'O' levels, delighted this desire to study had flourished at such an apposite time. Of course I was found out when my father came to ask how my revision was progressing, but his reaction was more bewilderment than anger and I think he thought I had been bewitched. I wasn't the only boy to draw Dan Dare. Keith Watson, an artist later to work on the real strip admits to this boyhood practice although he had enough natural talent to create his own images. In fact when he grew tired of his first job he used his skill to apply, in a series of drawings, for a place in the Hampson studio.

My Dan Dare fixation made a mess of my exam results but I still felt grateful for the fun I'd had. Many would say – my parents did say – this time spent over the carbon paper was time shamefully wasted but the strip afforded me an instant delight and I'm sure was filled with good influences. Perhaps I'm being fanciful or trying to justify this boyhood addiction but if pictures can have an influence on the soul – and some hold that renaissance art achieves that – could Hampson's possibly have had an effect on mine?

By 1975 I was a copywriter in a big advertising agency where I dreamed up a campaign using the strip cartoon technique. We were selling small cartons of orange juice and the idea was to create a serial which would run in women's magazines, featuring a boy who took the product to school to drink at lunchtime. Mothers, I cajoled my readers, put a bit of fruit in your kids' satchels. Free school milk had just been discontinued, the product we had to sell was pure fruit juice and anyway, I was in business.

Readers might suppose I was influenced by good old Tommy Walls who featured on the inside back cover of Eagle and indeed Tommy had been drawn in the early days by Frank Hampson. Walls' advertising people refused to buy the space unless he agreed to draw for them so who better, I thought, to draw my own character. Hampson had recently appeared on a TV show so I wrote to the BBC asking them to forward a letter to him. He replied in a few days turning the offer down, explaining the unremitting deadlines of Fleet Street were no longer for him. In fact advertising deadlines aren't nearly so unremitting as newspaper ones but his letter had been adamant and, since there were plenty keen enough for the job, I didn't press him. I came to think later he was afraid to accept my work lest he be unable to complete it to his own satisfaction and had refused it for that as much as any other reason. Of one thing I was sure, he could have used the money.

But having once been in touch with the man I decided I ought to meet him, partly to write a feature on him for my trade magazine. Another letter inviting him to lunch, led to our first meeting in January 1977. At a first meeting Frank Hampson is easy to like and my infatuation began at that lunch table. He shook hands nervously, his big frame slightly stooped, his beard greying, his craggy face betraying a formidable past and his tweed jacket a little too tightly buttoned, the result of a weight problem he's been battling all his life. His eyes were bright and twinkly, he soon relaxed over the meal and had me scribbling frantically into my notebook. His pride and enthusiasm about Dan Dare were obvious, his willingness to talk delightful and his intelligence and informed conversation had me clinging to every word. I didn't know at that time that he was studying for a BA with the Open University which he was awarded in January 1979.

It was after this conspicuously successful magazine article, and the stories it uncovered, that I felt the pricks of indignation. I was told many times that Hampson had been robbed of his birthright, the copyright of Dan Dare, was poorly off, which I could see for myself, and working as a technician at Ewell College drawing rapid illustrations to order for lectures on a salary of £3,100 a year – £400 less than Hulton paid him in 1955. It seemed on the surface that injustice had been done and that Hampson had been deprived of credit and income which in a better world would rightfully have been his. What, I wondered, was the truth of all this and how could I best find out?

I contacted Hampson again and over another meal told him I'd like to write this book, had drawn up a list of chapter headings and would like his permission and, hopefully, his collaboration in carrying out the work. He greeted the project with enthusiasm and believing his story would be incomplete unless it could include some examples of his work I wrote to the International Publishing Corporation, who own the copyright, for permission to reproduce certain frames from Eagle. This was refused. At the same time I began to detect a reluctance in the artist to talk at any length about creating the comic which surprised me in view of his openness at our previous meeting. But without pictures and without Hampson's co-operation a book seemed both worthless and impossible. I decided to let the matter lie and so meetings between myself and the artist ceased.

So great was the latent interest in his story that I continued to research his life and produce occasional pieces in my trade papers. I found I had picked up quite a following among members of the Astral Club, a group of fans who have been publishing newsletters and holding meetings since the early '60s in an effort to keep his memory alive. In 1982 IPC launched a new Eagle and at the press party, I met and talked with the man behind the new comic, John R. Sanders the Corporation's Youth Group Assistant Managing Director. Our conversation led to an immediate and unqualified reversal of IPC's decision not to release copyright on Hampson's pictures which appear here with Mr Sander's permission for which I would like to express my thanks.

My last article on Hampson appeared after this launch and I sent it to him and asked if I could see him again. Now we could use his pictures the idea of a book was practical and perhaps, I thought, he would be more willing to talk. A phone call from his wife broke the news that the artist had been felled by a massive stroke. He spent the Summer of '82 in hospital. Late in September he was discharged and by now it was clear that if a book were to come about it would have to be without putting Frank under pressure. To lift the burden of the story from his shoulders I began interviews with his friends and ex-workmates, Marcus Morris, Denis Gifford – an authority on comic art and artists – and others whose names appear on these pages.

One source of detail was the writings of Astral Club members who sought out Frank in earlier years and persuaded him to tell parts of his story.

In this regard I must single out Alan Vince who continues to write on Hampson and has an outstanding collection of photographs, letters, clippings and original artwork to which he has allowed me access; without his help and guidance this book would not be as detailed or well illustrated.

Other material is culled from the files of the Daily Mail, Guardian, Sunday Times, Daily Express and the National Newspaper Library at Colindale.

After gathering all together I prepared a wall chart, starting at Frank's birth and filling in details about each successive year, details often conflicting since few journalists are rigorous enough in checking their facts. (John Ezard of the Guardian being a notable exception). Only Greta Edwards has kept a diary of these events, which took place between twenty and thirty years ago and although everyone I spoke to searched their memory conscientiously, memories nevertheless fade. The press reports are more reliable but even Frank in his many interviews has put different dates on the same happenings and no doubt embellished here and there in an attempt to provide new copy. However he and his family were sent the manuscript and encouraged to correct any facts and I am content that the story here is as accurate as research and recall can make it. I am simply the reporter for I believe the details as they are recorded speak for themselves. To Frank Hampson, his wife Dorothy, unsung and for the most part unseen heroine, and everyone else who has helped in what was, quite simply, a labour of love go my grateful thanks. Now, fasten your safety belts.

Alastair Crompton

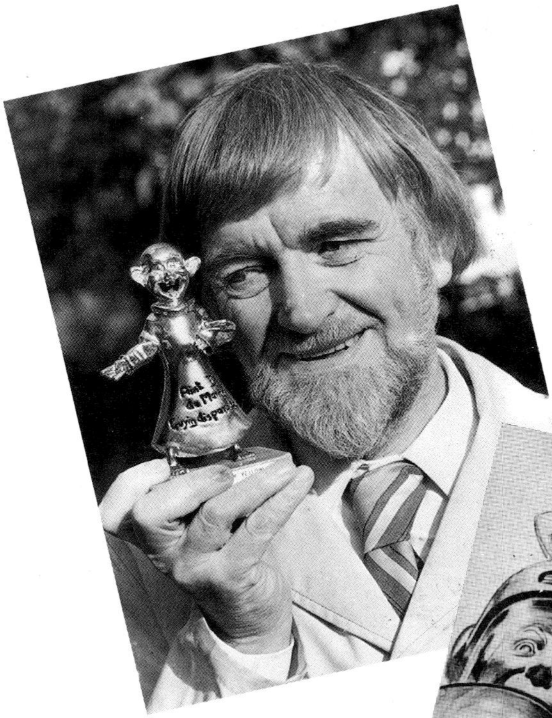

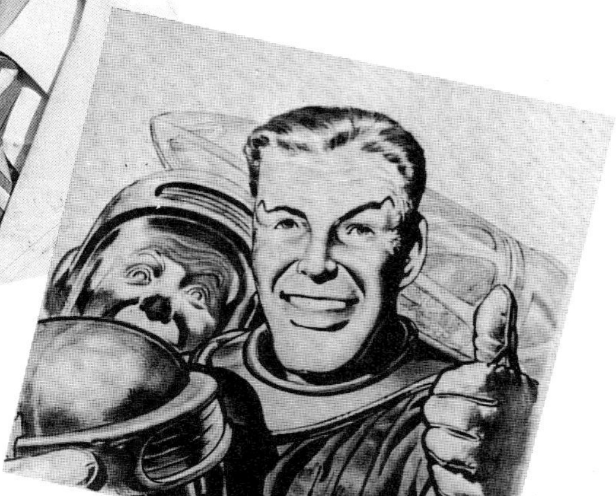

CONTENTS

THE BIRTH OF SPACE TRAVEL
17

A LITTLE HORROR IN THE NURSERY
28

THE SCHOOLBOY'S ROLLS ROYCE
46

THE CRUX OF THE MATTER
61

FRANK'S STUDIO AT WORK
83

ARRIVALS AND DEPARTURES
99

BEWARE TREENS
118

THE LAST GREAT STRIP AND THE LAST GOOD OFFER
133

NIGHT AND FOG
145

THE BEST IN THE WORLD
160

UP LIKE A ROCKET, DOWN LIKE A STICK
174

THE LONG GOODBYE
189

SUMMER LIGHTNING
209

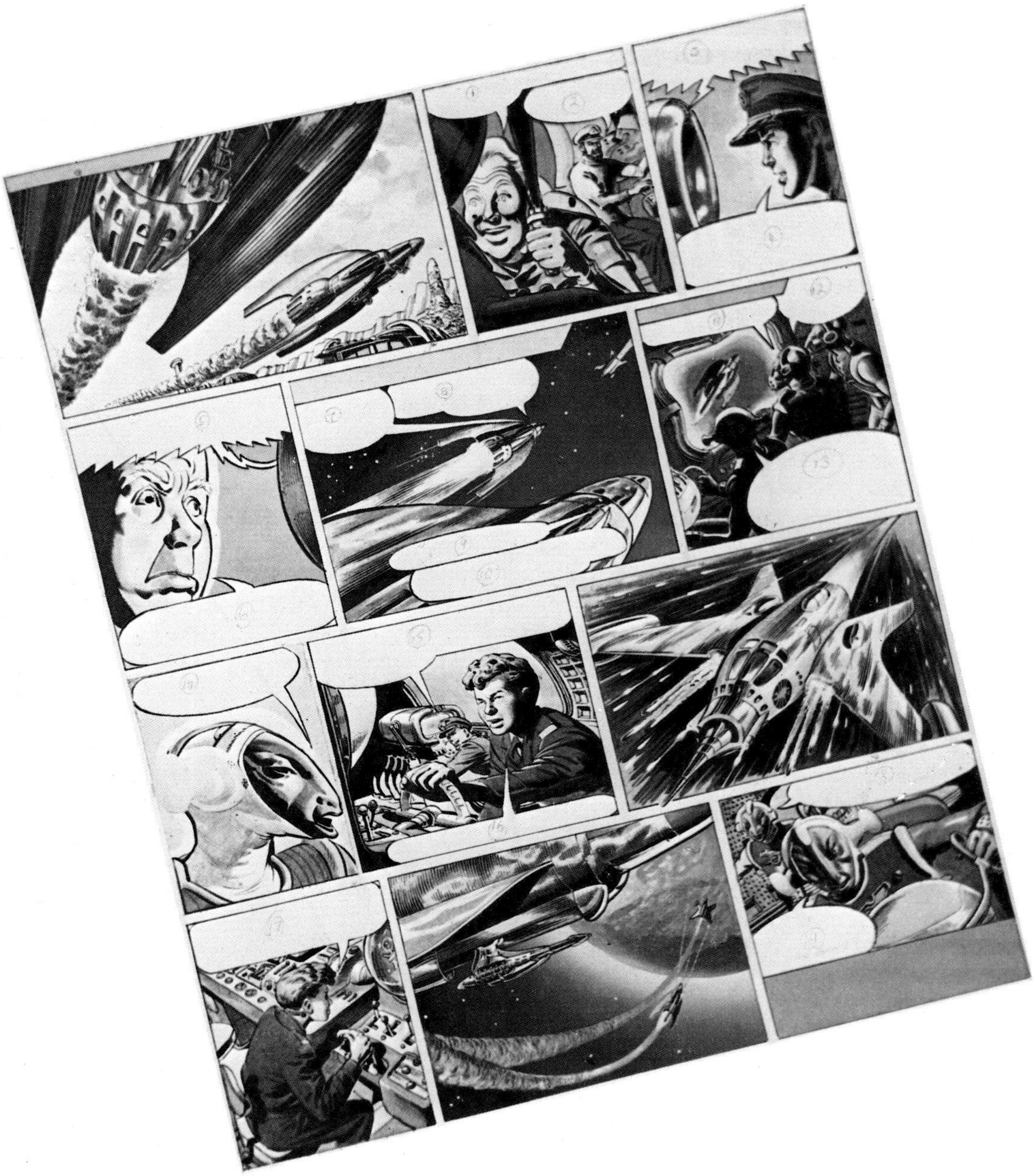

THE BIRTH OF SPACE TRAVEL

It's Christmas Eve 1918 and a twenty-three year old bobby on his beat round Audenshaw buttons his cape against the Manchester rain. Indoors by smokey coal fires, families celebrate the first Christmas of peace for four years. The churches are full of thanksgivers, and wives whose husbands will never give thanks again. The pubs are full of young soldiers, grateful the carnage is over and anxious to be out of uniform. The glistening streets are empty and constable Robert Hampson, tall, slim, and with a small moustache, is keen to be home to the tea mashing in the grate. He still has an hour to go but it's a quiet night, a peaceful night, in fact it's a very good night, for in their Audenshaw home his wife Elsie is nursing a new baby, born on December 21st, just three evenings ago. War ended and Frank began.

Grandpa was a railway signalman and although the railway workers were the cream of the working class, wages were low, three and ninepence an hour for a fireman on the Lancashire and Yorkshire Railway. Both railwaymen and policemen had to show employers evidence of a sound moral background. Some railmasters still insisted on their men going to church on Sundays and to be a bobby you often needed the nod of a local clergyman. These niceties did nothing to increase their pay but there was pride and security in the work and the respect of your peers and neighbours.

When Frank was three months old his Father decided to move and the family travelled some fifty miles west to Crossens in Southport, a town down the coast from Blackpool. Here Constable Hampson walked a new beat which took in the parish of St James in Birkdale, where twenty-four years later a new vicar, the Reverend Marcus Morris arrived. But at this time Marcus was only three years old, and living in some little better style than Frank in Emmanuel Vicarage, Preston, where his father was an Anglican priest. The Hampson family grew: there was a brother Eric and a girl, Margaret and the three children began their education at the local primary schools. When he was eleven, the hardworking schoolmarms of those days saw Frank into Southport's King George V Grammar School where he was joined some two years later by another artist who figures in this story, Eric Eden. At this time neither boy had any formal art training but Frank liked to draw and when he was thirteen, and just for fun, he entered an art competition run by *Meccano Magazine*. The editor laughed heartily at his comic illustrations, gave him a small prize and invited him to send in more. So began his first regular commission and his work appeared in that journal for the next two years.

Into the Hampson home at that time, from relatives who had emigrated to Canada, came a steady flow of Canadian and American newspapers. On the other side of the Atlantic there was a battle going on, and had been going on for years, between the two great magnates of the US Press, Joseph Pulitzer and William Randolph Hearst and each believed one of the surest ways to increase circulation was to produce giant Sunday Supplements. Each supplement could carry up to forty pages of strip cartoons, many in colour, and featuring characters like Dick Tracey, Li'l Abner, the Katzenjammer Kids, Flash Gordon and Buck Rogers, and three artists in particular caught Frank's attention and fired his imagination. One was Hal Foster,

Left When time allowed the unlettered pages were photographed in black and white for reference before leaving the studio. The blank balloons were numbered on the artwork in pencil to match the accompanying script, the lettering being done in London. From 'Rogue Planet' (1956).

who it is generally held created the first modern comic strip based on, and originally using, the stories from Edgar Rice Burroughs' Tarzan, which he began to draw in 1929. Another was Milton Caniff whose most famous creation, Terry and the Pirates, was begun in October 1934 and it is to Caniff in particular that credit belongs for bringing the techniques of the cinema, long shots, close-ups and panoramic effects to the comic strip. Caniff became a master of the skillful use of light, elaborate chiarouscuro effects and dramatic contrasts in black and white.

It was these two artists from America who Frank was later to say inspired him with the wish to draw strip cartoons. Caniff's work, a marriage between dialogue and plot, narrative and illustration was forerunner to Dan Dare and has now become the classic comic-strip style. Frank also enjoyed the spirit of chivalry Hal Foster brought to his second famous strip Prince Valiant, which he began in 1937. Son of a dethroned king who had come to seek refuge at King Arthur's court, Valiant was good looking, fearless and resourceful and Frank admired these characteristics and was later to build them into Dare. A third cartoonist, who by general consent had the most versatile talent of all was Alex Raymond who died in 1956. His pictures were precise, clear and incisive, he developed a harmony between his pictures and the plot and became brilliant at leaving his readers on a cliff hanger every three frames.

He had to do this with Rip Kirby a detective whose story was syndicated world-wide and appeared in many daily papers which only carried three frames at a time.

Frank made a careful study of the work of these men and observed there was nothing like it being produced in Britain. He learned how to fit pictures to words so dialogue could be minimised and that it was quite acceptable to cut from a complete figure in one frame to simply a hand reaching for a telephone in the next. He was reaching fourteen and studying for his school certificate exam. He just had time to sit the papers when he went down with a grumbling appendix and left King George V Grammar before the last day of term. He convalesced from the operation during the Summer holidays, learned that his efforts in the exam were successful and began to look for his first job. He joined the Post Office and was sent biking round Southport delivering telegrams. These bearers of important news – now lost and gone forever – were dropped on householders at almost any hour which meant Frank could be at work either during the day or at night. Nightshift left him plenty of time for drawing, much of it done on paper snitched from the police stationary cupboard. Robert Hampson watched his son practicing illustration and was impressed so he collected the best of the work and fixed a meeting with the Principal of the local art school. Together the policeman and the headmaster agreed an arrangement where Frank could attend life classes on those days when he wasn't on Post Office business.

In 1935, when he was seventeen, the boy delivering telegrams, was taken on to the GPO establishment and became the boy selling postal orders behind a counter. Under the counter he kept a sketch-pad on which caricatures of colleagues and customers appeared, then a Post Office Union official appeared, grinned at the cleverly drawn faces and persuaded the clerk to contribute to 'Post', the GPO's official magazine. On 25th July 1935 that prim publication – under the heading 'Humour' in case readers were in any doubt – printed Frank's first four-frame cartoon. He'd collaborated with a friend, and since it wasn't Frank's own script it wasn't up to the standard we came to expect later, but postmen were amused so once more Frank became a contributor to a regular magazine. A friendly trade union officer and a concerned and impressed art-school headmaster persuaded the cartoonist he should take art more seriously, so with the agreement of Robert Hampson, Frank came from behind the counter and enrolled full time at Victoria College of Arts and Science. This was in the Spring term of 1938.

Into the same art class Frank joined, came another young artist, Harold Johns, who had moved up to Southport when his father had accepted a headmastership there. Johns was born in Somerset and began art studies at Kidderminster. A mild, chubby and bespectacled character, Johns had a keen intelligence and had passed his GCE with a distinction, due in some part, no doubt, to Dad's post as a headmaster, and he was attracted to the tall, handsome Frank Hampson.

They were the same age, and although quite different in personality, Frank being confident and determined, Harold mild and diffident, they met, talked and worked together Frank concentrating on figure drawing while Harold learned to master watercolour.

There had been civil war in Spain and Frank could clearly see war with Germany was coming so he interspersed art training with drill and rifle training in the Territorial Army. A year later the school presented him with his National Diploma of Design (intermediate) and in September 1939 the War Office presented him with his call-up into the Royal Army Service Corps where he learned to drive trucks. Harold, who was drafted into the Yorkshire Huzzars, which later became the Royal Armoured Corps, trained as a tank driver, filling in as the CO's chauffeur. The two artists survived the war although Frank picked up a small scar over one of his eyes. His brother Eric, a merchant seaman, was torpedoed in mid-ocean and was lost with his ship.

Almost immediately Frank was sent to France then picked off the beaches at Dunkerque. Thereafter he rode convoys for a couple of years, but chafed at life as a squaddie and fought for a commission. He began to chafe at the army itself since his heart lay in flying but before there could be any chance of him getting into an aircraft he had to get into the officer's mess.

Finally, he was accepted for officer training and passed out with his lieutenant's pip, whereupon he requested a transfer to air crew training. The RAF Board accepted him, but the army wouldn't let him go. When Johns had learned to handle a tank, he began to train as a cartographer and in this job, and with the rank of corporal, he joined Monty in the Western Desert. He packed his paintbox in his knapsack, and painted a series of watercolours while he fought his way through Egypt, Syria and Greece.

Private Hampson was lifted off the beaches at Dunkerque; Lieutenant Hampson and Corporal Johns were landed onto the sand at Normandy, and in different units, fought their way through France and the low countries. When Antwerp was captured Frank's convoys loaded supplies from the ships plying munitions across the channel. He saw the doodle-bugs fly past on their way to London, and was later to write in a book about Dan Dare: 'On the quays of Antwerp you could watch the birth of space travel' Meanwhile Johns had been mentioned in dispatches and was awarded the British Empire Medal. Within a year after the end of the war, both men were demobilised. Frank came home to a wife (he had married Dorothy on 7th February 1944), and set up home in a council flat in Devitt Crescent, Southport; Johns returned to live with his parents; Robert Hampson retired from the police force with the rank of Detective Inspector: the three of them had to decide what to do with the rest of their lives.

For the ex-policeman, there was no hurry but Frank and Harold Johns were anxious to get on with earning a living. They both decided they were not sufficiently qualified to start as freelance artists; thousands of men were coming on to the labour market and those with experience and portfolios to show would obviously get the work first. Frank was keen to master the skill of drawing from life. Harold Johns wanted to become a better draughtsman and watercolourist. Both talked things over with their families and in the Autumn of 1946 both enrolled for three years at the new Southport School of Arts and Crafts.

These scenes are from the 1952 story 'The Red Moon Mystery' where Dan's own spacecraft, the Anastasia, crash lands at Space Fleet, stopping just short of the HQ buildings. We see here a table-top model of the crash landing area leading to the steps and facade of the building, built by Bruce Cornwell and Harold Johns. Hampson provided the earthquake effects with a hammer!

The location together with the model of Anastasia (probably made by Walkden Fisher who made the more solid models) were photographed from many angles, moving the Anastasia as necessary by means of threads attached to the model. These photographs were then used as reference for more than a dozen frames depicting the salvage of the ship which forms a pictorial sub-plot to the main story line over a period of three episodes.

21

> WE CAN'T EVEN IMAGINE THOSE JOURNEYS. TO GET FROM ONE STAR TO THE NEXT MUST TAKE SCORES AND SCORES OF YEARS — MORE THAN OUR OWN LIFETIME — EVEN AT THE COLOSSAL SPEED AT WHICH THIS THING CAN MOVE.

> WHEN THE WAR DANCE, OR WHATEVER IT IS, REACHES ITS CLIMAX, THE SOUND WAVES CROSS THE BORDERLINE TO FREQUENCIES THAT KILL NORMAL ANIMAL LIFE BY REVERBERATIONS IN THE BRAIN.

> AND *THAT* ISN'T SO STRANGE EITHER — THE GERMANS PRODUCED A SOUND TRANSMITTER THAT COULD KILL AT 50 YARDS AT THE END OF THE 39/45 WAR.

The art school, like the country, was in disarray; there was little equipment, not enough tutors, an unclear curriculum and one of the few matters that had been decided was that ex soldiers, who wanted to take up art, would be put into a class apart from other students, who were much younger and had neither job nor fighting experience. Frank and Harold were both twenty-six, Eric Eden (another artist who was later to join Frank's studio) was twenty-two, and it was not until they'd been in class several weeks that they got their own full time tutor. In fact, Southport School of Arts and Crafts was running a full recruiting drive; men who had taught there before the war had either been killed or decided to move to pastures new. The Principal had not only to completely re-staff his college, but also decide how his new students should be taught. The tutor in charge of the ex-servicemen was Raymond Geering, now retired, but still living in Southport.

He remembers Frank and Harold clearly, and has followed Frank's career with interest and affection. Here is his description of Frank at work:

'He was a tall, good-looking, athletic young man; very cheerful and never ruffled. Above all, he was industrious. He sat in his corner and never stopped working, although he was aware of, and acknowledged the rest of the class and enjoyed and contributed to the general conversation. He was, even at that time, an outstanding draughtsman, prepared to go to endless trouble to get a thing right. For example, he was once illustrating a scene taking place in the cockpit of a Sunderland Flying Boat. Any other student would have been content to make up the background; not so Frank. He left the class and popped round the corner to a well known press agency at that time, "Real Photographs Ltd." In ten minutes he was back with the very thing for reference.'

Frank hadn't been at art school three months, when Dorothy Hampson fell pregnant. He could foresee the time when she would have to give up work and began to think of ways he could increase his income beyond his college grant. He started to tout for small freelance commissions he could complete after the school day was over, but soon this wasn't enough and he consulted Harold on how the two of them could make more money. Together, they set up what Raymond Geering thinks was called a 'Commercial Art Partnership'. They were experimenting in silk screen printing, a cheap method of reproduction which can be used for pictures, sales literature and handbills, required in small quantities. Commercial success was the aim, and it took precedence over everything, including getting qualifications. What mattered to Frank and Harold was that they should become better artists, and then get busy earning money and recognition. Throughout 1947, Frank divided his time between art classes and freelance work, and it was inevitable that his intermittant attendance at school should come to the notice of the lecturers. Raymond Geering had no doubts Frank was an excellent artist and that if he based his efforts solely on getting through his examinations, it would be at the expense of his talent and income (the examiners, says Geering, were a purblind lot) but other teachers were less happy at the cavalier way Frank was treating his grant. One of the regulations governing grants at that time was, if the school examination was not taken, then part of the grant had to be returned. Frank asked Geering whether he really thought qualifications mattered and was told not to worry too much about getting letters after his name. They are only important, he told him, if you want to take up art teaching as a career.

Four years previous to all this, while Frank and Harold were still in the army, and Eric Eden working on farms, a new vicar arrived in Southport to take charge of St James, Birkdale, which has been described by a popular journalist at 'the richest parish in England.' It needed to be, because Marcus Morris was to get a deal of money out of it before he finally left for London and a career in publishing.

Frank Hampson and Marcus Morris, mid-1950s.

John Marcus Harston Morris was born on 25th April, 1915 and began his full time education at Dean Close School, Cheltenham. In 1934, when he was ninteen he won an Exhibition to Brasenose College, Oxford where he played hockey with some skill and took a Second in English and the Humanities. He planned to follow his father into the Church so from Brasenose went on to Wycliffe Hall (that most austere and puritanical of theological colleges according to *The Observer*) where, in 1939, he won a Second in Theology.

Marcus Morris had a good mind but he believed that all work and no play would make him a dull boy; he loved exhibition dancing and spent his Saturday afternoons in Oxford spinning round the dance floor of the Randolph Hotel with his then fiancé. It was this, he jokes, which stopped him getting a First. After graduating in 1939, he was appointed a Curate, and later, a Vicar. Two years after that, his first fiancé forgotten, he entered the whirlwind romance to end them all. After the very briefest acquaintanceship, he married a beautiful actress, Jessica Dunning and it says much for his sense of daring (and his sense of publicity) that he managed to get a photograph of his wedding into the Daily Mirror. It shows them, hand in hand, with the caption: 'He met Miss Dunning three weeks ago and they became engaged a week later.' According to the Mirror's reporter, Jessica Dunning also broke several wedding conventions (she had nothing borrowed and nothing blue) but then bridal jokes like that always make good copy.

Marcus spent time as a chaplain in the RAF, moved on to other parishes, including Weeley in Essex (population 1,000) and in 1943 arrived in Southport. One of the first tasks he set himself was to raise £5,000 for improvements to the church; this occupied him well enough for a couple of years, then he turned his attention to the Parish Magazine. He changed its name to '*Anvil*', because, he said, he wanted it to hammer out important issues of the day. And there were issues aplenty. The war had just ended; a landslide election had brought a Labour Government to power and the nation was intent on building a brave new world. Marcus took time to study journalism and magazine layout then based the style and size of *Anvil* on a journal of the time, *Lilliput*, which had been created by one of Hulton's editors, Stephan Lorant. (Lorant was actually a pioneer journalist, quite brilliant for his time, who also created and was first editor of *Picture Post*, which was to build Hulton's fortune during the Second World War). *Anvil* began modestly enough but soon Marcus was looking for more readers and to find them, he decided the magazine must be brightened up. Here's how he puts it himself:

'I had always been interested in journalism and for a long time felt the Church of England was not communicating as it should. It was not effective, either at publicising itself, or its message. In fact I was interested in winning a wider forum for Christian discussion, and got a group of friends together to form the 'Society for Christian Publicity'. I hoped it would eventually grow to have a considerable effect on the whole Christian movement.'

Marcus decided his magazine needed an illustrator and to find one he sought advice from a journalist who worked on the local newspaper, *The Southport Visiter*. Joe Crossley (now dead) directed him to Southport School of Arts and Crafts because, there, he said, was a young man looking for freelance work who, he'd been told, was very good. Meanwhile, on 24th July, 1947, Frank's son Peter was born. Now the pressure on Frank to make money was greater than ever. One of his wheezes was to enter a competition held by the Southport Borough Council. Their Publicity Committee was looking for ideas to promote the town as a seaside resort and offered a prize for the best poster. Frank went back to 'Real Photographs' and got some aerial pictures of the town including views of the promenade and yacht marina, from which he painted a highly detailed sky view of the sea front complete with hotels, promenade, buses, boats, gardens and pier, all thronging with holiday-makers. Over the top he put the headline: ENGLAND'S SEA SIDE GARDEN CITY. It delighted the Councillors who were pleased to award him first prize. The news, with a copy of the poster, appeared in the *Southport Visiter* on 29th May, 1948.

It's tempting to picture the first meeting between Frank and Marcus as a memorable affair, at which prophetic words were spoken and where each immediately recognised the other's qualities. In fact, of course, it was simply the local vicar popping along to the local art school to meet an ex-serviceman student who was looking to augment his income. It took place in the mid-afternoon, Marcus calling at the school secretary's office, wondering if he could see Frank. He was asked to wait until the class was finished, and when Frank came out Raymond Geering conducted the introductions. This is how Marcus tells it:

"When he came out, we were introduced and we talked. I asked if he would like to do some illustrations for my magazine, he said he would, and that was how he began to work for me."

Frank was being asked to contribute to a brave little magazine; Marcus was working hard to make it succeed and had won contributions from some respected writers, including Professor C. E. M. Joad, C. S. Lewis, The Rt. Hon. Harold Macmillan and a well known cleric, the Reverend Michael Scott, whose articles managed to get *Anvil* banned in South Africa. In addition Frank and Harold were continuing to build up their other contacts and soon had a nice little business going, so although Frank was still officially a student, his attendances at art classes became fewer and fewer. To him, at this time, Marcus was simply another string to the bow, another name to add to his steadily growing list of clients. He was, in time, to find an affinity with Marcus, but not yet. About hiring Frank in 1948, before any thought of Eagle had crossed either of their minds, Marcus has this to say: 'You must remember, I took Frank on as an illustrator for *Anvil;* I had not the least idea at that time what would happen to either of us in the decade to come.'

A LITTLE HORROR IN THE NURSERY

If you asked anyone in Fleet Street today to turn a parish magazine into a popular national magazine, they would laugh in your face. But in the autumn of 1947 that's what Marcus believed he could do; it was, of course, before the coming of four major TV channels, video-recorders, computer games and cable TV. The first job he gave Frank was to illustrate Anvil's front cover which Frank agreed to do for three shillings and sixpence a go. It says something for Marcus' skill as a journalist that he thought of illustrating the front covers at all. There were no pictures on the front of The Times or the Manchester Guardian. Talking about the work he did for Anvil, Frank says smilingly that he 'put on about half a dozen new readers.' In fact Anvil grew steadily and from being read solely in the parish began to spread first across Southport, then across Lancashire until in a year or so, it could be found all over the country, with a few copies even travelling overseas. A critic of the time was willing to recommend it as 'a Christian magazine on a par with the best secular publications.'

Within a few months, Marcus began to use Frank more frequently, to produce layouts and pictures for the inside pages, read proofs, and help supervise the finished artwork before Anvil was printed. Meanwhile, the clergyman was pushing his ideas about spreading the gospel in print amongst the more senior members of the Church, especially, those he could easily contact. Soon, he had support from four local Bishops, an Archdeacon or two and a number of the local vicars, including the Reverend Chad Varah, who was later to establish the Samaritans but, at that time, was editing the Blackburn Diocesan Magazine for the Bishop of Blackburn. So the Society for Christian Publicity was born, and a few days before Christmas 1948 called a press conference to announce its formation and aims to the world. On 20th December 1948 the *Liverpool Post* said this:

'A Birkdale vicar has been responsible for forming a new church society whose aim is to capture the popular reading public who seldom see religious periodicals. Styled The Society for Christian Publicity, the new organisation will endeavour to tap a hitherto unexplored field by producing magazines and other periodicals with appeal to all levels of public opinion among non-church-goers. Four Bishops, including the Bishop of Liverpool, are among the Vice Presidents. Originator of the project, the Reverend Marcus Morris told me: "The Society exists to do the kind of work not being done by any publishing company, producing Christian magazines and periodicals that will appeal to the ordinary man in the street." One idea is to attract readers of illustrated weeklies, girl's romances and other cheap fiction. *The possibility of running strip cartoons will also be investigated,*' (my italics).

From this, and the rest of the report, it is clear that Marcus and his friends had been doing a lot of talking. Where the money and staff were coming from to proceed with these ventures, however, was another matter. The Society had two things under way, *Anvil*, 'which has attracted much attention outside religious circles' and an organisation for improving diocesan publications. Their current aims were to keep pushing *Anvil*, and, when they got a chance, to produce a news sheet. What makes the report in the *Liverpool Post* interesting, is it is the first trace I can find anywhere of the mention of strip cartoons, although, since the Bishops, Archdeacons, Marcus and Varah wanted to get into virtually every kind of magazine eventually, it's quite possible that comics were thrown in for good measure.

However, there was a desperate need to improve comics, for at this time, Britain was being beset by the first of the horror comics, which were being shipped from the US as balast, and sold partly to satisfy the demands of the American Servicemen who were billeted over here. In his book "Boys will be Boys", E. S. Turner describes these American imports thus: 'The horror comics fell into three main categories: the pornographic, the sadistic and the necrophilious. Some of them contrived to combine all three appeals. The stories were told in strip form, with the minimum of legend thus enabling the horrors to be laid on more thickly.' From time to time, shocked Members of Parliament read out in the House, extracts from horror comics which came into their hands. Turner continues: 'There were plentiful scenes of mutilation, gouging, eye-pricking, face-treading, flogging and preparation for rape. The heroines' skirts were usually riding up their thighs and all had pumpkin breasts'. J. B. Priestly summed up the nature of the new cult with discernment and precision.

'This new violence, with its sadistic overtones, is not simply coarse, brutal from a want of refinement and nerves but genuinely corrupt, fundamentally unhealthy and evil. It does not suggest the fairground, the cattle market, the boxing booth, the horseplay of exhuberant young males. It smells of concentration camps and the basements of secret police. There are screaming nerves in it. Its father is not an animal maleness but some sort of diseased manhood, perverted and rotten.'

Priestly wrote that in the *New Statesman and Nation* in 1954. Marcus and Frank were onto, and protesting against American comics almost five years before. The protest, published as a raging article in the *Sunday Despatch*, came about as follows.

Having announced that his society was to publish new and exciting magazines, Marcus began to search for people who could help him to this end. He also began a search for financial support which was sadly lacking from the church authorities. He talked matters over with Frank and other journalist colleagues, the man he mentions particularly is Norman Price, and it was Price, who suggested that the best field in which to make profits was in boys' magazines. Frank and Marcus decided to investigate what they were up against in this field, and in their forays into comic buying, as well as picking up the British efforts like *Wizard, Adventure, Rover* and *Hotspur* (for the older boys) and *Dandy, Beano, Film Fun* and *Radio Fun* (for the younger) they collected some American and Canadian comics as well. In the British strips, the technique of illustration was to treat each frame as a 'stage' on which all the characters had to appear, and they simply changed positions from box to box – the boxes being generally all the same size, with the same perspective and without close-ups, cut-outs, or any of the variety and imagination used by Hal Foster and Milton Caniff. They had two other disadvantages; they were printed on cheap newsprint, in the most limited range of colours, which came off on your fingers. And they contained no *realistic* adventure stories, no heroes you could believe in, simply countless variations of Desperate Dan and Korky the Cat. The US and Canadian comics Frank and Marcus picked up were nowhere near as bad as those described by Turner and Priestly but they were bad enough. With a little help from Norman Price, Marcus began to write and on 13th February, 1949 – just a couple of months after the launch of the Society for Christian Publicity – Marcus' piece was published in the *Sunday Despatch*, under the headline 'Comics that bring Horror to the Nursery', with the word 'comics' in quotes to emphasise that in his view, they were anything but funny. The piece opens dramatically enough: 'Horror has crept into the British nursery. Morals of little girls in plaits and boys with marbles bulging in their pockets are being corrupted by a torrent of indecent coloured magazines that are flooding the bookstalls and newsagents.' (He could well have added fish and chip shops because you could buy the American comics there too). Marcus goes on to complain that these dreadful papers were being devoured by 'sons and daughters from seven to seventeen' – hardly the nursery years – that the Irish had banned them and American

FICTION · ARTICLES · FEATURES

THE ANVIL
APRIL 1949

6d

H. BALCON M.D. PSYCHI...

THIS MONTH
WHERE DO THE CRIMINALS COME FROM?
BY COLIN DALE

THE STRANGE CASE OF JOSHUA TEEK
BY MICHAEL HERVEY

The ORIGINAL Christian Magazine

FICTION · A
THE ANVIL
MAY

THIS MONTH
Maurice Moyal - R. R. Roseveare
H. R. D. May - C. O. Rhodes
ANVIL BRAINS TRUST

The ORIGINAL Chr...

UNFAIR TO STRIP CARTOONISTS

KEEDOINK!

THE ANVIL
FICTION · ARTICLES · FEATURES
FEBRUARY 1949 — 6d

THIS MONTH
Alec Robertson .. .. Canon J. M. Swift
C. O. Rhodes .. Michael Hervey .. Dewi Morgan
ANVIL BRAINS TRUST

The ORIGINAL Christian Magazine

Is Stalin winning in Asia?

A conte and wash drawing by Frank Hampson for a Southport Fashion House 1949.

and Canadian parents had successfully appealed for the protection of the law. In fact when he came to describe in detail this miserable material most of it was mundane stuff. 'A character murders a group of six policemen with a machine gun, chortling "Dis is fun"'. And 'Two little boys thump each other's noses and brandish pistols through seven drawings, to end with "Now yer know who's the toughest guy around here"'.

Marcus claimed that these comics, most of them printed in UK, led children to commit crimes of violence which in one case, led to a boy losing both legs, in another, to murder. But it's the end of the feature that astonishes, for it contains some paragraphs of the most dazzling prediction.

'I shall not feel I have done my duty as a parson and a father of children (sic) until I have seen on the market a genuinely popular children's comic where adventure is once more the clean and exciting business I remember in my own schooldays, not abysmally long ago (in fact Marcus was 33). Surely, there is adventure enough for any boy or girl in the lives of men like Grenville of Labrador? And some of the daily dangers St Paul met would make even Dick Barton look like a cissy. There is a healthy humour that does not involve a bang on the head with a blunt instrument. Children are born hero worshippers, not born ghouls. They will admire what they are given to admire. It is up to us – whether or not we go to Church each Sunday – to see they get a glimpse of what really brave men have done in this world, and share laughter that comes from the heart, not from the gutter.'

That was pretty phenomenal crystal gazing – only nine months after it was written Hulton Press were cabling Marcus saying they wanted Eagle.

'Comics that bring Horror to the Nursery' stirred up considerable interest. How did Frank and Marcus follow the piece up? In fact they were working on a strip to appear in a national newspaper, titled 'Lex Christian', a chaplain at work in London's East End. The venue meant he could be involved with children, crime and inner city problems but still do good deeds; the aim was to get the gospel message to as many people as possible and, hopefully, replenish the Society's coffers. The biggest newspaper Frank and Marcus could reach without much travelling was the *Sunday Empire News* which was edited by Terence Horsley and printed in Manchester. Horsley had spent his war years in the Fleet Air Arm, flew himself, taught others to fly and was later to write two textbooks on flight. He had worked on the *Daily Despatch* and *Newcastle Journal* and came to the *Sunday Empire News* in 1947. Apart from newspapers, his great passion was gliding. He was a prominent member of the Derbyshire and Lancashire Gliding Club and once kept a glider airbourne for 130 miles. His paper was already running two comic strips, but they were funnies drawn Beano-style.

The Sunday Empire News consisted of about ten broadsheet pages and Horsley aimed it fairly low intellectually. Marcus took the Lex Christian strip to him, and Horsley could see at once that its realistic treatment was quite different to his other comic material. He gave Marcus the impression that he was interested but dubious about the Christian overtones, not convinced they would go down easily with his readers. Instead of agreeing to publish, he armed Marcus with suggestions on how to make the strip more acceptable inviting him to make changes then come back and talk over the matter again. At least it was a positive start, Marcus left with the feeling he was getting somewhere and Frank began to make amendments to the strip.

But 'Lex Christian' wasn't making any money and Frank relied on extra curricular commissions to live. In an attempt to win more of them, he took his portfolio round the studios in Liverpool; the recurring theme from them was that the work was of a high standard and Frank should seek his fortune in London. One of the studio managers arranged

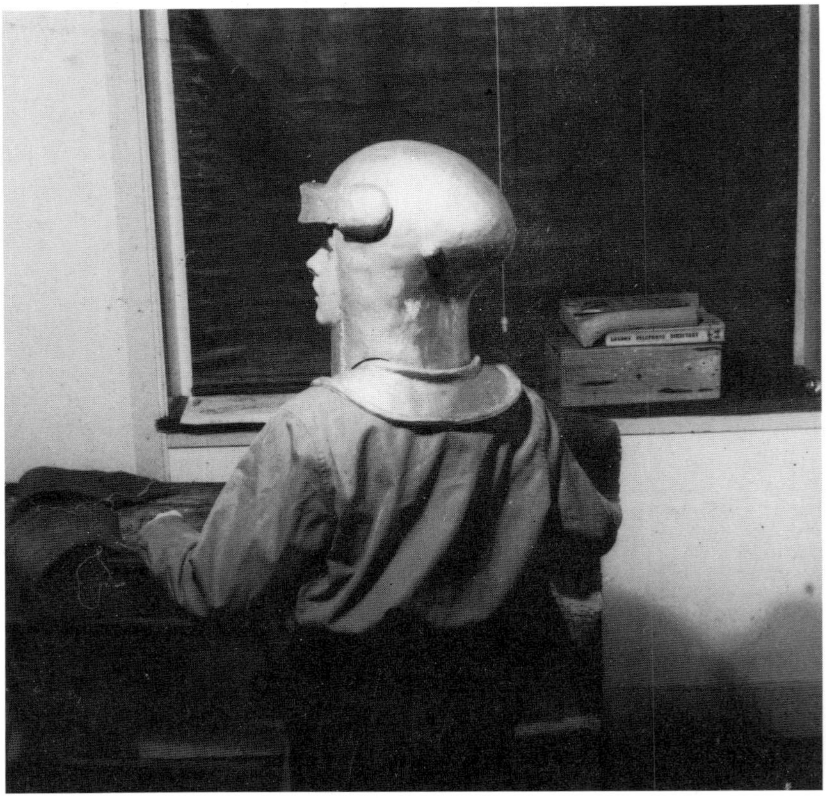
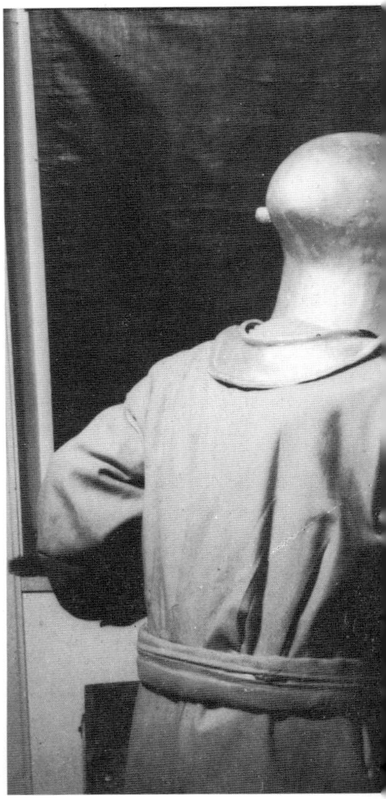
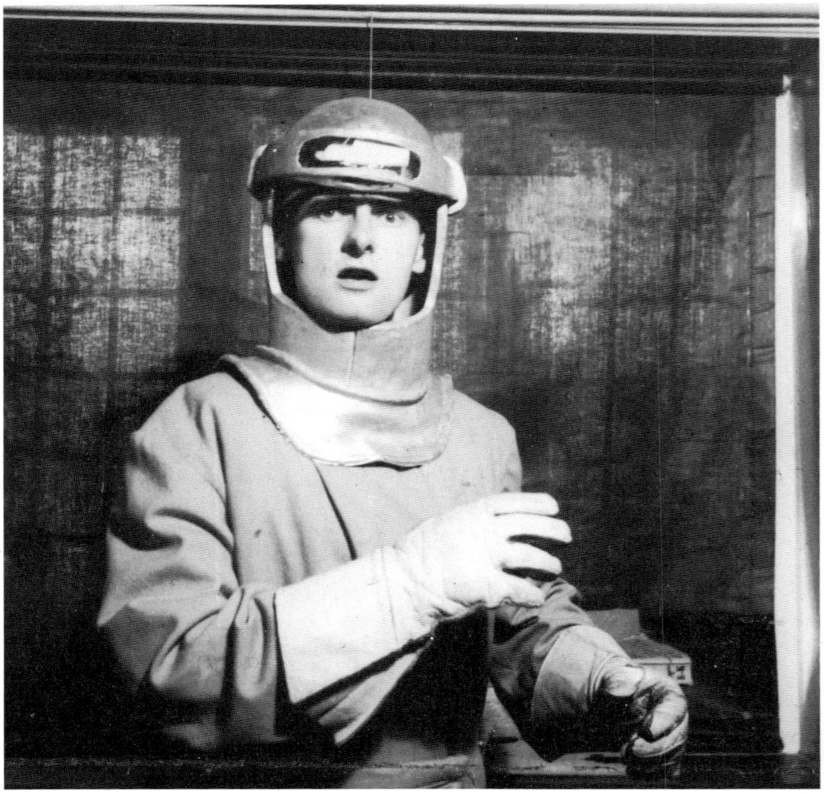
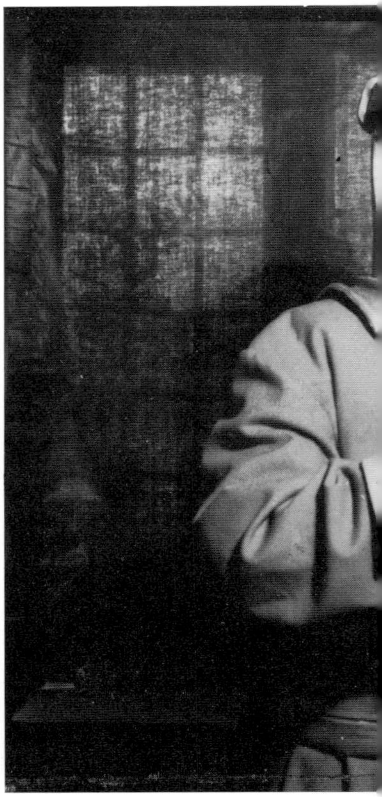

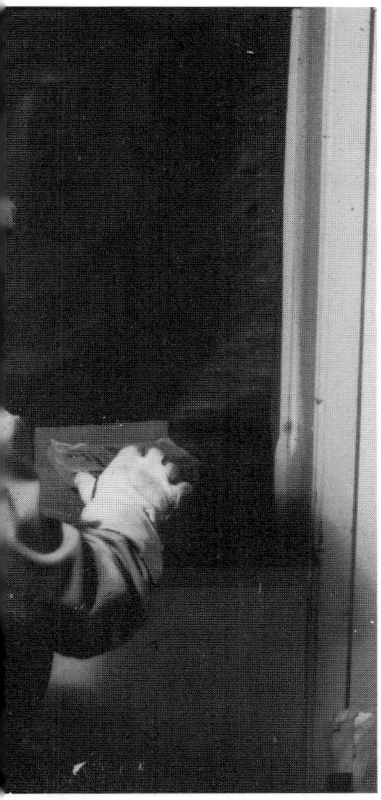

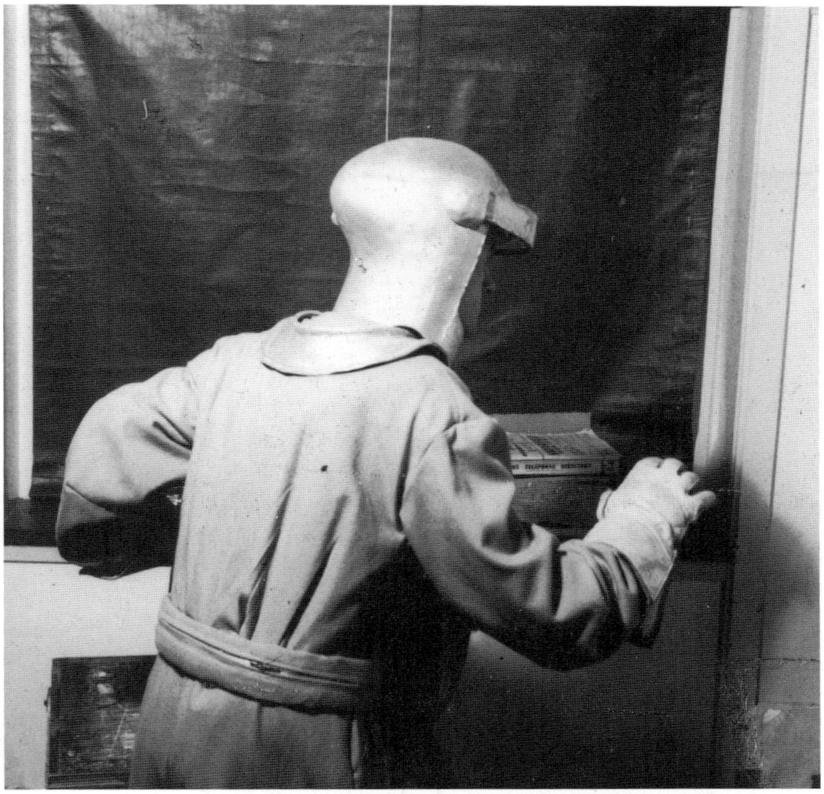
TELEPHONE DIRECTORY

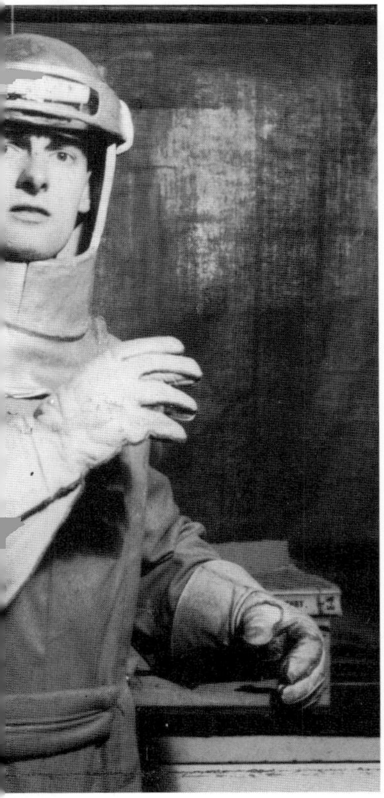

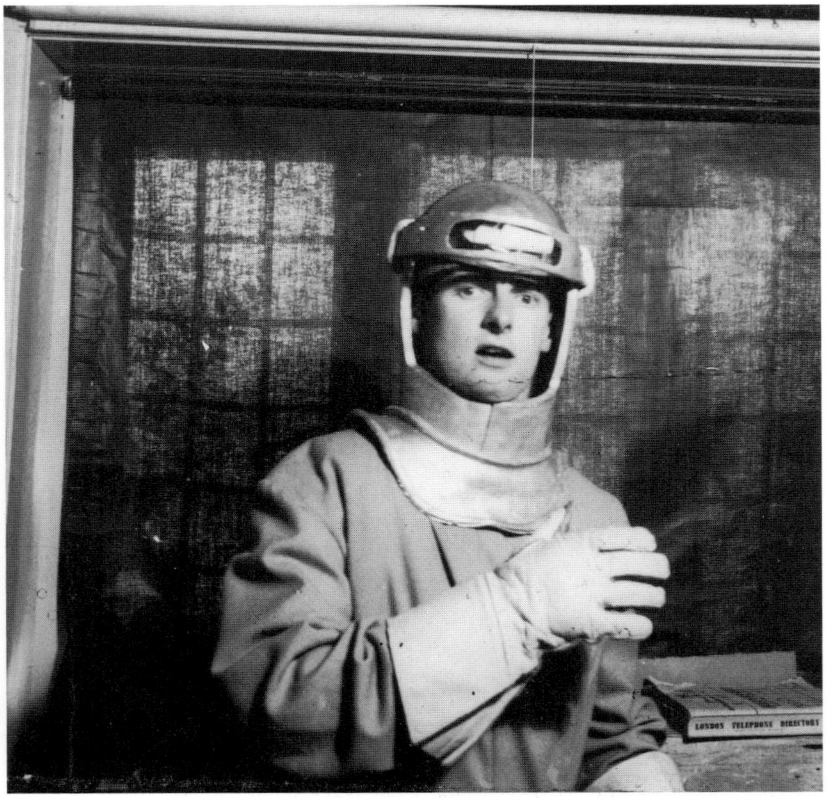
LONDON TELEPHONE DIRECTORY

Previous page and above *Max Dunlop, Part-time member of the studio, posing for the Dan Dare strip.*

37

THE BIRTH OF JESUS

And they came with haste, and found Mary, and Joseph, and the babe lying in a manger.

And when they had seen it, they made known abroad the saying which was told them concerning this child.

And all they that heard it wondered at those things which were told them by the shepherds.

St. Luke 2, vs. 16, 17 and 18

an appointment for him to see International Artists. Frank was delighted; this looked like the break he'd been waiting for, so forgetting about his classes, he bought a ticket South. In London he was told that his illustrations in charcoal, conté crayon and wash were saleable to magazines like *John Bull* and *True Story* and that International Artists were prepared to help launch him. But they stipulated that it would be necessary for him to come and live in London to be on hand when a commission was received and to become properly established.

Frank tells of his reaction: 'Back North I went, delirious with joy, to make preparations but on my arrival home, I found Marcus Morris there waiting for me. He wanted to employ me immediately, as a full time staff artist and said he would pay me whatever I was capable of earning in London. This seemed incredible to me. I pointed out I would probably expect to make £1,000 a year as a good illustrator which was a tidy sum in 1948. I further offered that, as soon as I was settled on a regular basis, I would gladly resume illustrations for Anvil, free of charge, as a contribution to the cause of the Society, for which although not particularly religious, I had acquired an affection and a loyalty.

'In the course of a long explanation however, it transpired that the Society, and he personally, were in dire financial straits. I was "his only asset" and if I "left him now he would be ruined". So eventually I agreed to try it out for a year, for £8 a week, rising to £12 (although the latter never came about). I became the Society's full time artist.'

About 120 miles south of where Frank and Marcus were working, someone else was trying to establish herself. Jocelyn Thomas, later to join Frank as one of the first artists on Eagle, was part way through her course at Hereford Art School. Jocelyn was born in Ballasalla, on the Isle of Man, a twin in a Parson's family. She spent her childhood in Norfolk, and her war years in the WRNS. She was now twenty-four and working for her National Diploma in Design. While in London, at the Slade School of Art, a 21 year-old willowy blonde was working for her Diploma in Fine Arts. She was Greta Tomlinson, also destined to be part of Frank's early team. A third member, Eric Eden, was watching Frank cope with the problems at Southport School of Art. While the Principal, John H. Mowells ATD approved of Frank's activities, one of the junior masters decided on a show-down, and told Frank he must either give up his NDD grant or his outside commercial work. Raymond Geering stayed on Frank's side and Frank, who wanted the best of both worlds, his grant and his freelance income, played for time.

Now fully employed by Marcus and the Society, Frank gave more attention to the 'Lex Christian' strip and, at the same time, began to think seriously about just how far a single story in a newspaper was going to get them on their way to becoming a major influence on children. Not very far was his verdict, and he talked things over with Marcus suggesting it would be a good idea to produce a dummy of something that Marcus could put physically into people's hands. Then came a bombshell. Terence Horsley of the *Sunday Empire News*, their only way into print so far, died tragically in a glider accident. According to an eye witness, his glider, an Olympic Sailplane had difficulty in getting airborne and bumped some rocks. Spectators shouted to Horsley as his plane became airbourne to return for an inspection but, apparently, he did not hear. When the plane approached Bradwell Edge, over a valley at a height of some 400 feet, the tail dropped off and it crashed. Horsley was killed instantly.

Left above *When illustrating the nativity, Hampson was not content to give the expected and using skilful lighting and composition leads the eye to the focal point of the stable door. A half-page colour illustration from the 1957 Christmas issue of Eagle.*

Marcus Morris writes: 'This (Terence Horsley's death) proved to be a turning point. I still recall a late visit to Hampson's house where I told him we should pack up the idea of doing a single strip for any paper and that we should be bold and resolute and concentrate our energies on producing an entirely new, original children's paper of our own. He agreed immediately.'

When did this visit take place? Terence Horsley died on 24th April 1949. The inference in the paragraph above is that Marcus made that call within a day or two of hearing the news. When I spoke to Marcus at his office at the National Magazine Company, I put the question to him: 'Just for the record, was the idea of producing a complete comic for children your idea?' The answer was an unqualified 'Yes.' Frank's version of events is as follows:

'The idea that eventually took hold after discussions with Marcus, myself and an "advisor", a freelance journalist, (whom I take to be Norman Price) was that the most profitable field in which to make profits (sic) to save *Anvil* and the Society, was in that of boy's magazines and for several weeks, Marcus tried to drum up financial support for this project without success. Meanwhile, although busying myself on *Anvil* and several other small projects, I grew increasingly convinced that we must produce several dummies of the proposed paper for Marcus to put, physically, into people's hands. I telephoned him (my house, where I worked, was across town from St James) to say that I was going ahead on producing the artwork for such dummies and he replied: 'well, alright, if you think it's the right thing to do.' So I started work on a sample page of the religious strip of the Life of St Paul for the last page of the paper – or rather – the last two pages originally, followed by two pages of Dan Dare.' Frank goes on: 'It seemed almost inevitable to me at the time that the front cover story should be science fiction, as it was such a flexible medium, and I wanted to build a character that would last a long time. Title, story, drawings and inventions were all mine, and after a few vicissitudes the paper, in recognisable form, and christened "Eagle" by my wife, was ready on my council house dining room table.'

Marcus has never made any dispute over the creation of Dan Dare. He says 'Dan Dare was entirely Frank's idea, and not only did he draw the strip, he wrote the story too.' But it is fair to say Marcus is the man always credited with *the creation of the paper*. So let us recap on the timescale of events with the published evidence in mind.

We find the first ever public mention of 'comic strips' (not, you will notice, a completely

The spread overleaf (page two, third instalment of 'The Man from Nowhere, 1955) demonstrates the standard working method that brought to the reader those two painstaking pages of Dan Dare every week for ten years. On the left hand page is Hampson's visual surrounded by some of the photographs taken for the final page, reproduced on the right from original artwork. In this instance the page was drawn, half-up and is stunning to observe at this scale. The photograph accompanying Frame 3 is of particular interest – from left to right, we have Frank Hampson (looking not unlike Dan himself), Don Harley doing his usual excellent Digby impression and Robert Hampson complete with artificial beard and full naval regalia as Commander Lex O'Malley. He also poses as Dan in frames 7 and 9 with Don Harley as the boatmen. This period, early 1955, saw the team settled in Bayford Lodge and the start of an era that produced artwork of a consistent high quality. Don Harley became very much Hampson's right hand man, to such an extent that some weeks featured the dual credit as shown here.

Dan Dare: The first Story 1951

Right Hampson was not only able to develop and draw characters with imagination and skill but could apply these abilities to his architecture and hardware, as shown here in this view of Space Fleet H.Q.

Below right A rare picture capturing Frank Hampson as the bombastic Dapon.

IF SHE STAYS ON COURSE, SEA JUST OFF THE NOR OF NIPPON. SWITCH OV AND TAKE A LOOK, SIR
SHE'LL SMASH TO SMITHEREENS WHEN SHE HITS THE DRINK
IMPACT ALTERED URSE A ACTION!
FAR BELOW, ON THE CALM WATERS OF THE PACIFIC, JAPANESE FISHERMEN PLY THEIR AGE OLD CRAFT....
AND AT SPACE
I WONDER WHAT IT WAS I SAW SHOOTING CLEAR OF THAT WRECK
IT MUST HAVE BEEN SOMETHING YOU ATE AT TONIGHT'S PARTY DIG!
BUT FAR AWAY IN THE IMPENETRABLE JUNGLE OF BRAZIL'S MATTO GROSSO A STRANGE OBJECT HAS ALSO EARTHFALL

Panel 1: IF SHE STAYS ON COURSE, SHE'LL HIT THE SEA JUST OFF THE NORTH-EAST COAST OF NIPPON. SWITCH OVER TO AUTO CONTROL AND TAKE A LOOK, SIR!

Panel 2: THE TUSCARORA DEEP IN THE PACIFIC! THAT'S WHERE I'M DOING MY NEXT SUBMARINE SURVEY!

Panel 3: I THOUGHT SHE MIGHT BREAK UP WHEN SHE HIT ATMOSPHERE.
SHE'LL SMASH TO SMITHEREENS WHEN SHE HITS THE 'DRINK'!
THE IMPACT HASN'T ALTERED HER COURSE A FRACTION.

Panel 4: LOOK!

Panel 6 (centre): FRANK HAMPSON & DON HARLEY

Panel 7: STAND BY FOR TOUCH DOWN!

Panel 8: I WONDER WHAT MADE THAT SHIP BLOW UP?
I WONDER IF WE'LL FIND ANY TRACE OF HER?

Panel 9: I WONDER WHAT IT WAS I SAW SHOOTING CLEAR OF THAT WRECK?
IT MUST HAVE BEEN SOMETHING YOU ATE AT TONIGHT'S PARTY, DIG!

Panel 10: BUT FAR AWAY IN THE IMPENETRABLE JUNGLE OF BRAZIL'S MATTO GROSSO, A STRANGE OBJECT HAS ALSO MADE EARTHFALL.

IN THARL'S FLAGSHIP, THE RADAR SCANNER SHOWS!—
GREAT THARL!— IMPERIAL FLEET APPROACHING.... CLOSING FAST FROM STARBOARD!
SAKIBOLTERRIMO— HE'S RIGHT! THEY'RE ON TOP OF US!
JUMPIN' JETS! THERE'S ENOUGH OF 'EM! WE'LL BE OUTNUMBERED TWO TO ONE!
THARL CALLING ALL SHIPS! BREAK OFF ATTACK ON KROOPAKS. PREPARE TO ENGAGE IMPERIAL FLEET— BATTLE FORMATION V/13— TURN & CLIMB...
SO THE STRUGGLE FOR POWER IN SATURNIA ENTERS A NEW PHASE AS THE RIVAL FLEETS JOIN BATTLE OVER THE STRICKEN CITY OF TITAN....
...AND THE GREATER WEIGHT & NUMBERS OF VORA'S FLEET BEGIN TO TAKE TOLL OF THARL'S LIGHTER SHIPS
ABANDON SHIP!
PLEASE PUT "IMPERIAL BADGE" OF SATURN & MOONS ON ALL "IMPERIAL" FLEET. (Similar to Voras Chest badge)
Ships in this frame are Imperial "Cruiser" (Green) + single seat fighter (blue)
Ship in following frame crimson one in top RH corner is Imperial Battleship.
These are the three types in Imperial fleet.
Battleship approx size of Zeppelin— much bigger than any of Tharls.
Cruiser approx size of a B.36 Bomber
Single seat fighter as shown by scale of head in cockpit.
∴ fighter in big frame is nearer "Camera" than either cruiser.
HAIL, WISE & MIGHTY VORA! ALREADY FOUR REBEL SHIPS ARE DOWN & THARL'S FLAGSHIP ITSELF HAS BEEN HIT TWICE!
HA HA HA, HO HO! I'LL WAGER THARL AND EARTH DARE ARE FEELING SORRY FOR THEMSELVES NOW!
BUT, IN FACT, "EARTH DARE" IS REALLY RATHER ENJOYING HIMSELF!
THAT'S THAT HOLE PLUGGED ANYWAY... HOW'S THE BATTLE, THARL?
'Q' SQUADRON REPORT 3 MORE SHIPS DOWN. 'PHOEBE' OUT OF CONTROL— DIRECT HIT. ENEMY CRUISERS MASSING AGAINST 'J' SQUADRON...
SAKIBOLTO!— THEY'RE TOO MANY FOR US! WE CAN'T HOLD THEM DOWN HERE...
SIGNALLER! ISSUE GENERAL ORDER TO FLEET... BREAK OFF FIGHT— GET UP INTO SPACE!
SWITCH TO PLAN P/S... BREAK OFF FIGHT!
THARL! WE CAN'T GIVE UP NOW! WE CAN'T ABANDON THE REBELS DOWN THERE IN THE CITY!
I AM DOING THE ONLY POSSIBLE THING, COLONEL!
BUT ON THE GROUND, WHERE FIGHTING HAS FLARED UP AGAIN...
GOLLY! WHAT'S HAPPENING UP THERE NOW? THE SHIPS...!
ALAS, I FEAR IT MEANS THE WORST, O PROFESSOR!
SACRE BLEU! THARL—'E IS RETREATING!
PULLIN' OUT!— LEAVING US WITH THE BABY!
AT THE MERCY OF VORA— AND HIS KROOPAKS!
THARL HAS ABANDONED US!

new paper for boys) in the *Liverpool Post* of 20th December 1948. On an unspecified date, Marcus and Frank take advice from journalist Norman Price. It is Price who says that the real money lies in a completely new paper. As a protest against the existing papers sold to children, and maybe also to test the reaction to a new comic, Marcus wrote his piece in the *Sunday Despatch*, which came out two and a half months after the official announcement of the formation of the Society for Christian Publicity. What is undeniable is that in the *Despatch* on 13th February 1949 Marcus actually promised his readers a 'genuinely popular children's comic' and specifically named St Paul as one of the characters to be featured.

However the only strip apparently ready to appear was 'Lex Christian', currently in the hands of Terence Horsley. Marcus and Frank were waiting anxiously his decision on whether or not he would publish. According to Marcus, Horsley's tragic death was the shock, or catalyst, that convinced him it was time to begin on a complete comic. Horsley died four months into 1949, on 24th April, and in September, five months later, Hultons telegrammed the clergyman to say 'definitely interested'. If work on Eagle began on Horsley's death, then copies of the dummies were ready to be shown to Fleet Street in just three months.

Frank specifically claims it was *he* who set to work on the dummies and that Marcus was dubious and would only say 'Well, alright, if you think it's the right thing to do.' Money and recognition were what Frank needed. Having made up his mind years ago that a strip cartoon artist was what he wanted to be, and having been convinced by a professional journalist that there was a market for a new comic, and the time was right to set about creating one, Frank saw no reason to delay. He was committed to working for Marcus and the Society for Christian Publicity for at least a year. He made up his mind to see how far he could get, working on his dining room table.

Marcus could be forgiven for being dubious. He was already committed to one strip – 'Lex Christian'. He also had the responsibility for producing *Anvil* every month, and this meant finding contributors, paying them, and getting the magazine on the bookstalls. And *Anvil*, despite its growth, was losing money and the Church authorities made no effort to help finance it. Any money that was forthcoming came from the local parish as Marcus's flock held jumble sales and garden parties to replenish the coffers. Marcus also had to find Frank's wages. The professional in the story, the man who, when the troika were looking for gold, put his finger on the map and said 'dig here', was journalist Norman Price. The man who devised the 'look' of the paper, drew many of the strips and found artists to help with the rest, was Frank. Marcus was not an artist and never pretended to be. But he kept faith, kept the money coming, contributed ideas, imposed a certain 'attitude' or editorial direction, and was of course, profuse in his encouragement. Frank said of Marcus that 'he put his money where his mouth was'. His parishioners were, as he puts it, 'beginning to think that I may be slightly bats'. His bank manager, although loyal, could be forgiven for feeling decidedly nervous. For without any guarantee that he would find a publisher, and with *Anvil* taking more and more from his own pocket every month, by the time Frank was ready to put something into his hand to take to London, Marcus had debts amounting to around £3,000.

Left Hampson supplied colour visuals for his studio team to use and this example, from 'Operation Saturn' 1954, shows the amount of work and detail he put into them. Members of his studio readily agree that with a little more finish they would have made better pages than those the team finally produced. This is certainly true of the period prior to 'Man from Nowhere' 1955.

THE SCHOOLBOY'S ROLLS ROYCE

If you're going to create a brand new comic, the first thing to decide is who you think is going to buy it. Frank and Marcus decided to go for boys between the ages of eight and twelve. Next, you have to check on the kind of comics they're buying at the moment. Frank and Marcus had already been through this exercise; the artist was unimpressed and the clergyman disgusted. Next, you have to pinpoint what you can offer that isn't currently being offered, and unless your business brain is as sharp as your creative powers, this can be a daunting task. Frank summed it up concisely: 'Into this scrap-yard of rusty old bicycles', he said, 'I'm going to drive a Rolls Royce.' The Rolls Royce being bigger than any bike, Frank chose a large page size for Eagle. It wasn't identical to the final version which came out measuring almost $14\frac{1}{2}''$ deep by $10\frac{1}{2}''$ across, but it was near enough, the printed version being determined partly by the regulations governing the use of paper, partly by what the machines could handle, partly by what would suit the artists and, finally, by what would clinch a sale: the comic was bigger because a giant page made it look better value.

Two things in particular were not being offered in 1949. The first was realism. Ever since comics began, around 1870, the characters in them had been comic. They had bulbous noses, cauliflower ears, pot bellies and flat feet, and the daddy of them all, a creature called Ally Sloper, who appeared in a paper called *Ally Sloper's Half Holiday*, and on which all subsequent comics were based (although this particular paper was designed to appeal to adults) had the lot. There was lots of scoffing ice cream and cow pies, lots of pratfalls, onto thistles, tin-tacks or through thin ice, there was lots of tying tin cans on to tails, punching, kicking and jumping on the bandaged feet of gout-riddled fogeys. Of all this kind of humour there was, in fact, too much, so Eagle made a point of offering none of it. But of another thing there was too little, and that was bright, blazing, spectacular, rainbow-wide colour, so Eagle made a point of offering colour in abundance.

Next, Frank and Marcus took a look at the relationships between comics and their readers, and they discovered *anonymity*. Only very rarely did an artist actually sign his strip and this meant creators could get away with producing any old nonsense without fear of harming their reputations. And the editors of existing comics signed themselves 'Your chums', or 'The Editor', possibly because editors changed so often that a steady relationship was impossible – though a pen-name would have solved that – but, thought Frank, principally because the editors of children's papers simply didn't respect their readers enough to bother to introduce themselves. Both these defects Eagle rectified. Artists *had* to sign their artwork if they were to draw for Frank. This meant they had to put their reputations on the line, and the readers could, therefore, be sure of decent work. And part of the concept of Eagle depended on Marcus establishing a relationship with his readers, the better to mould their still malleable personalities. Marcus guessed nothing would better ensure the acceptance of Eagle by parents, teachers and other guardians of the nation's morals than for them to see a clergyman was editing it. In the early days, the old-stagers of Fleet Street were greatly amused that a churchman should be editing a comic and some wrote Marcus off as a nine-day-wonder; the wonder was to be around, and in the boss's chair for nine years.

With few exceptions, the strips in Eagle were based on characters the boys could believe in and were drawn firmly from life. Nobody had flat feet (although there were lots of jokes about them in PC49, a character borrowed from the BBC) and only a very few of the villains

Frank Hampson surrounded by admirers in the 1950s.

'Rob Conway', 'The Great Adventurer' and 'Tommy Walls' all drawn by Frank Hampson.

49

had cauliflower ears or Pinnochio noses. Let us say, argued Frank, that an artist is commissioned to draw a cowboy strip. He has to get the cowboys' clothes authentic; the guns, saddlery, ropes, spurs and other accoutrements must be right for the period. If there's going to be a battle with Indians, the artist must decide which tribe of Indians, in which State, at what time of year. If the fight takes place in winter, is there to be snow on the ground? And if there is, and the US cavalry come to the rescue, will the troopers be allowed to ride with their gloves on? If they do, an officer must give an order to remove them before firing starts, since troopers' gloves were too thick to pass through the trigger-guards of their rifles. To get all this detail right, the artist must undertake some considerable research, this takes time and money.

So Frank decreed, much to Marcus' astonishment, that one artist should be employed to produce one page of artwork per week, and the wage should be £30 (if you allow for inflation, that's more than most get today). Marcus was thinking, originally, more in terms of around £3 (claims Frank), but Frank insisted that the more generous figure would allow the man to do a proper job and not have to take on other work in order to stay above the breadline.

Once you've decided the kind of comic you're going to launch, you must give it a title. I would like to have discussed with Frank the different titles he considered. Sir Thomas Hopkinson seems to remember the one first suggested to Hulton was DRAGON. However, EAGLE was the name finally agreed, and this was thought of by Dorothy Hampson. She was sitting in church and her gaze rested on a large eagle-shaped bible lectern of glistening brass at which the parson was reading the lesson; the wings of the bird were spread to support the good book and that's how the thought arrived. At the same time, Marcus had picked up an attractive brass ink-stand at a White Elephant stall; it, too, was in the shape of an eagle and Frank used the inkwell on which to base his drawing of the masthead. The lettering was done by Berthold Wolpe of Faber and Faber and the typefaces for the front cover were chosen by typographer Rauri McLean, an advertising agency man who, not surprisingly, picked a face called cartoon bold. It was McLean who suggested that the golden eagle should be flying over a large, squared-up scarlet background.

There has been a lot of rationalising about how Frank arrived at Dan Dare. It can be looked on as a logical thought process from "Lex Christian", a parson in the East End, to the Parson of the Fighting Seventh, which became the Interplanet Space Fleet, whereupon the parson became a colonel (at the age of twenty-six to boot). But that's imposing a logical sequence on what was a purely creative process. Somewhere along the line, Frank's mind leapt sideways and he began to play with the idea of a lady detective called Dorothy Dare. Dorothy discarded, he began to think about how he could create a character who would live for years. To one journalist he said: 'Obviously, the main challenge was to find something spectacular for the front cover. It was a toss-up between a cowboy story and a space adventure. The great thing about science fiction is you can keep changing the venue; if things get bogged down on Venus, there's still the rest of the universe to explore. The fifties were a time of terrific technical development so sci-fi was enjoying a boom. And anyway, there was no way I could draw horses.' To another writer who interviewed him Frank said; 'I felt the prognostications about technology were too gloomy. Attitudes were so pessimistic, with The Bomb, the Cold War and rationing in the forefront of everyone's mind. I wanted to give hope for the future, to show that rockets and science in general could reveal new worlds, new opportunities. I was sure that space travel would be a reality. I had seen the innards of the V2 rockets while under attack in Antwerp and had been taken by the beauty and precision of the working parts. It seemed to me, somewhat ironically, as we were under constant bombardment by these machines, that here was the birth of space travel.'

To a third journalist, he expressed the same ideas, slightly differently: 'I wanted to hold up in science an example of adventuring, like the empire-building sagas of G. A. Henty I had read as a boy.

'It was Marco Polo discovering China simply brought up to date. You could visualise different types of civilisation, their history and their culture. Dan Dare was an exciting looking surface story with as much detail as I could get into the backgrounds, so it could be read many times instead of skimmed over once.' In the end, when he had told the story so often he was finding it difficult to provide writers with new copy, he boiled the tale down to one pithy sentence. 'Dan was the man I always wanted to be; Digby, his batman, was the man I saw myself as.' And Frank always said that with a smile, and in the manner of a man who'd said it more than once before and knew it would make good copy.

Interesting as it is to read these explanations, the truth is they are rationalisations, told to journalists many years after the event; in fact long after Frank had stopped drawing comics for anyone. Even if he were in superb health today, and had total recall, it is doubtful if he could tell what his thought processes were; ideas come in flashes, not in logical steps. Frank worked on Dan Dare for nine years and over that time, he imposed a logic and discipline on his creation, partly to ensure continuity, partly because events in the current stories were introduced so they could be referred back to (and possibly used) in future stories and partly because, having a rational frame of reference made it easier to explain the "rules" when a new artist or researcher was taken on. It's been said that Einstein glimpsed his theory of relativity in a flash and spent the rest of his life explaining it; Frank's pictures of the future jumped into his mind, in the early period at least, faster than he could write them down, they were tiny quantum-jumps of the imagination and how or why they happened not even he can say. To give you an idea of how singular they were, Eric Eden tells the story of how one of the RAF Establishments, he thinks it was at Farnborough, used to buy and read Eagle, searching through Dan Dare for new ideas as a spur to their own thinking. Eden himself was once approached by an aeronautical designer who borrowed various pieces of Frank's reference material, in the belief they might help him on spacesuit work he was doing at the time.

When all the thinking was done, the drawing had to begin, and Frank realised he couldn't possibly do it all himself. What he did do, however, was to sketch out dummies of the first three issues; at first the plan was that Eagle would appear fortnightly although later Hulton decided on weekly episodes. Frank drew Dan Dare on pages one and two, and The Great Adventurer on the inside back page and the back cover. He also created a black and white strip, Rob Conway, featuring a young airforce cadet who gets involved in a search of a secret city, but this strip was very much a filler and Frank never signed it (despite his rule that artists should put their names to their work).

In the beginning, the three dummies were sketched out in black and white, but it became clear that if a number of publishers were to see the work simultaneously, then copies would be needed. Frank and Marcus got the black and white drawings printed by the *Southport Visiter*, up to a dozen copies of each of the three issues.

Then Frank, together with Harold Johns, coloured the printed copies with water colours. Frank also contacted other artists to help, including the (then unknown) cartoonist Norman Thelwell, and L. Ashwell Wood, who devised the idea of the exploded drawings which appeared on Eagle's centre spread. Boys were later to snip out these cut-aways of ships, planes and trains and pin them onto corkboards in the class room or on the bedroom wall. Chad Varah was enlisted to write adventure stories, and Marcus found Macdonald Hastings and persuaded him to become Eagle's 'Special Investigator'. Says Marcus: 'He was a very

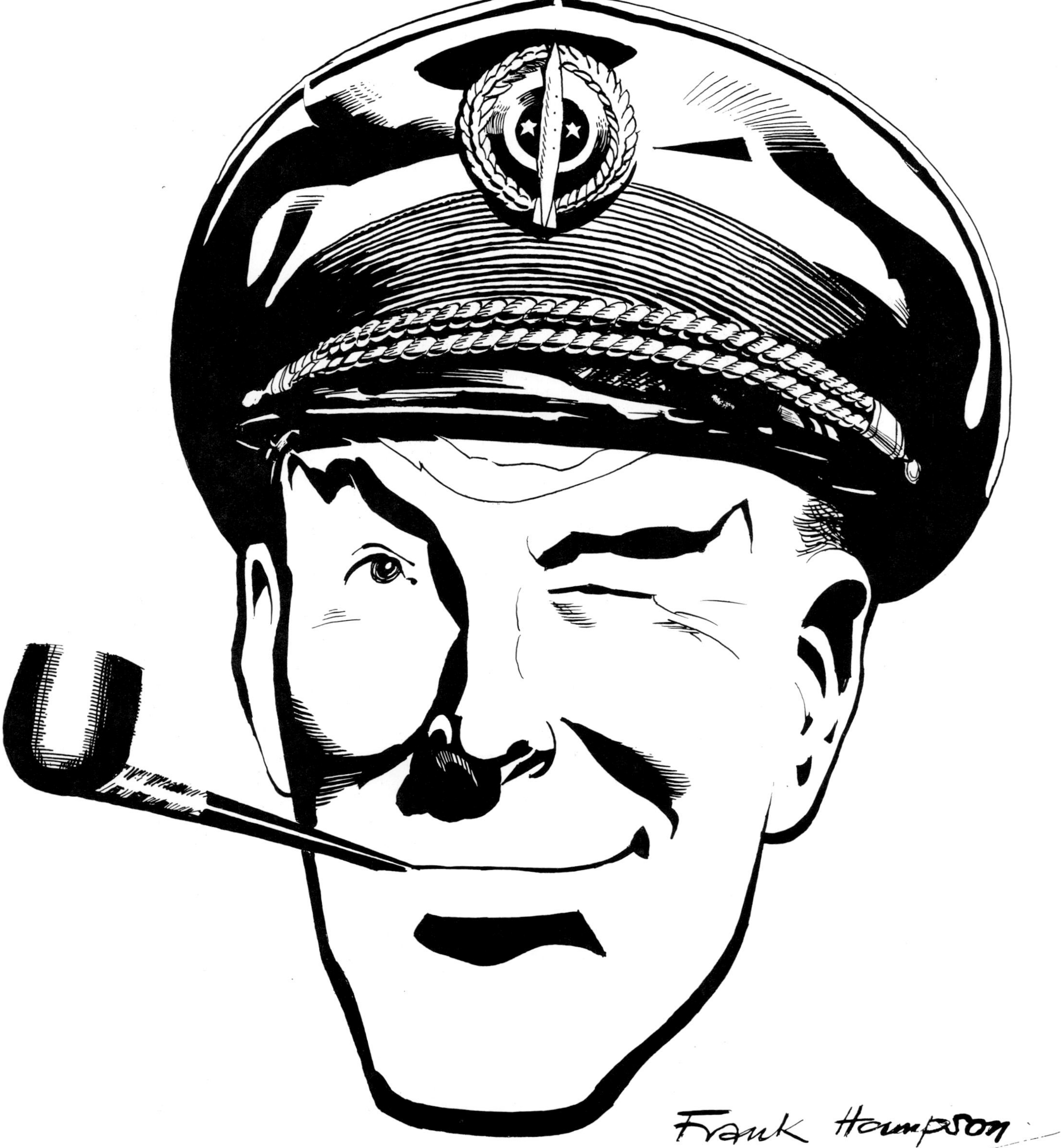
Frank Hampson
20

courageous man. An intrepid man; liked adventure; liked doing things; exciting things. A fine man who produced some very good material. And his character fitted in very well to the whole idea of Eagle.' Despite his frequent references to how dangerous the tasks were that Marcus set him (and he travelled half the world, took on some amazing escapades and often suggested his editor was trying to kill him), Hastings died at his home in Basingstoke in October 1982.

Working on the assumption that Frank really began to put his back into the dummies in early May 1949, after Terence Horsley's death, and Marcus' report in the Observer* that they were ready to take the comic to London that summer, it took the two men three months to create Eagle. Frank's final examinations at Southport School of Art also arrived around this time and he had either to take them, or repay part of his grant. Eric Eden says Frank took time off from preparing the comic to produce 'about six square inches of elegant penmanship' which were submitted to the examiners in an attempt to persuade them to award him a diploma. They dismissed the work with disdain, as not being sufficient evidence of his ability as an artist. So although Frank didn't have to cough back any cash, he is down on the school records as 'Hampson. F. (NDD – Failed).' The failure didn't stop the school following his subsequent career and they have a book of clippings which records his progress to London. Eric Eden also took the exam and failed. Their tutor, Raymond Geering writes: 'Frank did not deserve that treatment from The Board of Examinations in Art, but the system, as it was then, was incapable of recognising his gift.' It has the ring of a teacher hurt when a favourite pupil fails to do well. We can hardly blame the examiners if all they saw was a postcard-size piece of penmanship. Eric Eden says: 'Frank's easiest way out was to tear himself away from his baby just long enough to comply with the regulations.'

It was now time for the pair of comic-makers, working in tandem, to have a change-round; Frank stopped pedalling for a bit, and Marcus began the search for a buyer. He pointed his wheels towards London, which was surprising since probably the biggest of the comic publishers was D. C. Thompson, whose headquarters are in Dundee, traditional centre of jute, jam and journalism. Thompson produced not only *Dandy* and *Beano*, but *Adventure*, *Rover*, *Wizard* and *Hotspur*, weeklies which those in the trade liked to described as the 'Big Four'. But London offered a choice of five publishing houses which (in alphabetical order) were Amalgamated Press (who published the phenominally successful *Champion*) Hulton Press, Odhams Press, George Newnes and the Mirror Group. Of these five, Hulton were easily the smallest, having only seven publications under their flag, two of them controlled circulation magazines not available on the bookstalls but distributed by mail, often without charge. The other five were *Picture Post*, launched a few weeks before the outbreak of World War Two, *Lilliput*, a general interest magazine for men, *Housewife*, which was (Hulton wrote) 'for the woman who believes that in a home, brightness and beauty are as necessary as bread and butter,' and two farming journals, *Farmers Weekly* and *Agricultural Review*. A separate division of the company produced educational films strips and a variety of books.

Marcus has been to some pains to nurture the impression that finding a buyer for Eagle was a long hard slog. In fact, the paper was finished in August, Marcus left copies of the dummies at Hulton in September, received a telegram from the publishers a fortnight later (or so he told the Observer in 1954) and the deal was signed and sealed in November 1949. Which is not to say Marcus didn't trog round Fleet Street, although looking at the list of people he called on, which he gives in his anthology '*The Best of Eagle*' he could have saved some of his shoe leather. His visits to the general manager of The Times, the personal assistant to the editor of The Sunday Times and the proprietor of the Daily Telegraph could hardly have

---

* *Observer:* 24th March 1954.

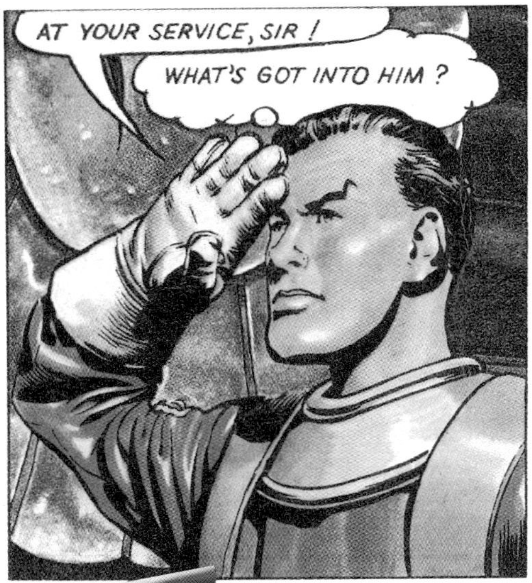
AT YOUR SERVICE, SIR !
WHAT'S GOT INTO HIM ?

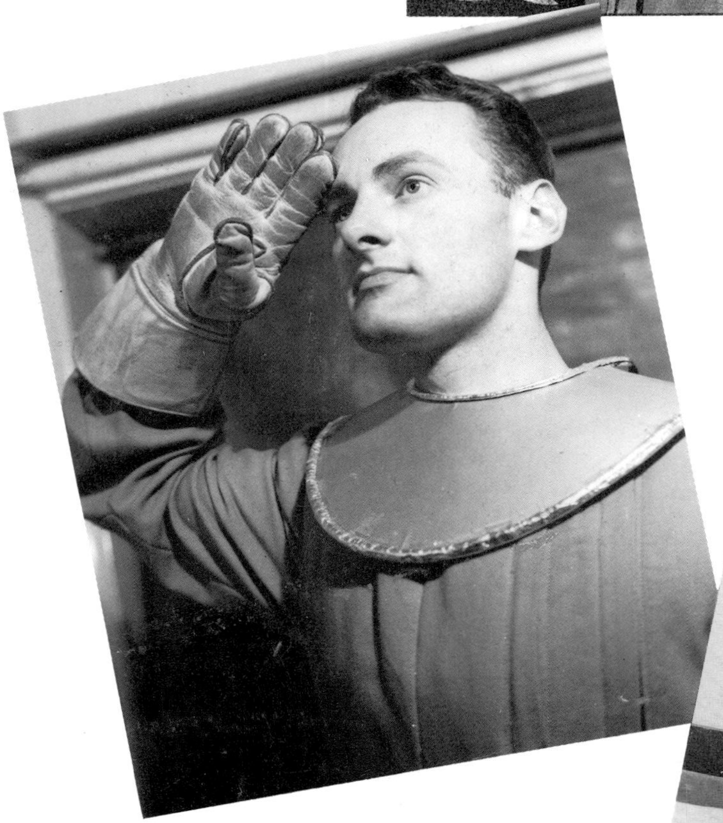

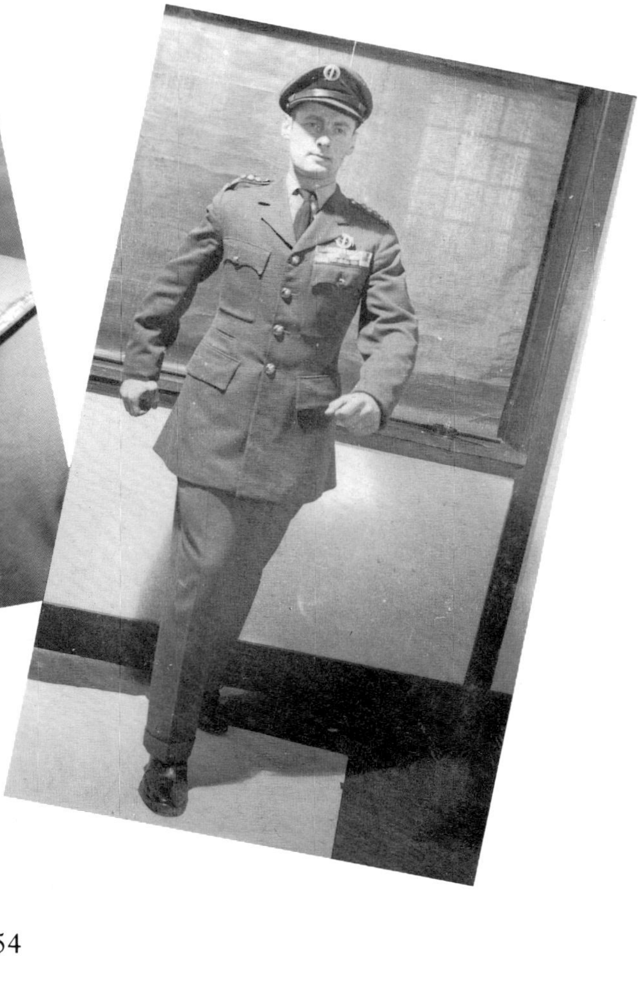

Dan Dare 'look-alike' Max Dunlop, a part-time member of the Hampson Studio, posing as the Space Fleet hero in scenes from 'Phantom Fleet' (1959) (far left) and 'Reign of the Robots' (1957) (above).

been expected to bear much fruit. He should have done better with Montague Haydon who was the director of children's publications at Amalgamated Press. Amalgamated were big rivals of D. C. Thompson, and an exstaffer recalls seeing Haydon with copies of the Eagle dummies. Apparently what put Haydon off Eagle were the very qualities Frank and Marcus had so carefully built into it. There was too much colour, the illustrations were too good and the page size too big. Haydon was used to producing his comics on the cheapest paper, which, if an artist fudged his drawings, absorbed the errors, so it hardly mattered anyway. The religious strip – and remember that originally there were two pages of it – cut no ice with Haydon either, and he dismissed Marcus without too many words, giving him the impression 'that I was an impostor, even a mild kind of lunatic'.

In 1955 Hulton Press printed their version of how they bought Eagle in a staff magazine. At that time it, and it's sister papers were on the street and riding high; Eagle was also selling in Holland and Norway and *Girl* in France. It reads as follows:

'It was in 1949 that a clergyman walked into the offices of Hulton Press with a large folder under his arm. He had obviously been walking for a long time. He looked tired enough to have walked all the way from Southport, where he told us he had come from. Certainly, he gave the impression that if we weren't interested in what was in the folder, there was no doubt that he would have to walk all the way back.'

'But as he opened it and explained what it was all about to the directors, the expression on their faces told quite clearly that he wasn't going to have to walk anywhere for some little time – unless he felt he needed the exercise. He was showing them a dummy for a new kind of paper for boys, called Eagle.'

'When the clergyman was gone, the directors rushed to the conference room for a copy of Crockford's to see if this parson was real. He was, Eagle was duly born and the name of the vicar, Marcus Morris, was soon a household word. The formula for Eagle is now unquestionably the most sought-after and imitated production in the field of boy's and girl's papers. It contains no ideas of crude or senseless violence. Its features all provide exercise for the young imagination. The adventures of Dan Dare, Chief Pilot of the Space Fleet are a good example of the level on which Eagle exists.'

There is more in the same self-congratulatory style (which I shall spare you) since it was written as a bit of PR to spur on the Hulton staff; more to the point, it isn't very accurate. A much more rewarding account is given by Tom Hopkinson (now Sir Thomas Hopkinson) who was, in1949, struggling with Hulton's *Picture Post*, which he had taken over in the wake of its founder-editor Stephan Lorant. Hopkinson was being bombarded with complaints by Edward Hulton, expressing anxiety over the Communist danger, and his conviction that *Picture Post* was too left-wing. At the same time Hulton believed that *Picture Post* had lost all its vitality, and that readers found it dull, uninspiring and out of touch (familiar criticisms if a proprietor wants to get at an editor). Discovering Eagle was, for Hopkinson, some welcome light relief. He writes:

'In the Spring of 1950 (sic) two incidents took place within Hulton Press. The first had nothing to do with my difficulties, but provided one of the last agreeable interludes I would experience. I was summoned one day by Maxwell Raison and John Pearce, who had been brought in as his assistant manager, to have a look at the dummy for a new publication which had arrived by post (this report is in conflict with the (PR) story that Marcus delivered it by hand) and they placed in front of me the paste-up of a magazine for boys quite unlike any I had ever seen. Its title at that moment, I believe, was *Dragon*, which would be changed to Eagle before it actually appeared. Unlike most dummies this was not an amateurish affair, with one or two pages carefully drawn and the rest hazily roughed in. It was complete from first to last with coloured drawings to scale and all the captions and articles readable and in place. But what chiefly distinguished it was the impression that the Editor understood what he was doing. I knew – and still know – very little about boys aged eight to twelve, but I could see that the editor had mentally identified himself with them, and appreciated what they wanted almost without having to think.

'Well – what d'you make of it?' Raison asked.

'I've been looking at dummies on and off for the last fifteen years', I said, 'but this is the first I've ever seen of which I'd say "Hire all the people who produced it, and start publishing as soon as possible"'.

'We can't do that', objected Pearce. 'He's a clergyman somewhere near Southport – the Reverend Marcus Morris'.

'Well he seems keen to become an editor' I answered. 'so the thing is to hire him a good curate or two, and let them run the church services while he gets on with the magazine.'

'Such was my first contact with Marcus Morris, who over the next few years would produce a succession of highly successful children's papers *Eagle, Girl, Swift* and *Robin* – all precisely adapted to the age and sex of their young readers as well as to that particular decade – before moving on to wider fields and becoming Managing Director (sic) of the National Magazine Company. When he turned up in our offices Morris proved to be slight, fair-haired and outwardly hesitant but soon revealed the essential streak. When I said that his plans in general looked excellent – particularly the long-running serial on the adventures of Dan Dare, that space-age pilot still remembered with enthusiasm by millions of middle-aged men – but that the adventures of St Paul at the back of the paper seemed incongruous, and that something better might surely be found to take its place, he replied, 'If that is not included then I shall not produce the magazine.'

'Hastily I backed down to admit St Paul's adventures. Morris himself I nicknamed "Father Martini", not because of any propensity to drink, for all I know he might well be a teetotaller, but because – well-dressed, controlled, decisive, – he appeared all set for publishing success and therefore for the life of high finance, good restaurants and first-class aeroplane travel which not many clergymen, I think, find themselves in a position to enjoy.'

That's all Hopkinson has to say about Marcus and Eagle, his problem of the moment being how to persuade Mrs Edward Hulton to let him retain control of his magazine, and not hand it over totally to her husband 'Teddy'. In a letter I asked Sir Thomas for his views on Frank and his contribution to the 'positioning' of Eagle in the market, in other words the fine tuning that made it so right for eight-to-twelve year-old boys. 'I doubt if I ever met Frank Hampson: if I did it can only have been to shake hands.'

As we all now know Hulton's General Manager Maxwell Raison and his assistant John Pearce who launched the first Eagle promotion took Hopkinson's advice to 'hire all the people who produced it.' Two weeks after the dummies arrived at Hulton, and they'd held their meeting with Sir Tom, they shot a telegram to Marcus at his home in Birkdale. According to his report in 'The Best of Eagle' it read: DEFINITELY INTERESTED DO NOT APPROACH ANY OTHER PUBLISHER.

Of course, Marcus had already approached other publishers, but none of them had expressed real interest and Marcus had returned disconsolate to Frank, exhausted at trying to run his parish and, at the same time, establish himself as an entrepreneur. I asked him if he had ever despaired: 'We often got to the stage when we thought we would never break through,' he replied, 'but, in the end, I was sure that what we were doing was worthwhile, and

58

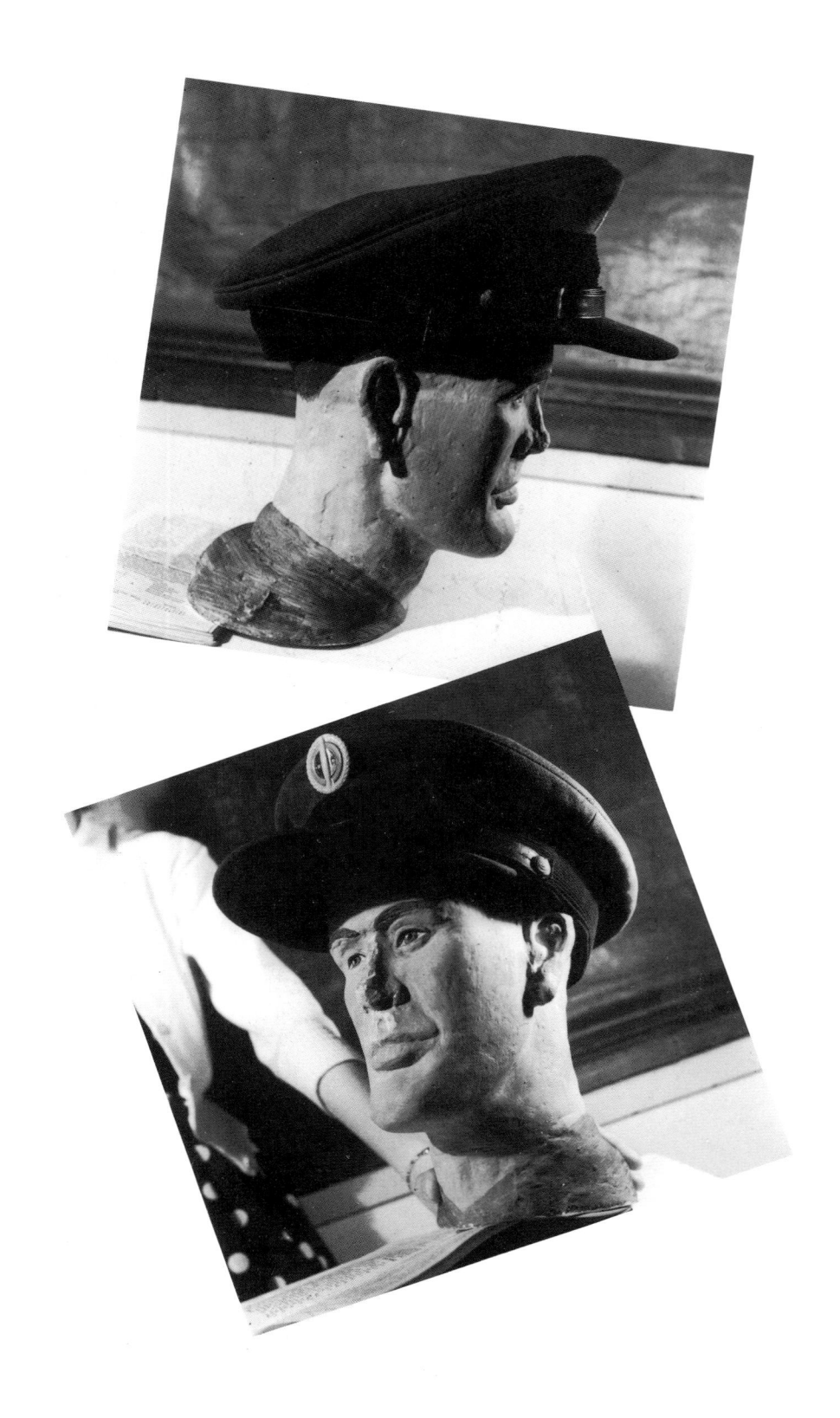

the right people would turn up to help us do it.'

When Hulton's telegram arrived the group were ecstatic. Marcus took them all out to dinner to celebrate, and next morning Frank was nursing a hurt. During the meal, Marcus raised his glass and turning to Jessica Dunning said: 'I couldn't have done it without my wife.' But there was, apparently, no public thankyou for the contributions made by Frank and Dorothy. Harold Johns was nursing a hurt head: he went into his class at Southport School of Art the next day, apologising to Raymond Geering because he couldn't concentrate. Geering and his class had known for some time that Frank and Harold had a scheme going, but knew none of the details, for the two had been circumspect. But now Harold told them about Eagle and its acceptance, and (says Geering), a silence of amazement fell on the class.

Whilst Frank worked on the dummies, he was being paid as a full time artist for the Society for Christian Publicity and let himself believe that, in a sense, the comic belonged to them and he and Marcus were acting on their behalf. Hulton, when Marcus went to see them, went right down the line. He was soon appointed editor, and was told how to alter the paper so it would be right for printing (changes included the reduction of The Great Adventurer strip to one page). Hulton also engaged an advertising agency to help them launch the paper.

That Hulton were serious was never in doubt. Whether or not they gave Eagle the best possible chance of success you can judge by the following facts. In Southport they had a small team of artists, none of them with professional experience, working to turn out four different strips. In London they had 60,000 schoolboys clamouring to join the Eagle Club with thousands more applications arriving every post. On the Eagle editorial staff in London, four weeks after the comic was launched, there was only Marcus and three other people, not one of them with any previous experience of juvenile publications, working like fiends to produce the copy for issue number ten.

Left A life-size model head of Dan Dare complete with cap sporting the badge of the Interplanetary Space Fleet.

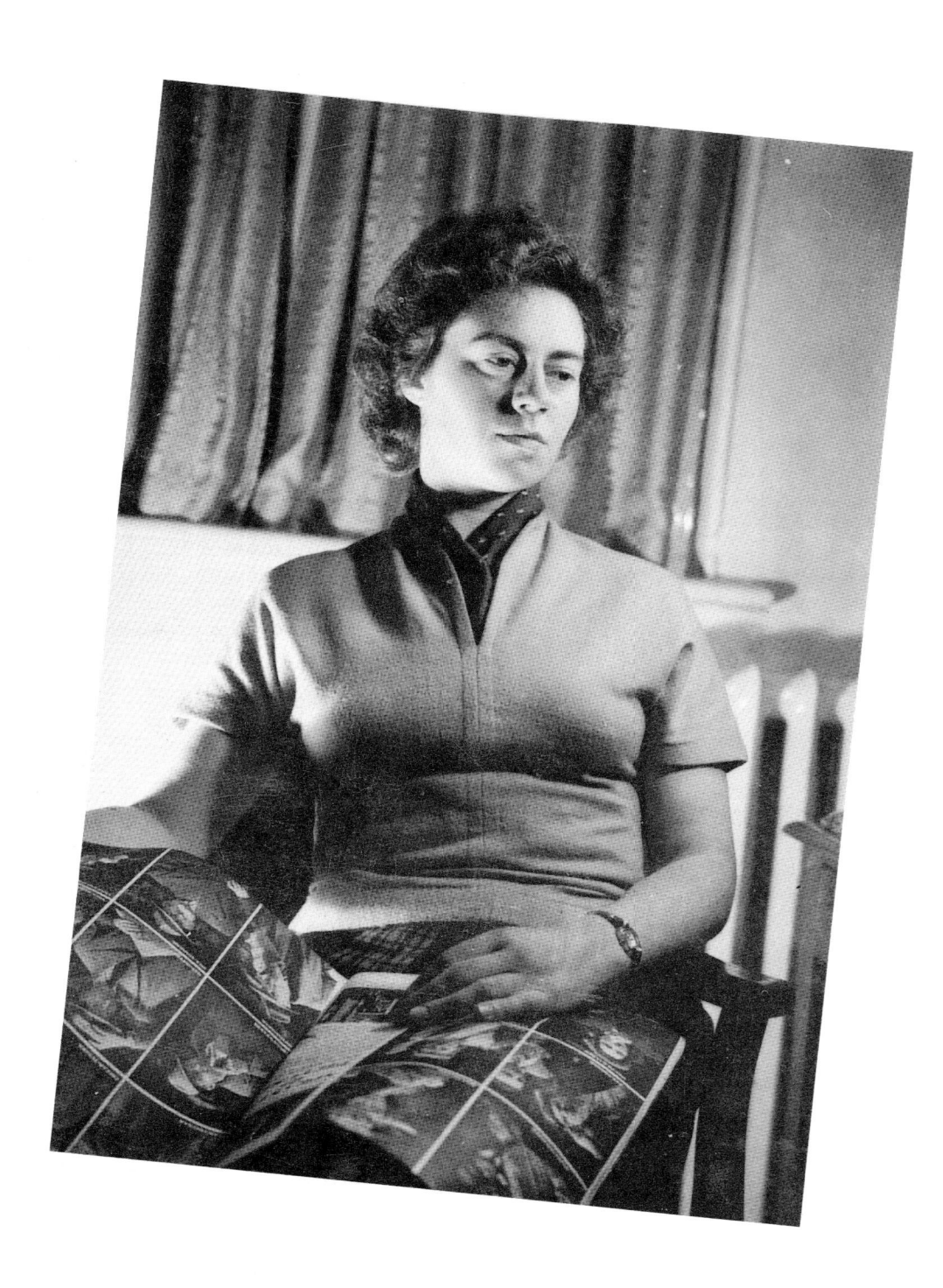

Jocelyn Thomas

THE CRUX OF THE MATTER

'The principal factor in my success has been an absolute desire to draw constantly. I never decided to be an artist. Simply, I couldn't stop myself from drawing. I drew for my own pleasure. I never wanted to know whether or not someone liked my drawings. I have never kept one of my drawings. I drew on walls, the school blackboard, old bits of paper, the walls of barns. Today I'm still as fond of drawing as I was when I was a kid – and that's a long time ago – but, surprising, as it may seem, I never thought about the money I would receive from my drawings. I simply drew and drew.'

That's not Frank Hampson writing. It's a letter from an American cartoonist, Winsor McCay, to one, Clare Briggs. But it puts into a nutshell the way Frank thought in 1950, and the attitude with which he went into Eagle and Dan Dare. Show him the letter today and it'll probably produce a twist of the lip and a bitter smile, but back at the beginning the world was wonderful and there was nothing Frank wouldn't do to make Eagle the best comic the world had ever seen. Even the bit about money was true, as we shall see when we investigate the copyright problem, which in a year or so, was to become the rock on which all his hopes foundered. For the record, Winsor McCay was thought to be the greatest comic innovator of his age. His wonderful 'Little Nemo in Slumberland', a masterpiece of elegance, simplicity and poetry, was created in 1905 and interrupted in 1911; re-created in 1924 and finally disappeared forever in 1927. Its plot is very simple: each night Little Nemo is carried in dream to Slumberland, and each morning he is brought back to daily reality by the harsh shock of awakening.

Frank was to face the harsh shock of awakening but not for a year or so yet. The prevailing problem after Hulton accepted Eagle, was to set up some kind of studio in Southport and find the artists to work in it. His first move was to rent 'The Bakery', a ramshackle building in Botanic Road, Churchtown, a corrugated shed from which, until it closed down, the locals got their daily bread. It had two things going for it: a glass roof through which the light poured making it ideal for artists to work in, and a peppercorn rent of fifteen shillings a week. It also had bad things about it: rain as well as light came through the roof, there was no proper heating, the door wouldn't shut properly and even the side gate, to get into the place, was falling apart. It still stands today, used as a workshop, store and garage. This, Frank decided would be a good place to gather his team together. But how to do that? He and Marcus decided to launch a recruiting campaign in magazines likely to be read by young artists and some of the national newspapers. They couldn't advertise the fact they were preparing a national paper for boys; that would have set Fleet Street on the trail at once, and they might well have been beaten to the launch by a rival publishing group. So the advertisements danced round the subject, saying simply that the employers were working on a 'new venture' and artists who might be interested should send samples of their work to Southport.

Frank and Marcus studied the portfolios they received and sent rail tickets to the most likely applicants. One of the first to arrive was Jocelyn Thomas, who had completed her course at Hereford and was looking for her first job. She saw the advertisement in the *Daily Telegraph*, picked some of her best specimens and waited to see what would happen. Frank invited her North, to see first himself, and then Marcus. Jocelyn takes up the story:

'It was agreed then and there that I should join the team. I'm not sure of the exact date; late 1949 or very early in January 1950 – I'm almost sure it was January. Certainly Frank had

'The Bakery', virtually unchanged today.

Above *Frank Hampson, Joan Porter, Bruce Cornwell and Jocelyn Thomas outside 'The Bakery', early 1950.*

taken over the bakery by then. I started a week later and did some of the early Dare pictures over work sketched in by Frank. I also did a lot of the colouring and after a month or so began to concentrate on the religious stories on the back cover. Perhaps Frank thought a parson's daughter was the right kind of person for such work.'

The next to join was Joan Humphries (later Porter), who was quickly christened 'Humph', a colour artist who had seen the advertisement in the local newspaper and soon became an invaluable assistant. She helped to colour the strips, did a lot of the research Hampson insisted on, and made up the costumes.

Greta Tomlinson, fresh from Slade Art School in London, found Frank's advertisement in *Advertiser's Weekly*. This is how she tells the story:

'As soon as I saw what Frank was doing, I couldn't wait to be part of it; his illustrations were superb and I'd never seen anything like them. Of course I knew they were for a boy's paper, but what it was, who was publishing it and when, I wasn't told. Nor did I know the money Frank was offering; it wasn't until I'd taken the job I found I'd only get four pounds, ten shillings weekly. About three pounds of that went on my digs so I found myself stretched even to get my shoes mended.'

Greta was interviewed on 6th February 1950 and started work on February 20th. At the same time Frank took on Harold Johns full time as he had finished at art school. Frank knew what he could do, and understood how conscientious Harold could be. In fact Harold went out of his way to please Frank, but so did they all.

Then Bruce Cornwell came, and he was a different kettle of fish. Bruce had 'been around' as Eric Eden puts it, he knew what it was like to earn your living with a pen and was less in awe of Frank than the others, who were in their first jobs and glad to have them. Bruce was expected off the mid-day train at Southport and Robert Hampson, who had quickly become part of the studio, now he was retired, was detailed to pick him up.

'You can't miss him' said Frank, 'tall, Canadian, carrying a big bag and obviously lost.' But 'Pop' Hampson did miss him and it wasn't until Greta was out at lunch that she saw this lean, lanky man with a giant hat, belted camel coat, pale blue ankle-length slacks and 'brothel-creeper' shoes struggling up the street with his portfolio. When she ushered him into the bakery, policeman Pop got zero for observation.

Those were the six people who put together the first six months' issues of Dan Dare, The Great Adventurer, Rob Conway and – a strip that arrived quite late on the scene, sponsored by Walls Ice Cream. Walls had bought a page in colour, provided it was drawn by Frank, or, as they put it, 'the artist who drew the chained-foot frame in the St Paul strip.'

Meanwhile, Marcus was in London tying up the contract with Hulton. There has been criticism about the way Marcus handled the business side of the affair at this time.

He seemed to sign away all the rights of the artists, and his own rights, in order to get Eagle on the road. To understand this properly, it's important to know what it was like in Fleet Street at the time. Newsprint was at a premium, it wasn't rationed but it all had to be imported, mostly from Canada, which cost precious dollars. The amount of newsprint coming into UK at that time was only 40% of what it had been before the war, and the national papers had only recently reintroduced the six page paper. This meant that only a limited number of advertisements could be accepted, and there was, therefore, a limit to the income advertising provided.

Moreover, Fleet Street, at that time, was reluctant to take on any new projects and one reason for this was the agreement that existed within the Periodical Proprietors Association. They had decided among themselves that they would not offer newsagents any magazine on a

Joan Porter

Greta Tomlinson

sale-or-return basis, because – it was argued – if you were able to send out copies sale or return then you would send out more than the shops were likely to sell. The sure way to make a retailer order papers cautiously is to refuse to refund him money on copies he's left with. That meant print orders were kept low; the publishers themselves only ran as many copies as they were certain they could sell; nothing would come back unsold, for pulping, thus precious newsprint would be saved. All very laudable and logical and quite in keeping with the times (butter, bacon, sweets and so on were all still on ration). The important part of this story is that it was an agreement between traders, nothing to do with the Government and not enforceable by law.

Remember too, that Fleet Street often displays a parochial suspicion of projects not hatched within its own narrow confines. Here was a country vicar asking the press Lords to sink a fortune into a comic which contained, amongst other things, a serialisation of the Life of St Paul. The horror comics were a menace, sure, but wasn't this going to the other extreme? There was one other factor that made Hulton brave in taking the risk. The quality of Eagle meant that it must be printed photogravure. They didn't know of presses available, and, in the event, costly new machinery was imported from Germany, always in the forefront of printing technology. The presses were delivered to Eric Bemrose, printers in Long Lane, Liverpool.

Hulton did not own Bemrose, who were part of The News of the World group although they hired themselves out to any publisher they could agree terms with. So there was a lot going against the launch of Eagle and it says much for the courage of Hulton that they were prepared to go ahead. What did they want in exchange?

Naturally, they expected to own the new paper, lock stock and barrel; to have it any other way would mean that should Eagle be a success, Marcus, Frank and anyone else who owned the copyright, could take it away and run the comic for themselves. What was Frank's attitude towards copyright at that time? Marcus says that he and Frank never discussed the matter, neither during the time they were preparing the dummies, nor when Marcus was offering them round Fleet Street. Nor, insists Marcus, was the question of copyright brought up when Hulton said they were interested. Nor did the publishers raise it during the signing of the contracts. Marcus didn't think of it (or, at least, not directly) and Frank didn't mention it either. These are Marcus' exact words:

'I do not think it would have been possible when I did the deal with Hulton Press to have the copyright of Dan Dare vested in Frank Hampson. I can't say for certain, since the question of copyright never arose either with Hulton Press or Frank Hampson. Eagle was a highly speculative publishing venture, but after its success it is only too easy to look back and feel one could have done better.'

But if Marcus didn't think of the copyright directly, surely he must have thought he and Frank deserved some kind of reward for originating the idea? After all, Marcus had spent £3,000 on Eagle and his other publishing ventures, and this was highly speculative at the time. Isn't the entrepreneur entitled to be reimbursed for the risk he takes, and the money he lays out in hope of a much greater return? Moreover, Frank hadn't just put in his many hours at the dining room table. The fact that he was able to draw as he did, was due to hours of studying the American Artists and practicing their techniques for years. And what about the meticulous thinking-through of the marketing proposition, the care taken in analysing rival comics, spotting the gap in the market, and producing a product tailored precisely to fill that gap? That was business thinking of a high calibre, and deserved financial recognition as well as merely picking up the ball and running with it, however costly that running might, at first, appear to be.

Harold Johns

So what did Marcus ask Hulton for when he was discussing the financial terms? 'I did ask Hulton Press for a royalty which would have been shared between us (Marcus and Frank?) but this was turned down. If I'd thought of getting a good lawyer, possibly a better deal could have been done. I myself received nothing for the idea or the dummy, so never made any money out of Eagle, or the other comics (that stemmed from them).

The artists who worked with Frank have given a slightly different impression. Marcus, after all, was in debt to the tune of £3,000 and has emphasised the fact on a number of occasions. Did Hulton do nothing to help him with this? If studio gossip, rife at the time, is to be believed, the money it cost to print the Eagle dummies, and all Marcus' other debts, were settled by Hulton.

Also Marcus still had *Anvil* on his hands, and this was now a national magazine, whether it was making money or not. Marcus says: 'I sold *Anvil* for a nominal sum to the *Church Times*, which was then, and I believe is now, the leading Anglican paper. They intended to carry it on, which for a time they did, but it never made money so in a year or so they closed it.'

Moreover, Marcus was appointed Editor of Eagle, and presumably, he agreed a fair salary for the job. Here is Marcus' last word: 'As I say, the question of copyright never arose, but I was not in any position to make demands either for myself or anyone else. It has to be remembered that I was desperate to find a publisher having already approached about twenty without any success and I was heavily in debt because (a) I owed money to local printers who had produced the dummy and (b) I was paying Frank Hampson and his assistants more than I was earning myself as Vicar of St James', Birkdale. So I, alone, was taking all the financial risk of the project.'

The risk was soon enough transferred to Hulton Press; how seriously did they measure the project, and what money were they prepared to put behind it? As we shall see, quite a bit. Their biggest outlay in the early stages was on Eagle's advertising campaign. They hired an agency, Coleman Prentice and Varley and Gordon Metcalf took charge of the account. Hulton set aside £30,000 for the promotion, which, at 1950 prices, and bearing in mind that it was a magazine they were launching, and not a detergent, was a good round sum. What did £30,000 buy them? A total, according to the advertising trade press, of 107 million advertisements! (Remember, that's counting every page or poster site where an ad appeared.) They ran large spaces in the *Daily Express, Radio Times* and *Picture Post* – the first two were the largest circulation papers of the day and Hulton owned the *Post*. There were pages in *The Leader*, presumably to get to the opinion formers among the general public. There was also a direct mail campaign to teachers, the clergy and – God knows why – the Woman's Voluntary Service. To reach the kids, because few of these advertisements would get to them, they issued a million coupons worth three old pence, which meant if you took the voucher to your newsagent you could get a copy of Eagle for nothing. There were also slides at the Saturday Morning Picture Shows and packs of cars touring the streets with Golden Eagles mounted on their roofs. To get to the grass roots, they bought space in forty-four of the leading local and provincial newspapers. Not bad for a start. Finally, outside the newsagents, they posted double crown posters announcing in big red and black letters – 'Hunt the Eagle. Bring your tokens here.'

What was the advertising in the press like? For the most part, dull as ditchwater, not managing in the least to communicate the kind of breakthrough Eagle represented. A trade commentator at the time wrote: 'Only one aspect of Eagle disappoints me and that is its own advertising. I don't think I've ever seen such penny-plain advertising for such a threepence-coloured book. The spaces are magnificent, full pages and half pages, even some double page

Robert Hampson, every inch Sir Hubert Guest, is fondly remembered by the studio team as a kind and gentle man. 'Pop' Hampson had the unique ability to hold impossible poses longer than anyone else! Extremes of lighting were sometimes used to create extra depth in a face.

71

spreads, all demonstrating how to spend £30,000 in a few easy lessons. One stirring caption is: 'Get this coupon off today!' and another 'Hurry, hurry, hurry for Eagle!' The biggest feature is the coupon. I cannot understand why a greater attempt has not been made to sell the book. Apart from a brief recital of the contents very little is said.' (This was P. G. Allen in *The Newspaper World*, 18th May, 1950.)

It's easy to understand now why Hulton felt it was so necessary to protect their investment, and why, in the small print, the matter of copyright was all tied up. In fact not to have covered so basic a point would have been foolhardy in the extreme. But it's worth noting that Marcus hadn't got any legal advice whilst he was talking to his future employers. Maybe, (as he says) with the benefit of hindsight, a better deal for both he and Frank might have been arranged. One last point: Frank may not have thought at this time about who owned anything, he was too excited and too busy making Eagle work to think seriously about the business side of things, and, no doubt, trusted Marcus to look after his interests. When did he learn that the copyright wasn't his? Not until the paper had hit the street, and after he'd been hit himself with one or two powerful knocks, including the change of publication date, which had been tentatively arranged, but was suddenly brought weeks forward, and left the artists with such a logjam of work, they hardly saw a night's sleep. Here is Frank's version:

'*The Anvil* had been sold, and The Society for Christian Publicity vanished. Slow to adjust, I waited to see, now we were apparently down to a collection of individuals, what was to be done for me, and I waited and I waited. I went to see the Hulton Press Management who upped my pay (details later) presented me with a service contract confirming that the copyright of Dan Dare belonged to them, gave me a lot of assurances and vanished. I felt alienated. Every time I blinked something vanished. *The Anvil*, the SCP, the Hulton Press Management'. What was Frank earning when he started work for Hulton? It's hard to be absolutely sure, for the salary altered according to the work taken on. In the beginning, he claims he got £25 a week, which increased to £30, the fee he had recommended artists on Eagle should be paid. But with the arrival of Tommy Walls, the rate went up to £50 for that page only, so it was not unnatural that Frank took responsibility for that strip. In practice, of course, all the artists were drawing part of all the strips. When Greta Tomlinson worked on Tommy Walls, she got an extra £2 a week, making her wage £6.10 shillings. It seems that in the beginning, Frank's salary settled at £1,500 a year, Harold Johns', £10 a week, not bad for an artist in his first job, (the average wage for a new worker in a studio was around £7). Bruce Cornwell probably got more (I haven't been able to ask him because he was reluctant to talk at all about his time with Frank, despite a couple of lengthy letters from me, explaining the book and asking for an interview). When Eric Eden joined, he got £10 a week, and I assume Jo Thomas was getting the same as Greta; there's no reason to believe otherwise since both had similar qualifications and no previous work experience. When Eagle was launched, however, Frank went to talk to the Hulton management. He may well have explained he was writing the scripts for Dan Dare and The Great Adventurer, and taking full responsibility for the overall art direction of the paper. At any rate, Hulton increased his salary by £1,000 a year, to £2,500. They also found him a writer.

Since he was only thirty two, in his first full-time job, and the year was 1950, £2,500 was a very good salary indeed. In fact, although Frank is unlikely to agree, Hulton Press, during the ten years it owned Eagle, were uncommonly generous to the artists. Hulton were the first publishers ever to allow the creators of a comic to develop a studio system. Instead of having one artist and one writer responsible for a strip, with, more often than not, the writer producing the script with only rare meetings with the man who would draw it, Frank had

Bruce Cornwell

Eric Eden, posing in Space Fleet uniform.

Model of the 'jepeet' which moved on a gyroscopic ball, used by Dan and Digby in the first story 1950

between seven and nine people working together, at first in Southport, and later in Epsom, creating a number of strips (in the beginning) with writers and artists in the one place. However, writers didn't last long with Frank. The first was with him for six weeks, joining at episode eleven of Eagle and leaving at episode seventeen. He asked Frank to have a bite with him, and over that lunch, broke the news that he didn't know where to take the Dare story from the point they'd reached. Frank was disgusted, and then and there, decided to take his runaway success and go it alone. He was to write the complete plot and dialogue for the Venus story, and the Red Moon Mystery, not giving way to another writer until Marooned on Mercury, which was taken over at short notice by Chad Varah. Eric Eden, who was first to help draw Dare, and under the Fleetway regime to write him, says in fact this is by far the best way to work, because the creator can then produce exactly the right expression to go with the dialogue; if there's a wry joke in the story, then Digby, for example, can have the right wry wink and smile to accompany it.

Two and a half thousand pounds may have been a handsome income, but Frank worked like a lunatic to earn it and took most of the studio along with him. Their day officially started at nine, but rarely ended before ten or eleven at night and there was no overtime added to the wages. Here's Jo Thomas on the subject:

'We frequently found ourselves working flat out, especially towards the end of the week when it seemed we'd never get the pages finished on time. So it was a case of 'Who'll stay on this evening?' and evening always turned into night. Often we had to keep each other awake, talking a lot, usually nonsense in the end, so we could keep going. Once we had to summon a taxi and pack Greta off at the last moment clutching the still wet precious cargo, on her way to the printer.

'Frank, of course, worked longer and harder than any of us; being his baby, he couldn't leave it alone. Robert Hampson – who we christened 'Pop' – was a tower of strength during these sessions. He'd be telling jokes as the sun came up and since he was always lighting and re-lighting his pipe, we'd josh him about the smell of his tobacco. He became our father figure, loved and admired by us all, and he was always around, "just in case"'.

Greta Tomlinson says much the same thing, emphasising again that Frank didn't ask the other artists to do anything he wasn't able and willing to do himself:

'The work-load was horrendous and Frank a perfectionist; every detail of every frame had to be just-so. In no time at all, he asked if I would like to do some overtime. Everybody laughed, saying I'd regret it but I was as committed as the rest and wanted to do my share. From early morning till late at night, I worked on the different strips but the wages remained the same until I took on part of Tommy Walls. That got me an extra £2 a week. No one worked harder than Frank. He refused to spare himself, and we were fired by his imagination and couldn't wait to see what he would come up with next. Once he pencilled out a whole episode and gave us each our frames to draw; then he went back to his desk and changed the whole thing. He'd had another idea, a better idea, so he spent the day working on that and next morning we had to throw all our work away and start again. In those early days, he would often change the story a bit, just to get in an idea he'd had, and, of course, some of them were ingenious. Take the "Jepeet", the little one-wheeled car that appeared in the first issue. It ran on a gyroscopic ball, which made it perfect for banking, and it was a concept he'd had in his mind for years.'

Right *A 'special' by Hampson celebrating all the Eagle characters for the 1957 Christmas edition.*

THE EDITOR'S CHRISTMAS NIGHTMARE

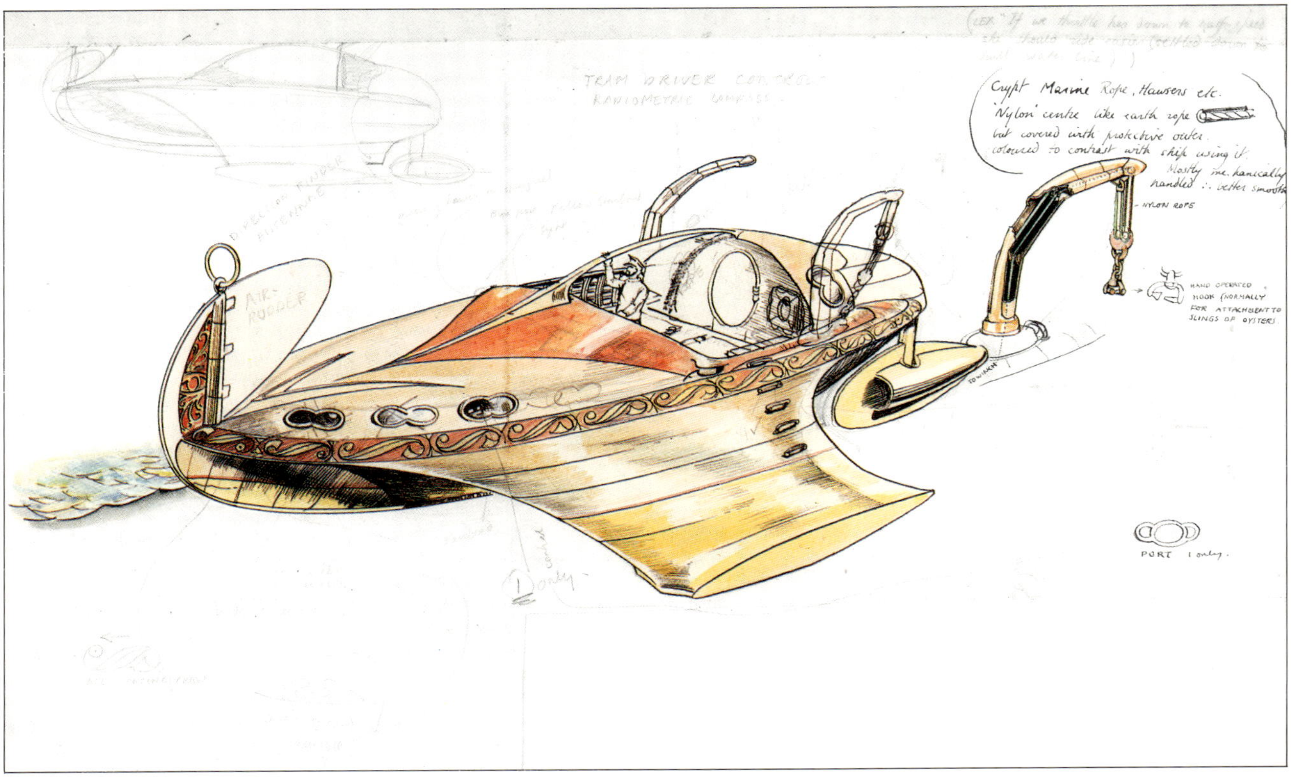
TRAM DRIVER CONTROLS
RADIOMETRIC COMPASS
Crypt Marine Rope, Hawsers etc.
'Nylon' centre like earth rope
but covered with protective outer
coloured to contrast with ship using it.
Mostly mechanically
handled ∴ better smooth
NYLON ROPE
HAND OPERATED
HOOK (NORMALLY
FOR ATTACHMENT TO
SLINGS OF OYSTERS
AIR-RUDDER
TOWINCH
PORT 1 only.

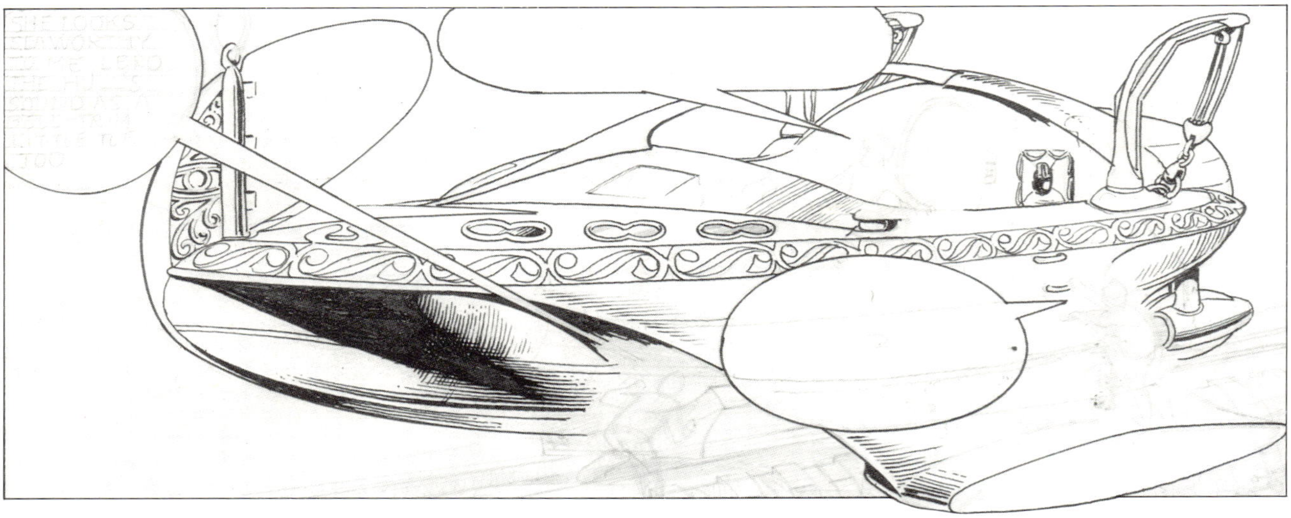

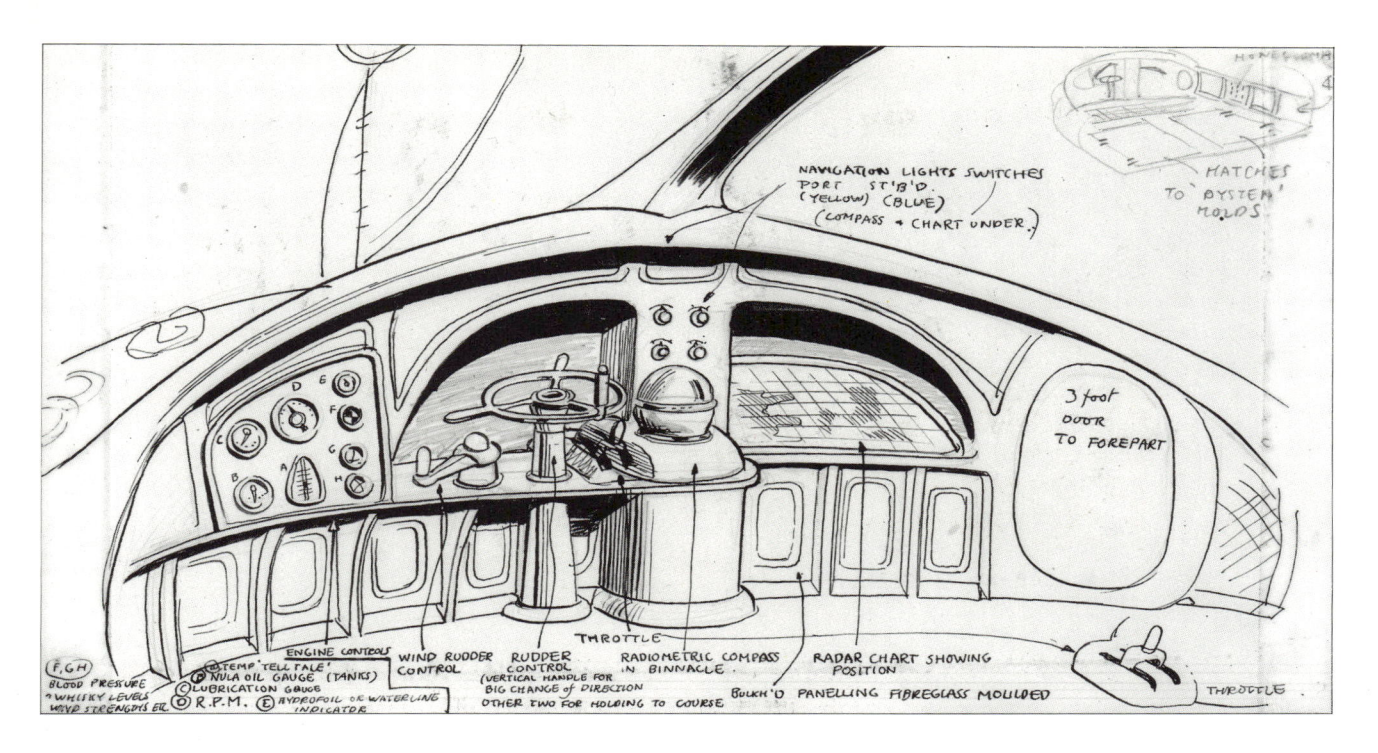

For Hampson, it was not enough that his hardware appeared authentic; he had to establish to his own satisfaction how his designs might actually work. These conceptual drawings for an Incan pearl-diver's boat (from 'Rogue Planet' 1956) illustrate the care and detail that went into conceiving just one vessel, even down to how the hawsers should operate. This exquisite boat displays Hampson's ability to design to the highest aesthetic standards beyond anything remotely expected of a comic strip.

A superb front page from 'Reign of the Robots' (1958). The original shown here, has a delicacy of line and brightness that never survived the printing process which dramatically changed the colour and thickened the line work. This page also demonstrates another unique feature of the Dan Dare strip – the use by Eric Eden of the airbrush. From 1955 to 1959 he used it mainly, as here, for space backgrounds. His airbrush work demonstrates a high degree of technical proficiency and creativity.

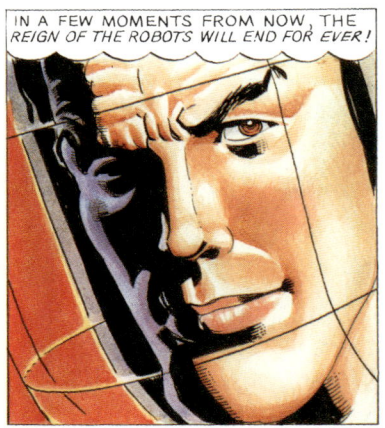

Around the beginning of March, 1950, rumours began to circulate in Fleet Street that the *Daily Express* were going to launch a new paper for boys. How did they get wind of Hulton's plans? Simple: about twenty different publishers had a chance to glimpse at the Eagle dummies when Marcus was looking for a buyer. The fact that he got short shrift from them was mainly because of the problems Eagle posed in the printing. But once Hulton had made the decision and started to look around for advertising space (and it became clear how much money they were prepared to spend on the promotion) it's quite likely that a number of people had second thoughts and – since Frank had pinpointed the market need – realised that a quality paper wasn't such a bad idea. Whether the rumours were true didn't matter, they put the wind up the Hulton Press management, who had no wish to be pipped at the post. So they gave out that due to production difficulties, the launch of Eagle was to be postponed (a story easy to believe, since printing problems were what everyone expected, and got). According to the General Manager, John Pearce, the *Express* relaxed. Instead, however, Hulton brought their launch date forward, some say by three weeks, Frank says it was more like months, and on April 14th, 1950, the first issue hit the street. It was Eric Bemrose, printers, who had the problems; the new German presses were still being bedded into the floor when the print run began.

But the printers problems were nothing compared to the tizzy Frank's Southport studio found themselves in. Frank claims the paper went to bed when final artwork had been completed for only four issues; you can increase that to six, for there was a six week gap between the delivery of artwork to the platemakers and the issue reaching the streets, principally, because of the large amount of retouching to the photographic plates when the pictures were photographed, in preparation for their transfer to the gravure cylinders. But it meant that the artists were right up against the dead-line and there was no leeway for mistakes, which explains Jo Thomas' tale of Greta being shipped off in a taxi at the dead of night. Dorothy Hampson also has a tale of Frank taking artwork to the printers and actually completing it on the train journey. Frank puts the position graphically enough: 'I found myself in the driver's cabin of an unstoppable train.' It took Bruce Cornwell very little time to decide not to ride with him. Bruce had come up from Middlesex to join Frank and six months after he arrived, he resigned to return to his wife in Ruislip. Frank decided to replace him with a student he'd worked with at Southport School of Art; Eric Eden came in the August or September of 1950, when the summer sun was belting through the glass roof making everyone hot and tired. But if you were tired, there was no question of going home. Frank had shipped into the Bakery a camp bed, so after the necessary cat-nap, the (hopefully) refreshed artist could be up and back at his desk again. Pop Hampson became self-appointed caterer and morale booster, bringing in snacks and sandwiches, brewing endless pots of coffee and tea, telling jokes and reminiscences and joshing them all along, until, as the dawn broke and the dawn chorus started, Frank would grumble: 'Tsk, tsk, them dratted birds again' Another day had started, and there weren't going to be enough hours in this one either.

EAGLE — BRITAIN'S NATIONAL STRIP CARTOON WEEKLY

FOURPENCE

EVERY FRIDAY

EAGLE

29 SEPTEMBER 1950 No. 25

AS DAN DARE AND HIS COMPANIONS STRUGGLE THROUGH THE WILDS OF VENUS, THE WORLD'S GREATEST NEWSPAPER HIGHLIGHTS SUSPENSE AND FAMINE-THREAT BACK ON EARTH

DAILY WORLD POST

No. 17,777 ONE PENNY EUROPE : TEN CENTS PANAMERICA : FOUR ANNAS ASIA : ONE SUT PANAFRICA

PUBLISHED SIMULTANEOUSLY IN LONDON, NEW YORK, SAN FRANCISCO, TOKIO, DELHI, BAKU, ROME, BULAWAYO, SYDNEY AND MARSVILLE

LATEST EDITION — MONDAY 28 SEPTEMBER 1995 . . . . . THE HULTON PAPER — LONDON

VETERAN SPACEMAN IN MISSING EXPEDITION

SIR HUBERT GUEST, K.C.B., O.U.N., 65-year-old controller of the International Space Fleet, who accompanied the Space Expedition to find food on Venus. Sir Hubert, knighted in 1980 for his lifetime of service with the Fleet, was in the first ship to land on Mars in 1965. He has made over a hundred space flights.

STILL NO NEWS FROM VENUS

RADIO SILENCE BLANKETS DARE'S ROCKETS AS "RANGER" RETURNS TO EARTH

Space Station XI, Monday, 3 a.m.

SPACESHIP "Ranger" landed here an hour ago minus the three Rocket Ships which it carried to within 3,000 miles of Venus in the latest attempt to reach the mystery planet and find food to banish the threat of starvation from Earth.

Tired and worried-looking Captain Hunter, of the "Ranger", boarded a Helicar to the United Nations World Government Headquarters at New York. Thirty minutes later the following bulletin was issued from U.N.W.G.:—

"The Prime Minister regrets to announce that there is as yet no definite information of the success or otherwise of the Rocket Ship expedition to Venus.

In view of the partial success achieved in getting through the Ray-field, a further expedition will be fitted out with Rocket Ships.

The fate of the members of the present expedition is problematic.

The *Ranger* will return to orbit the planet in case any kind of signal is sent out by survivors."

COMMENT

DARE'S ROCKET THEORY JUSTIFIED?

There seem to be grounds for cautious optimism in the 'partial success' reported in the Government bulletin. The fact that the Rocket Ships built to Colonel Dare's specification did succeed in penetrating the mysterious Ray-screen which has taken such a terrible toll of previous attempts, is the first piece of good news which has come from the planet.

The sad fact that through a radio blunder this brave and brilliant officer and his equally courageous companions may have lost their lives must not be allowed to diminish the importance of their achievement for mankind.

Captain Hunter arriving in New York

TENSION MOUNTS IN FAMINE TROUBLE SPOTS

PEKIN, SUNDAY (*delayed*). Central and Southern China is in an explosive condition tonight according to messages reaching here from Canton, Hong Kong and Shanghai. The Teleview communications system has broken down, presumably owing to deliberate interference and messages are being transmitted by radio. Rioting is reported from many provinces as a result of the complete collapse of the food rationing arrangements. Ration cards have not been honoured for over two weeks in some cities.

SENATOR DEMANDS VITAMINEAT PROBE

World Senator Hartwell of North England has called for a U.N. Congressional enquiry into the activities of Vitamineats Inc., the giant International Company which makes and markets the well known Vitamineat Food Substitute Tablets. Charging the Company with using inferior ingredients and making excessive profits, the Senator also hinted that the sabotage of food supply arrangements may be charged against the combine.

Mr. Lucius K. Kettlewell, Chairman and Managing Director of the Company, commented last night, "the Senator had better be careful."

Read **EAGLE** (Incorporating 'Lilliput')
EVERY FRIDAY 4d.

MRS. DIGBY SAYS "HE'S ALIVE ALL RIGHT"

WIGAN, Monday.
Interviewed in her Westbank St. home this afternoon, Mrs. Digby, wife of the only "Other Rank" member of the expedition, seemed very confident of her husband's safety. "He'll be all right," she said, when our reporter spoke to her in the parlour of this typically Lancashire home. "Albert's been in plenty of tight spots before with Colonel Dare."

Mrs. Digby and family at their Wigan home

OTHER NEWS

MASS CHANNEL SWIM BY EGYPTIANS

An entire company of the Egyptian Army entered the water at Cap Gris Nez yesterday evening to swim the Channel in formation.

SUCCESS IN EAST AFRICA— PEANUT ARRIVES IN LONDON

There was a touching ceremony at the Strachey Memorial in London yesterday when a whole unblemished peanut was handed to the Minister of Food by a delegation representing equally the native tribes in the groundnut area and the survivors of the Strachey scheme.

"AS GOOD AS A MEAL"

Vitamineats
The perfect chemical substitute for food
One tablet equals a good American dinner
VITAMINEATS INC., New York, London, Delhi

COME TO MARS

- Winzersport in the vast natural playgrounds
- Swim in the warm waters of the ancient canals
- See the magnificent earth rise.

You leave the worries of this world behind literally when you step into the luxurious "Spacebird" class liner at the start of a holiday that is thrilling — exciting — different.

"IT'S OUT OF THIS WORLD!"

"SPACEBIRD" TO **MARS**

ENQUIRIES: SPACETOURS, 42 SHOE LANE, LONDON

FRANK'S STUDIO AT WORK

No strip has ever been as inventively or creatively drawn as Frank Hampson's Dan Dare because Frank intended it that way. He believed he was a good artist, how good he wasn't certain, all he knew was that when he drew he came alive and the more detailed and carefully he drew, the more alive he came. He says now that he set out to be the best; Eric Eden suggests that beneath this apparent confidence lay uncertainty, which drove him on to be more scrupulous, more meticulous, more precise in his figure drawing and more detailed in his backgrounds so in each frame the eye could discover some new pleasure, some new idea whenever the reader returned to study the comic. There were two levels to Dan Dare, Frank says, the normally apparent one which was the storyline; the eye could run over the speech balloons to see how far the adventure had developed that week. Then there was the *pictorial sub-plot*, which meant the boys could go back to the beginning and study the artwork frame by frame. In the later years, the story often gave way completely to the sub-plot, for after Frank stopped writing his own material, neither he nor Hulton could find an equally talented writer to replace him.

Frank worked, principally, from live models; each of his characters was based, however roughly, on one of the artists in the studio. Dan had Frank's hair, nose and the unique Dare eyebrows were developed by Frank taking the scar just above his own eye and joining it to the eyebrow itself.

Digby, chubby and cheerful and with big, round wide-open eyes was partly Frank's Batman from his army days and partly Harold Johns. Sir Hubert Guest, boss of the Interplanet Space Fleet was every inch Pop Hampson with his distinguished face, tall, slim figure and blimpish moustache. In fact when Frank used a photograph of his father to illustrate one of the front page frames, it was Sir Hubert to the last detail, and dressed in Frank's old army uniform with his hat and epaulettes plastered with scrambled egg, he became an authentic and inspiring figure. Greta Tomlinson was Professor Peabody, young, blonde and with a slightly imperious air which came from her well-off middle class background and her slightly nervous sensitivity. Hank and Pierre, the American and French Pilot Captains were taken from Bruce Cornwell's and Eric Eden's posed figures – although not at first – since, in the very beginning, before he got his studio system properly worked out, Frank had to create them out of his own head. Raymond Geering says he could find characters from Frank's art-school days dotted all over the strip, each drawn with a delicious secret humour which was Frank's forte when he created minor parts. All the faces were carefully different so the reader could tell who was who even when the explorers were dressed in heavy-duty space suits. That was the thinking at the beginning, when Frank was bursting with ideas and couldn't get them onto paper fast enough.

He now says the Venus story was an analogy of the Second World War, the good Earthmen and Therons with their cultivated lifestyle and love of home and family, against the emotionless Treens, scientific automatons who sacrificed everything to efficiency and worshipped the intellect at the expense of heart and hands. A nice idea it is, but I suspect it's born of post rationalisation.

After a year to so, Frank developed a complete studio system, backed up by reams of research and reference sheets. He had models built of the space ships and plaster of Paris heads made of the principal characters including Dan, Digby, the Mekon and the principal

Treens. He mocked up space suits and helmets, had a model of the deep space station which cropped up in a number of the stories and a layout of the space fleet headquarters, which he then photographed, retouching the photograph to fill in details of the administrative areas, the departure lounge for ferries into space, the engineering workshops, car parks, launch pads and ramps, even an area at the far end of the complex for the rescue services. This modelling was done by Walkden Fisher, Bruce Cornwell and Eric Eden. When they came to think about the Mercury story, Walkden Fisher was told to come up with some 'fantastic' terrains for the surface of the planet. He developed rock surfaces like drooping treacle, lakes of molten lead, crags, crevices and caves filled with glorious colour. Frank didn't use them for long, complaining that they weren't fantastic enough; happily Harold Johns found them useful when he took over the Mercury story full time.

To this mass of reference material, created to guarantee continuity, Frank added reams of research. He used the works of Chesley Bonestall to create the surfaces of other planets. Bonestall's paintings were based on the writings of Willy Ley, a rocket scientist the Americans grabbed from Germany where he had been working on the doodlebugs. At his elbow, Frank kept a set of the Encyclopedia Brittanica to help him get his technical and geographical details right and when all had been completed, the strip was sent to Arthur C. Clark, the well-known science fiction author. That arrangement didn't last long, as this letter from Arthur's brother, Fred, confirms:

'I know Arthur used to receive the Dan Dare strip regularly, for checking, but I don't think he ever found a mistake in it. In the end he suggested to Frank Hampson that as the standard of the work and research was so high, they were wasting their money getting him to check it, so from then on, Arthur had to buy Eagle for himself to keep up with what was happening.'

Marcus, with his penchant for good clean Christian fun, even had a consultant child psychologist, James Hemmings, to check that the gory bits, such as they were, wouldn't disturb innocent minds. I don't suppose Disney worried about such niceties when he created the witch in Snow White, or the forest fire in Bambi, but Hulton accepted that this was part of Eagle's ethic and paid up willingly enough.

Finally, there was the creation of the strip itself and this was carried out with an almost pathological attention to detail. The artist's week ended on Friday, when the complete artwork had to be sent to the platemakers. For most of the studio, the weekend was then their own, but Frank would sit down and work out the next episode. He sketched out each frame in pencil, then inked it in, then – more often than not – coloured it, and many of the artists have told me, individually, that this rough layout was almost good enough to use as finished artwork, and with a little touching-up would certainly have been. Already, in its first stage, it was beter than almost all the other drawn material that appeared in Eagle. But for Frank, this was just the beginning. When everyone came in on the Monday morning, the photographic session began. Frank would divide his rough into frames, and everyone would pose in the positions in which the figures were drawn, first donning uniforms or space helmets or holding sticks or model guns, so that whatever Frank had sketched out could be checked to be anatomically possible. Shots were taken of the groups of artists, standing in the positions Frank had chosen, and care was taken to identify the source of light. Click, click, the shots were taken, sometimes three or four in each position, 'Treens' standing on boxes to get their height right, Digby upside down if he was coming out of a Telesender, Lex O'Malley caught mid-fight, swinging a hairy fist at a protruding jaw if the story was mid-way through a melée. This photographic session could take up to two days; a lot of the time was spent getting dressed, undressed, or bunching up more tightly to get the grouping in proportion to the

A studio member wearing a Treen mask.

EAGLE
THE HEADQUARTERS OF THE INTERPLANET SPACE FLEET. SOME YEARS IN THE FUTURE
IN THE LAUNCHING CONTROL ROOM
"KINGFISHER'S READY TO GO, SIR HUBERT
RIGHT DAN
HELLO KINGFISHER FLEET CONTROLLER HERE. WE'RE GOING TO GIVE YOU THE GUN NOW. GOODBYE AND THE BEST OF LUCK
AUXILIARY ROCKET BOOST
THEY'LL NEED IT!
DANGER SPACE SHIP TAKING OFF DO NOT PAS THIS POINT
KINGFISHER
WELL, THERE SHE GOES, SIR — I WONDER IF SHE'LL EVER COME BACK?
SHE'LL NOT BE IN THE DANGER ZONE UNTIL THIS TIME NEXT WEEK, DAN— ALL WE CAN DO UNTIL THEN IS WAIT ..... AND KEEP OUR FINGERS CROSSED.

drawn frame. It was tiresome, irritating and quickly became boring, and more to the point, it knocked precious hours off the time left to do the finished drawing.

Come Wednesday morning, the developed photographs could be matched up to Frank's frames. His instructions then, were to take the very best from his drawing, which normally concentrated more on expressions and facial characteristics that couldn't be photographed, and the best from the photographs, checking the source of the light and getting the folds of the clothes, the angles of the weapons and positions of the fingers right, and marry the two into the finished drawing. Frank would take some of the frames, normally those on the front page, and, in particular, the big frame opposite the masthead, and the other artists would share page two between them. This was because the front cover was what the punters saw first when they were buying the paper so Frank put everything he'd got into that. In particular, he concentrated on the big picture because the 'Eagle' masthead said 'this is the paper you know and love' while the big picture said 'and here's an exciting new episode, the best yet'. The best yet was one of Frank's aims; he was always trying to improve, or, at least, ring the changes on anything he'd done before. He had three rules for the big picture which normally occupied about a quarter of the page, but when Frank felt expansive, he could stretch over the whole front cover and fill it with the most intricate detail. His principle rules to maintain interest were that the first frame had to be (i) highly dramatic, with the story at a key point in its development (ii) if this were not possible, and often the story would lag in places, then the picture had to be technically or scientifically ingenious, and he was often put to designing ambulances, fire-fighting appliances or hover jets to cover up what may otherwise have been a fairly conventional opening; (iii) if those situations weren't appropriate, he would go for humour, and use a character (not always human, be it noted) who was doing or saying something funny.

Eagle hit the street in a blaze of trade comment, not all of it favourable, because Hulton had deliberately broken the Periodical Proprietors Association agreement not to offer copies on sale or return. They argued in their defence that the newsagents should not be expected to shoulder all the risk of the new venture, and they qualified their rule-breaking by promising that the sale or return arrangement would be maintained for four weeks only. To check how big a print run they should produce for the first issue newsagents were sent, a few weeks in advance, an incomplete dummy and asked how many copies they thought they'd be likely to sell. It was the paperboys who flipped and from an estimated 250,000 before the preview (much lower than the standard initial run of a modern-day comic, which is nearer 360,000) they upped their first printing to nearly a million (it's unlikely that Eric Bemrose could have produced many more anyway, for men and machines worked round the clock for a week), the new photogravure press producing $3\frac{1}{2}$ copies per second. Since Hulton had distributed a million three-pence-off vouchers from cars riding across the country, they virtually gave the first issue away. Here's what P. G. Allen said in his column in *Newspaper World* four weeks after the launch:

'We ought to be grateful to Hulton's for letting their Eagle loose on us. The beating of its powerful wings has disturbed lots of little prejudices and regulations that were roosting too complacently. And we have had the pleasure of Mr Harold Wilson's enlightened views, which must have been disappointing to those who thought he was going to give the bird the bird.*

Left *The front page of* EAGLE NO. 1 *that formed part of the sample dummy sent out ahead of publication to the newstrade to gauge likely sales. The absence of 'Dan Dare, Pilot of the Future' titles makes this of particular interest.*

---

* I searched Colinwood newspaper library to discover what Lord Wilson said about Eagle, but failed to find the quote. I then wrote to his Lordship asking if he had any press cuttings, which would tell us what he said. Although Lord Wilson's secretary acknowledged the enquiry, I never did discover the peer's comments – my query arrived during the Summer and on return from holiday Lord Wilson had more serious matters to attend to.

THERON TREEN DAN

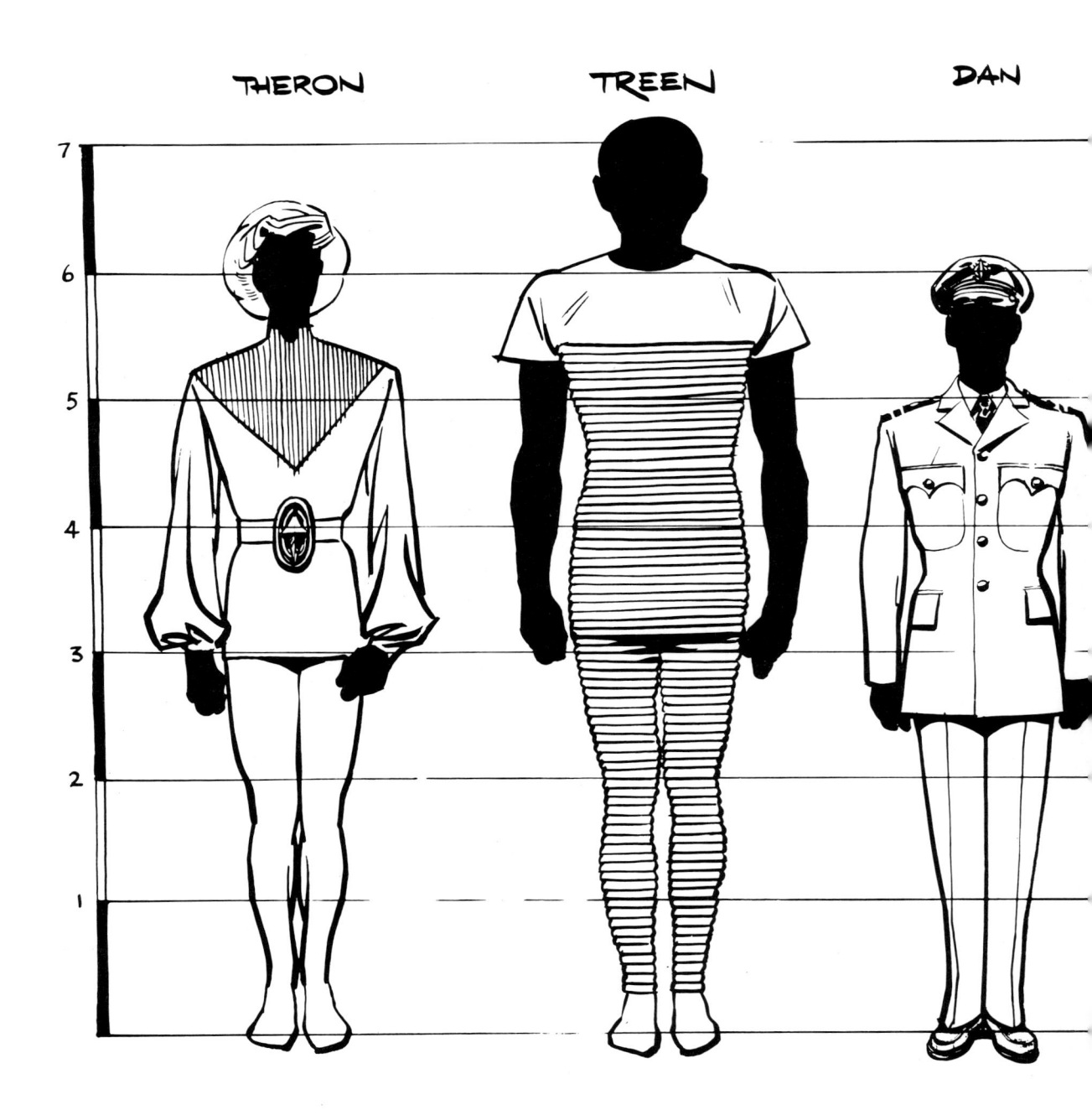

88

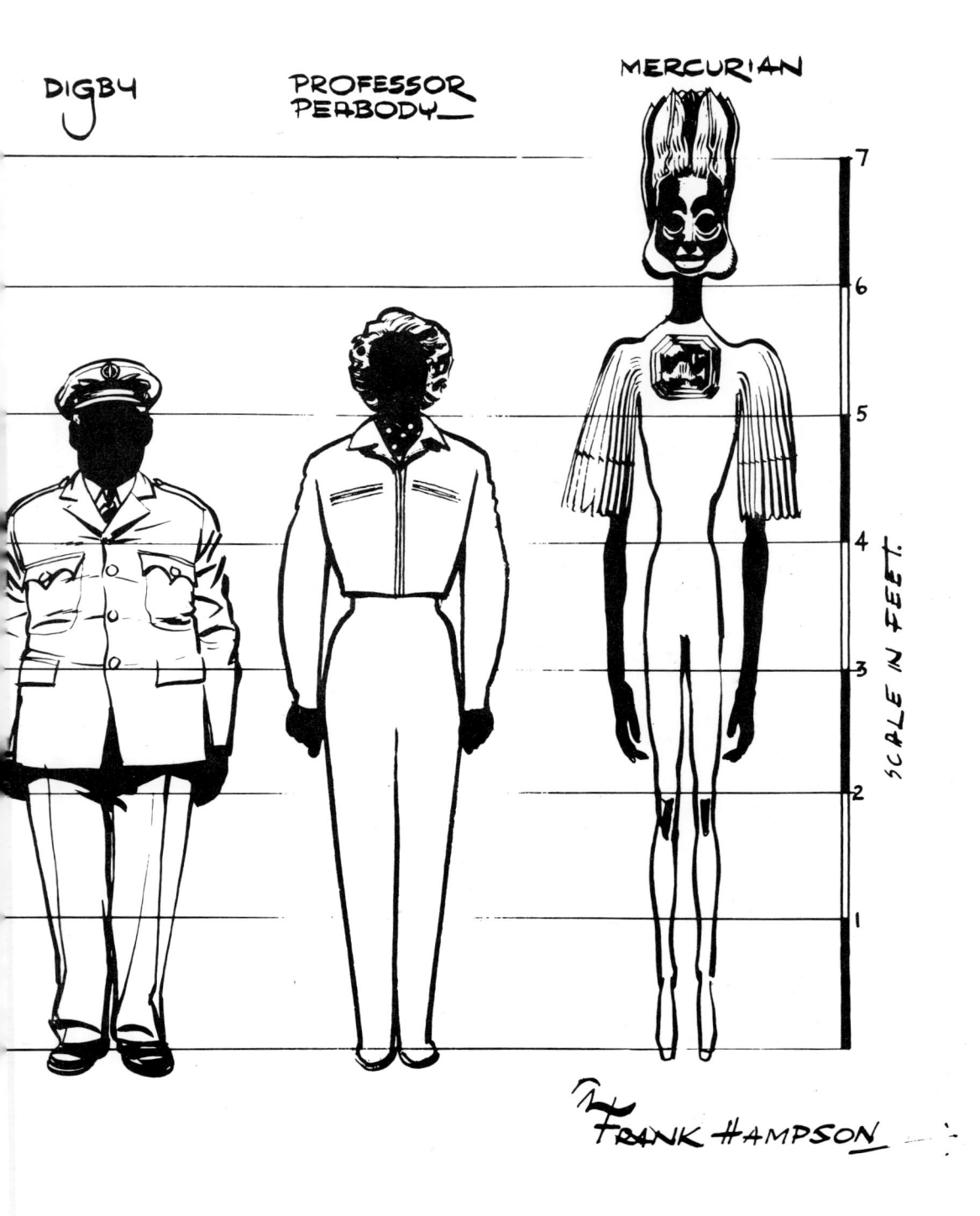

Above and overleaf top *These reference sheets, just a few of the many Hampson produced, show the inventive thought that went into the strip, anticipating by decades the 'Art of Starwars' and its companions.*

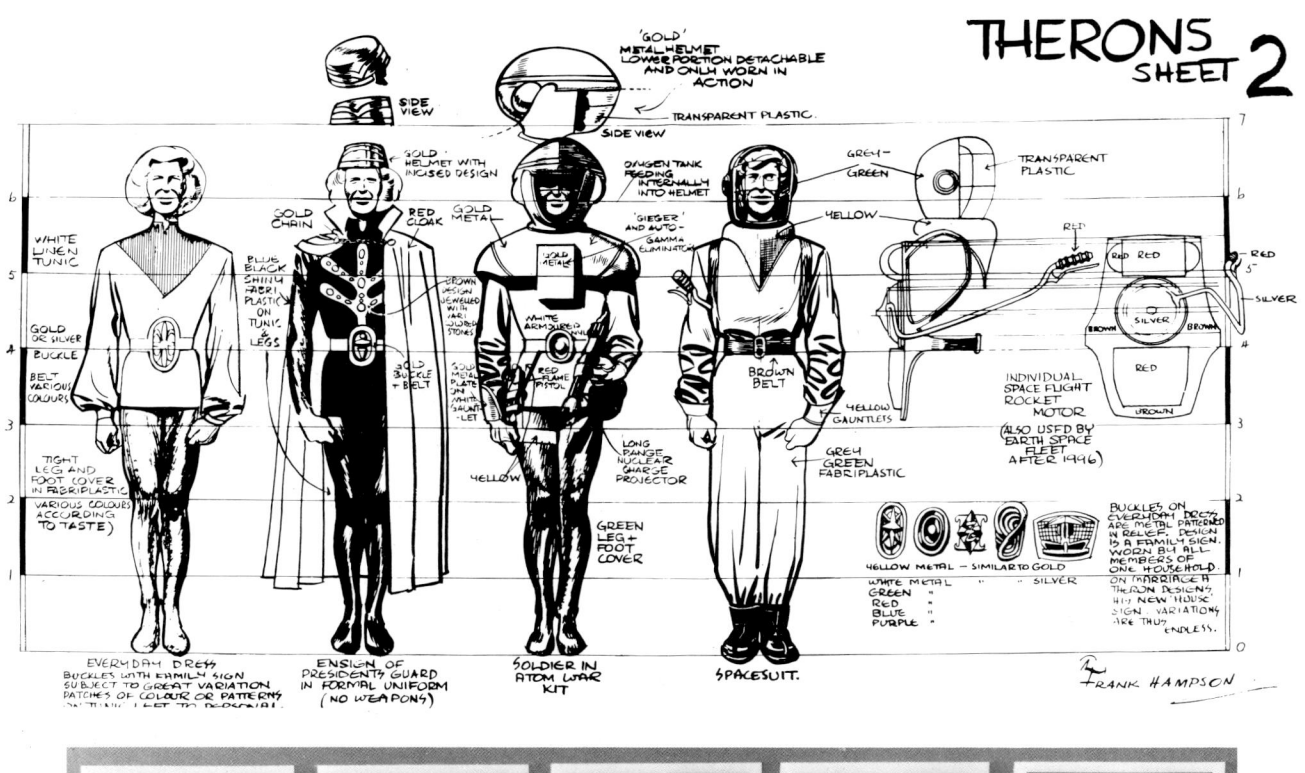

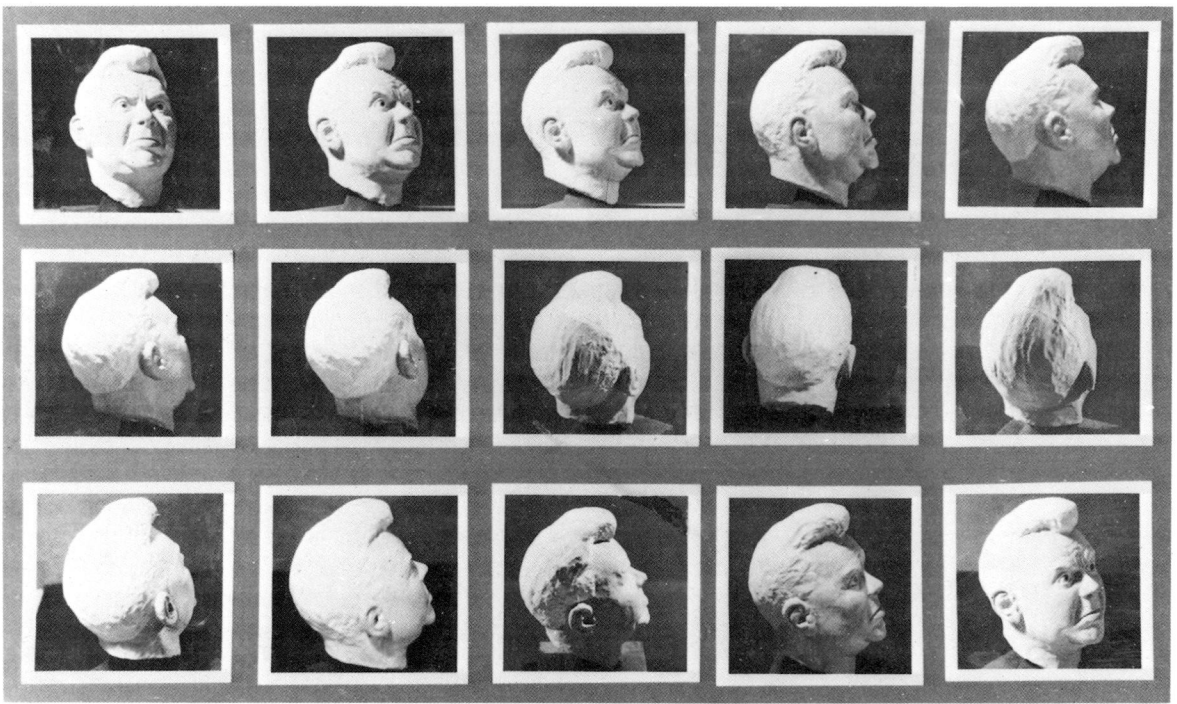

Model bust of Digby. Reference sheets such as this were compiled for all the key characters of the strip.

'Most advances in this world have been initiated by rebels and we should have a proper portion of them in our national life if we are to remain alive.... We should congratulate Hulton's on the birth of this new journal and, although it would, perhaps, be indiscreet to wish it many happy returns, we can hope that it goes on with the same measure of success that it appears to have at the moment.'

On 30th of March, however, *Newspaper World* had taken a less sanguine view of Hulton in it's main leader. The piece began on a welcoming note:

'Although the publication of a new children's comic weekly may not be regarded as a publishing event of outstanding importance, the launching of the Eagle in this field by Hulton Press has several facets of more than usual interest to the periodical publishing business. The print order for the first issue is one million copies and a circulation of 500,000 is guaranteed, so this weekly can claim to be the first mass selling periodical to be started by one of the leading big periodical publishers since greater freedom to sponsor new publications was restored. And it has quickly come in sharp conflict with one of the arrangements – the ban on returns – made among periodical publishers in membership of the Periodical Proprietors' Association to reduce the wastage of paper to a minimum.'

But later in the column, the tone turns to a reprimand: 'Nevertheless their action will no doubt arouse controversy and Hulton will have to face criticism. The departure from voluntary agreements, even in exceptional circumstances cannot be overlooked lightly for it undermines confidence. In a highly competitive field like periodical publishing, once that confidence goes, then the door is opened for resort to all kinds of promotion practices which might only have harmful repercussions on the publishing business as a whole.' Finally, however, there is a recognition of the need for compromise; 'But as so much is at stake, it is essential that any arrangements that are made should be flexible enough to meet changing conditions or exceptional circumstances so that no party is left with any sense of injustice or grievance.' In other words, Hulton have broken their agreement, there's nothing any of us can do about it, so let's wish them luck and hope they won't do it again.

Hulton may have given away the first week's issue of Eagle but they weren't giving away the advertising space. Advertisers could buy into the comic at the launch at the following rates: A whole page in colour, £600. A whole page in black and white £350, and smaller spaces on a pro-rata basis. For this money you were guaranteed half-a-million readers, an underestimate as it happened, for although the print run didn't stay at just below a million for long, the circulation quickly settled to 750,000; that was the number of copies sold regularly, not the number of children who read them. Eagle also offered a special service to advertisers who wanted to produce their promotional material in strip cartoon form. If you used a strip, you not only got reduced rates but were offered the services of an Eagle artist free to produce the required number of frames from any script supplied. The idea was that a comic strip would benefit the advertisers since it would attract boys who might think initially, that it was a non-advertising part of the paper, and it would help Eagle in the sense that it disguised the advertising (which was not available in comics like *Dandy, Beano, Wizard* and so on – if you exclude those classified ads that offered cheap foreign stamps 'on approval'). Some advertisers did take up the offer, and at the time Eagle was launched, a total of sixteen separate companies were running strip campaigns, though not all of them, of course, were in the comic. Both the rates and the arrangement proved highly attractive to makers of children's products, and after only eight months, and with the circulation having not moved one whit higher, the rates were increased to £750 for a colour page and £500 for the same area printed black and white.

It took Hulton thirty-nine weeks to put up the advertising rates, but less than half that time

For artists in the Hampson studio 'fights' such as these were all in the line of duty.

> THEREFORE I SHALL KEEP MY WORD TO YOU — YOU WILL NOT BE KILLED BUT SENT TO WORK WITH THE ATLANTINE CONVICTS IN THE POLAR MINES. THERE YOU MAY HAVE A FEW MORE YEARS OF LIFE.

The studio team posing for a frame of the first Dan Dare story. From left to right, Frank Hampson, Joan Porter, Greta Tomlinson, Robert Hampson, Harold Johns and Eric Eden.

to put up the cover price. In mid October 1950, just seventeen weeks into the life of the comic, they upped the cost of a copy from 3d to 4d, and when that had no deleterious effect on the sales, upped it again to 4½d. With the advertising rates and cover price pushed as high as they dared, Hulton began what they called 'a magazine-product tie-up and promotion programme on a scale never before seen in Britain'. Translated, that meant that in six months they had issued licences to over twenty manufacturers to make toys, clothes or anything else they thought appropriate, bearing either the name of the comic or a character that appeared in it. The first of these products was a 'Riders of the Range' jigsaw, and Marcus, with his eye, as usual, on promoting the ethical side of the paper arranged that the first hundred or so of these jigsaws to leave the factory would be sent, free, gratis and with the Reverend's compliments to children's hospitals throughout the country.

By 1957, Hulton Enterprises, a department specially set up for the job, and headed by John B. Myers (an ex-J. Arthur Rank employee) who seven years earlier, had told Marcus he couldn't help him publish Eagle, had issued over 200 licences for Hulton games and toys, linked not only to Eagle, but to *Girl, Swift* and *Robin*. Horlicks had been licenced to sponsor a Dan Dare serial on Radio Luxembourg which was based entirely on Frank's Venus story, and for which the author received £250. And Hulton were able to boast (and it was a boast, for there was no control at all over the quality of the material licenced) 'Product Packaging carrying the distinct Eagle Emblem on a red background, will become known as a symbol of quality in the toy world'. Of these licences Frank was to say later: 'The quality of most of this stuff was disgraceful, for the people who owned the copyright sold to anyone.'

Sweat and blood were being spilled in the Hampson studio but it was paying very nice dividends indeed for those with the opportunity to reap them. Which brings us to a major sticking post in Frank's story. The creation of Eagle and the other prestige comics made a lot of money for Hulton, and presumably, the manufacturers who tied-in their merchandise with the publications. Eagle itself created an advertiser's showcase with their introduction of 'Shop Window', a feature which regularly highlighted the sponsored goods. Frank claims that, at one stage, when he became disgruntled over money, he had a chat with the Hulton accountants and asked how much Dan Dare had made for the publisher and other manufacturers that year: the answer (he says) was around a million pounds.

So Marcus and his associates had turned their comics into a flourishing business; did Hulton spend their money fairly as far as the artists were concerned? Frank Humphris, who drew 'Riders of the Range' for a number of years during the Hulton regime has no complaints. The work was hard for him, despite the fact that he was a Wild West enthusiast, able to combine this hobby with the way he earned a living. His writer, Charles Chilton, seemed to place the Eagle strip fairly low on his list of priorities so Humphris was often left having to condense the script, and sometimes even re-write it, in order to have enough space left, or the right kind of scene to draw. But the work was regular, and the money good for the time; Marcus had his little foibles, including the idea that since the goodies in the *Saturday Morning Picture* serials always rode white horses and wore white hats, then Jeff Arnold must do the same, however out-of-place the dress was in real cowboy life, but on the whole, Humphris was treated fairly and with respect, and expressed only one regret. He didn't own his own artwork and had to make a special request to the publishers in order to have a few sheets returned to him, to keep as souvenirs.

With the Dan Dare studio, Hulton were more than generous, compared to any other publishing house producing comics. The normal procedure seems to be to let an artist create a character, pop along and sell it to the department in charge of juvenile papers, and then go

The marketing of Dan Dare and his fellow Eagle characters represented one of the biggest UK merchandising operations of the decade.

Eric Eden and Don Harley.

Don Harley

away and keep cranking out sheets of artwork at the lowest fee he will accept, until the publisher decides the readers are bored, and cancels the artists livelihood, usually with a minimum of notice. There is no redress and no court of appeal for a living abruptly cut off; if the artist can't produce and sell a fresh idea then too bad for him. Artists don't have a union (although some of them are agitating and working to form one), and have no muscle with which to negotiate higher fees. The fact is, they enjoy churning out drawings and will continue to do so for the lowest possible wage until the wife rebels at having to make ends meet on a pittance, and the artist decides to chuck it all in and drive a bus. That's the normal life of the average artist, working for the average comic virtually anywhere in the world, with a few exceptions – men who have so great a following amongst readers that publishers *must* treat them with respect.

Eagle was not an average comic, Frank was not an average artist and the studio he set up was quite exceptional. He may have felt, and Hulton most certainly did feel, that since Dan Dare was the strip that sold Eagle, and because of it the comic was making a great deal of money, then a studio complete with researchers, photographic facilities, odd-job helpers and tea-makers was not just permissable, but necessary. Hulton are the only publishers to have paid for, and tolerated such a complex and expensive system for producing just two pages of artwork each week, however good it was. They did not use the studio the way Frank wanted them to, which may even have been the best way and led to making even more money out of Dan Dare than they were making already. But they were providing the cash, and leaving the artists to get on with the strip with the minimum of supervision or interference, and presumably saw no reason why they should pay out more to finance Frank's personal ambitions, however laudable. What those ambitions were we will discuss later. Bearing in mind the quality of the comic they created, the quality of artwork they paid Frank to create, and what happened in 1959, when they sold out to Odhams Press, Hulton's were good employers.

Robert 'Pop' Hampson

ARRIVALS AND DEPARTURES

It was an exceptionally hot day, Wednesday 9th August 1950 when a large black limousine pulled up at Euston station and the chauffeur walked to the arrivals platform of the express from Liverpool Lime Street. A group of curious artists were surprised when he met them at the barrier and helped carry their cases to the car. Surprised because they hadn't expected such regal treatment when they got to London; curious because there were rumours that they were on their way to a large house in Epsom which would be Frank and Dorothy's home and where the others would work in separate rooms during the day. They wondered what it would be like, how many rooms it contained and who the housekeeper was that – again they'd heard whispered – Hulton had hired to help look after them. This house was the result of pressure Frank put on the publishers to find his team better accommodation than the old Church-town Bakery, which that summer had felt more like a greenhouse with the sun grilling them through the grimy glass roof.

Not that anything had been confirmed. At an earlier stage, Frank had suggested that they take over some existing studios which he knew had recently become vacant. They consisted of a house with nissen huts which had been properly converted and contained up-to-date equipment the artists needed. This suggestion wasn't accepted however, and it was decided the team should come South but the rumours talked of a place Hulton had been given permission to turn into a studio above, with living accommodation below. And, in fact, that part of the story was true; Marcus had applied to use part of 'The Firs' (as the house was named) as a commercial studio and according to the local paper Epsom council had agreed.

The big limousine moved off, the chauffeur picking his way to the South side of the Thames, down through the more dingy outskirts of Clapham and Battersea, crossing the Surrey border and heading for Epsom downs, and the racecourse where the Derby is run every year. The car finally left them at a hotel where, they understood, they were to sleep over that, and the following, night.

One member of the team remained in Southport. Pop Hampson had appointed himself guardian of the studio files and the precious models which the artists drew from. Pop supervised the packing, checked that the breakables were properly wrapped and protected, and labelled everything so that when the time came to unpack, nothing would be mislaid and the reference system which had been carefully built up over the year could be re-established in the new premises quickly and easily. In fact the rumour proved only partly true. The artists did start to work in 'The Firs' but it was Marcus and his family who lived there; Frank, Dorothy and young Peter Hampson had a house, Bruce Lodge, backing onto the downs close to some stables where, late at night, you could hear the horses pawing the ground.

There was disappointment expressed. Not that 'The Firs' wasn't a delightful place, but it did not have all the amenities Frank had hoped for, there was little space to take photographs and no dark-room facilities in which to develop them. Moreover, it was not long before the artists felt themselves getting under Jessica Dunning's feet. She had four young children and a puppy to look after, was jealous of her privacy, resented the artists need to use one of the kitchens to brew tea and coffee, and soon began to feel her home was scarcely her own. Moving South did not relieve the pressure of work. The average day still began at nine, and more often than not, continued until two or three next morning. Frank was as obsessional as ever about detail; he once asked Greta Tomlinson to draw a picture of a character water-

GRAB THAT SPACE FLEET FLAG, TUBBY — WE'VE GOT TO SET UP A RALLYING POINT AND OVERPOWER THE GUARDS.

...ES AT SPACE FLEET CONCEN- ...AWAY AT THE THERON RE- ...TERS ON VENUS . . .

Life-size models were made of all the main weaponry, including shown here, the Treen flame-thrower and flame projector pistol.

100

skiing. Four times, Greta drew the scene and four times Frank rejected it because the wake from the boat and water-skis didn't look as he thought it should. He accepted her fifth attempt but when she saw the frame pasted down on the final artwork, Frank had stuck a speech balloon over the wake she had worked so hard to get right.

The long hours did nobody any good. Eric Eden, Harold Johns, Jo Thomas and Greta used to complain over their coffee that surely such prolonged work was unneccessary and there were suggestions that if only Frank could get his administration a bit more efficient, the hours could have been reduced. Frank, too, was suffering, and popping Dexadrines to keep alert. From his point of view, he needed every minute to work on his pictures; channels of communication came a long way second. But the strain was beginning to show. Jo Thomas walked home to her digs one evening, tears of self-pity streaming down her face, weak from exhaustion and wondering why she put up with it all. Greta Tomlinson fell into bed in the small hours of Sunday morning, and when she awoke late in the afternoon, picked her way along the corridor to her bath side-steppping imaginary pools of fire. She'd spent most of her day in bed, and knew that if she was to be fit enough to start again on Monday, she should have a good meal and fall back between the sheets again.

Eric Eden had a chance to put the problem to Frank when the two men met to talk over some details in the strip. Frank called the meeting, and when he'd said his bit, Eric took a deep breath and asked: 'Is it really necessary for us to work these unconscionable hours?' Frank's face darkened and his lips pursed. Was this some kind of conspiracy? He'd suspected something was going on behind his back; was Eric's question the first sign of revolt? And was Eden the ringleader, bringing the matter up on behalf of them all? Well it had to be nipped in the bud. Frank was master in this studio and if he worked until he was ready to drop, at least the others could show they supported what he was doing. Frank was in no mood even to discuss the matter, and something may have been said to the effect that if Eric didn't like the way he was working, there was always an alternative. In fact Frank gave his fellow-artist no alternative. Within the week a letter of dismissal arrived from Marcus, saying 'there is no longer any further work for you of the kind you have been doing'. Eden insists he was not ring-leader in a conspiracy and, as far as he knew, there never was any revolt; simply the artists muttering together in a perfectly natural objection to having to stay at their desks until late in the evening, virtually every evening. But he left, and found himself work in what he describes as a miniscule advertising agency where he admits he wasn't happy. It was Bruce Cornwell who replaced Eric; Bruce had left the studio in Southport in protest against the workload, and come back to live with his wife and young son at his home in Ruislip in Middlesex. This house was twenty miles from Frank's studio, but Bruce was willing to make the motor-bike trip every day provided Frank would let him away at five-thirty. So the arrangement was agreed. At the same time, Eric Eden moved into Bruce's home to live with him for six months whilst he was settling down and looking for digs.

Early in 1951, Frank was invited to give a lecture at Epsom School of Art and in the audience, a student, Donald Eric Harley, admired the drawings, photographs and slides with which the talk was illustrated. Harley had spent many years studying art, some of them under the tuition of Sir Stanley Spencer; he was in his final year, already laden down with certificates and diplomas, and made a mental note that Frank's studio was nearby, and a possible source of work. When he graduated, Don Harley found it hard to find the kind of job he wanted and returning to Art School one afternoon to chat things over with his erstwhile fellow students, the suggestion was put to him to go and talk to Frank. He did, and Frank took him on for a couple of weeks, paying Don out of his own pocket. This had become rather a habit

Keith Watson (left) in 1959 posing for a frame in 'Terra Nova'.

since Frank was choosy about who worked with him and to take someone on formally then ask them to leave a few weeks later was bad PR for Hulton. However, Harley was just what Frank was looking for. He was by far the most skilled of the artists in Epsom (Frank aside) and the only one who could draw from models and photographs *direct into the frame*, without the sketching out before-hand that the others did before attempting the final picture. Don was quickly taken on permanently to join Frank, Bruce and Jo Thomas at Bruce Lodge which was now the main studio, while Harold and Greta remained at 'The Firs'. The studio was about half-way through the 'Red Moon Mystery' and Don can still point out the first frame he ever had printed in Eagle.

Don's arrival took much of the figure-drawing away from Jo Thomas who was not sorry, since she had found a beau in Epsom and was soon to get married. She told Frank her plans; the ceremony was held in a church in Epsom in March 1952 and Jo and her new husband left immediately for India. A week or so later, as the 'Red Moon' was drawing to its close, and Walkden Fisher was building models of the surface of Mercury for the next story, Frank fell ill. He developed trouble in his inner ear, which disturbed his sense of balance. He only had time to tell Fisher that his Mercury models weren't fantastic enough before he had to give up drawing the strip. It was taken over by Harold Johns and the story was written by Chad Varah, although Frank continued to get a credit at the bottom of the strip for having devised the characters. Johns was grateful enough for Fisher's models of the surface of Mercury; the lakes of molten lead, and landscapes that oozed like technicolour treacle proved useful to him.

Frank came firmly back into the saddle at the launch of 'Operation Saturn' and was credited as drawing the first twenty or so episodes by himself Then the story was taken over by Don Riley and the work spread much more evenly among the other artists. Looking at the finished artwork today (and I saw some offered for auction at Christies – only to be withdrawn from the sale a few days before it was due to take place) it's easy to pick out the frames that Frank drew, and the work done by the others.

Harold Johns and Greta Tomlinson worked closely together in 'The Firs', but there was friction building up there and matters came to a head when Jessica Dunning confronted Greta one day and accused Frank's people of being a group of jumped-up artists who were lucky to have their jobs and didn't appreciate what Hulton was doing for them. That was the end of working in Marcus' house and Greta and Harold moved out to a place in Epsom town; later they moved again to an office in London, and later still to a studio in Banstead, over an Estate Agents office.

In 1954 an outside publisher approached Harold Johns and asked whether he would take on another strip. Harold was interested since it meant a chance to do fresh work but felt he couldn't agree until he had squared things with Marcus. Harold didn't want to leave Eagle, and felt if he got Greta to help him with the new work, the two of them could cope and still continue with anything Frank gave them. Marcus didn't like it but instead of telling Harold 'no' he squeezed him for assurances that Eagle's artwork must be given absolute priority; provided it didn't suffer then Harold was free to do as he liked. Delighted with a chance to do something on their own, Harold accepted the extra strip and he and Greta began to work on it. But Marcus was not happy, and may well have said as much to Frank. A few weeks later, Marcus rang Harold and asked him to come to Shoe Lane, the Eagle editorial offices, for a chat. Not realising anything was amiss, Harold persuaded Greta to join him for the hour-long journey to London. She could do some shopping in the West End, and pick up Harold after Marcus had said his bit. But in the reception later that morning, Greta only had to glance at Harold to see something was very wrong. Marcus had pulled no punches, told Harold that he

Marcus Morris, Alan Stranks and studio member in full Dan Dare outfit, outside Bayford Lodge, home of the Dan Dare studio.

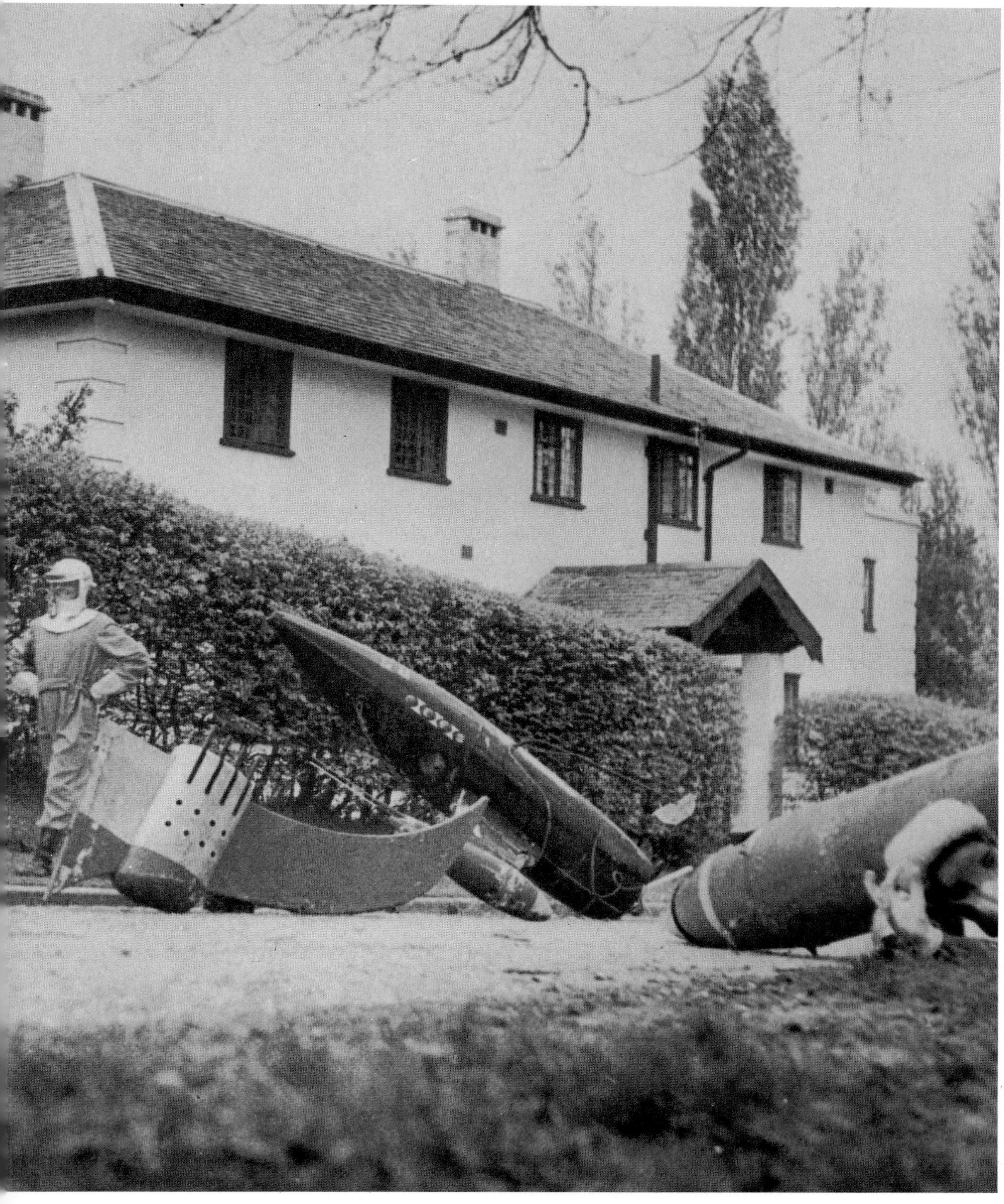

was disloyal to Hulton, who had given him his big chance, brought him to London and treated him so well. Accepting work from a rival was little short of treachery, and Harold must go. And Greta could join him; there was no further work on Eagle for either of them.

Dismayed and bewildered, Harold went to Frank in the hope he could get Marcus to change his mind. But Frank claimed there was nothing he could do. If Marcus had told him to go, go he must; there was no chance of Greta being reinstated either. And go they both did, each with one week's wages. They negotiated with the landlord to take over the rent for the Banstead office themselves, and set out to win freelance work. They took on advertising, sales brochures and work for other comics.

Although Harold was to stay in Banstead until the early sixties, he never worked for either Frank or Eagle again. Greta, who did not go to see Frank after her dismissal, later turned her hand to fashion drawing and was offered a job with one of the first of the new commercial TV channels. She worked in London for the next two years but in 1956 followed her future husband to the Middle East and they were married in Bagdad the same year. Greta travelled the Arab world until 1969, always sketching and painting.

In 1955 Frank wrote to Eric Eden asking if he would like his old job back. There were lots of apologies about the first firing and an explanation that although there was indeed a conspiracy, Frank had now discovered that Eric wasn't part of it. Eric, never believing for a moment the theory, was miserable at his advertising agency and agreed to come back.

By this time Frank was established in his new studio home, Bayford Lodge in Epsom, an imposing house of character which was to be an effective and permanent base for the Dan Dare studio until the end of the 1950s. The whole of the ground floor of Bayford Lodge was given over to the studio with Frank, Don and Eric each having their own rooms. In addition there was a room devoted to photography with darkroom facilities. The upper storey provided living accommodation for the Hampson family.

Frank had, by now, recovered from the ear trouble and the first of his serious illnesses, and his team had begun work on the 'Man from Nowhere' trilogy, in which Frank was to produce some of his finest artwork. The story was written in collaboration with Alan Stranks, an Australian who had first written PC49. Stranks was the only writer Frank ever felt completely at home with on Eagle and although the storylines began to be much more padded and the dialogue less terse and to the point, Frank seemed to compensate for the weaker words with finer and more detailed pictures.

Almost every frame in the strip was now drawn from either Frank's sketches or photographs; usually a combination of both.

Frank had one of the bedroom floors removed so that Joan Porter could take sky shots of the posed artists looking down from the room above, or ground-shots with the artists standing in the bedroom and Joan shooting up from below. Joan was also responsible for the running of the studio and producing a balanced colour-plot on Hampson's visuals. Colour work requiring tonal modelling was done by Frank or Don and Frank preferred to complete large close-ups of characters himself. After the colouring was completed, one of the artists had to go over almost all of Frank's black inking a second time, to reinforce the lines which had become faded by being covered by Pelikan inks. Keith Watson, who joined the studio in 1958, was given this job on his first day, and in his own words, 'made a complete hash of it'. He then went down with flu', had two weeks off, and when he came back, apologised to Frank for ruining the artwork. 'You didn't actually ruin it,' Frank replied, 'but you had a bloody good try.' Later Keith was to ask the artist who usually re-drew the black parts how he managed with Frank's fine cross-hatching work 'How do you go over that?' The reply was 'I don't.'

Don Harley as 'Digby'.

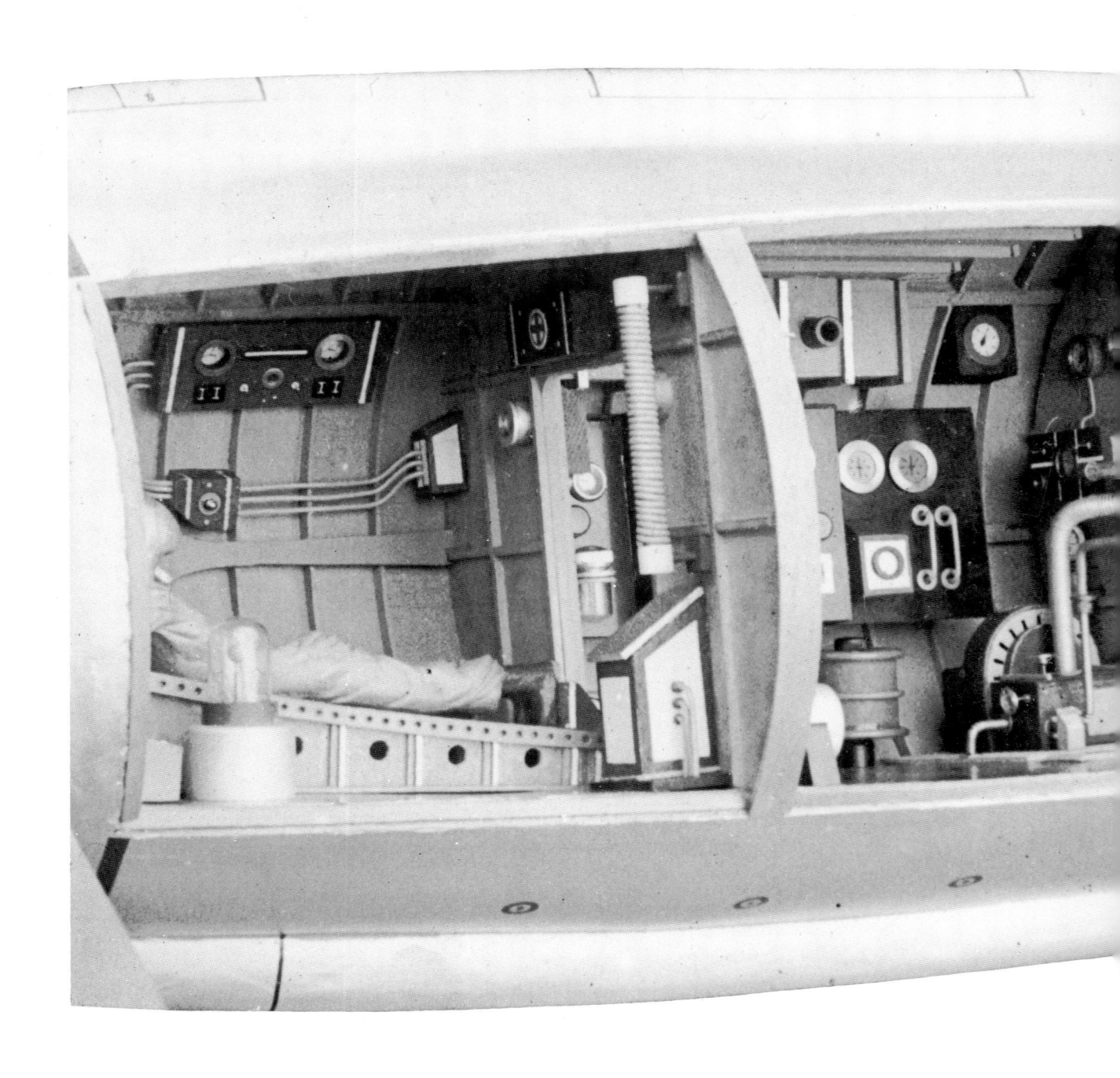

Above *Large model of a spaceship showing interior detail and pilot.*

Above right *Don Harley, Frank Hampson, Eric Eden and Joan Porter.*

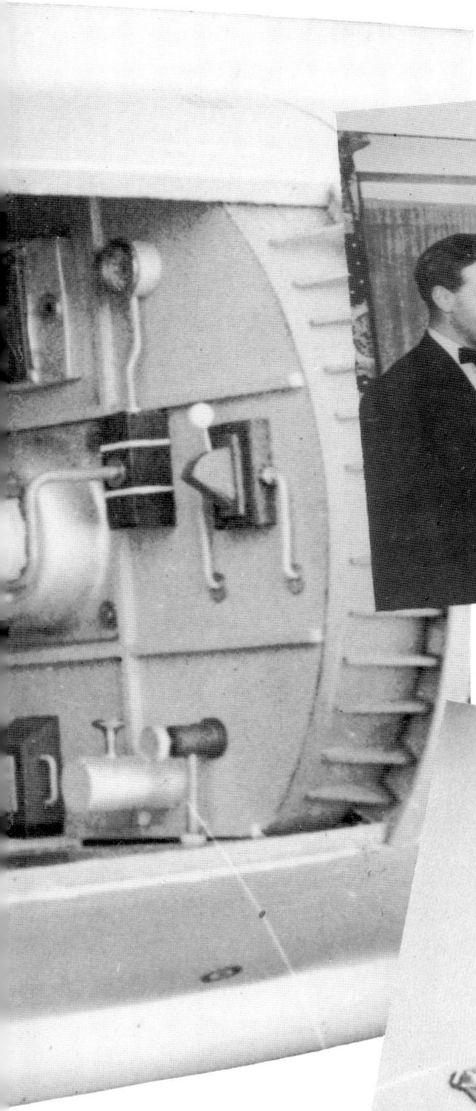

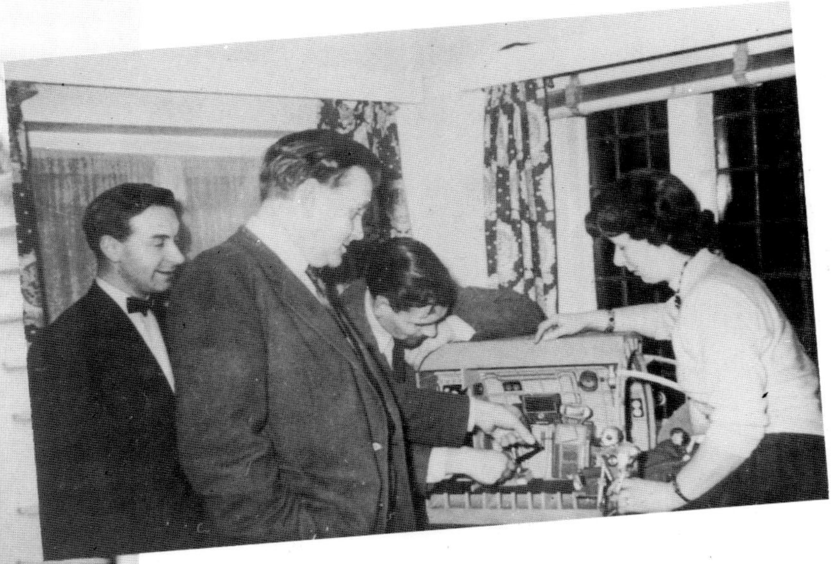

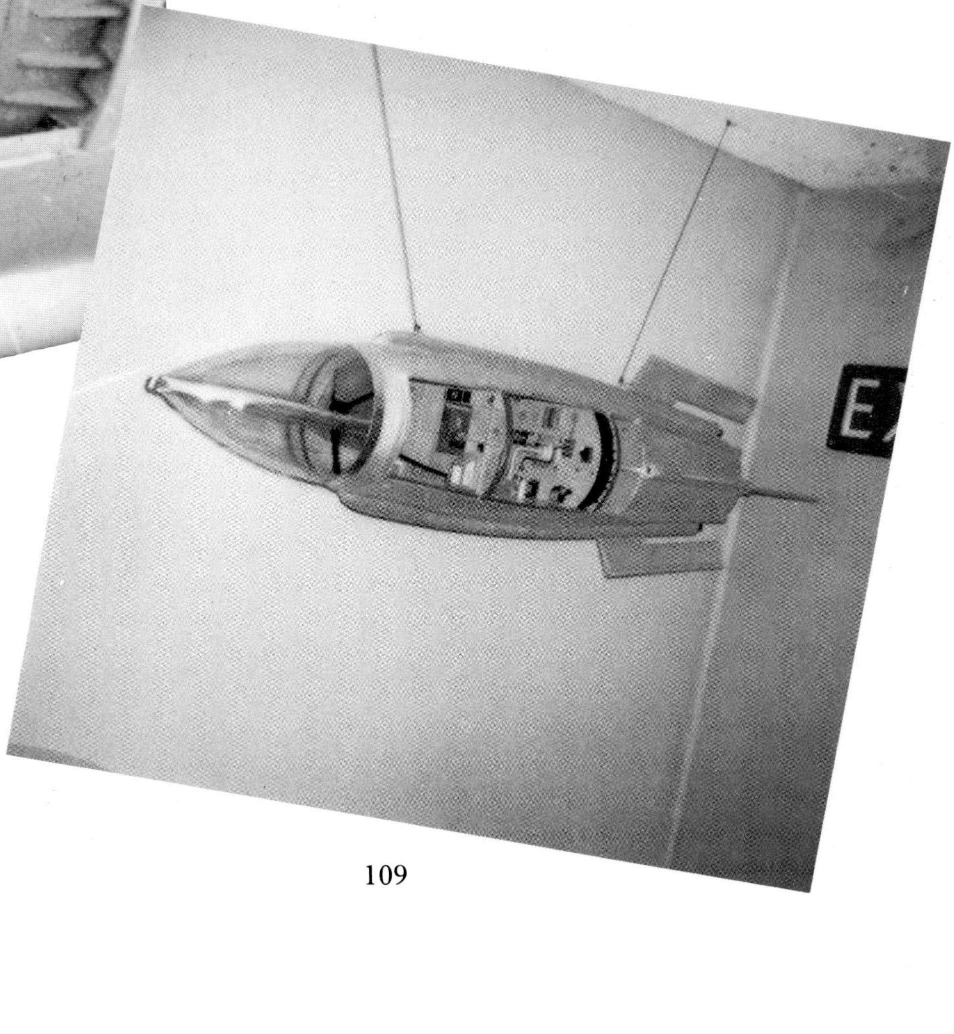

Keith had no art training at all but was handy with a pen and applied for the job by drawing a strip cartoon of himself applying for a job. Time passed, and Keith was wondering whether Frank had forgotten all about him when he was finally accepted into Bayford Lodge.

As well as the people we've met in this chapter there were a number of other artists and assistants Frank used over the years. There was a period when a great deal of the finished drawing was put out to Desmond Walduck, at first so that Frank could get his studio established when he moved from Bruce Lodge to Bayford Lodge, later in an attempt to get him off the deadline. Joan Porter highlights the situation: 'Time was the universal enemy – there was never enough of it for Frank's perfectionist ideals. His concept for the "Dan Dare Studios" meant incorporating a flow of on-going ideas and work, apart from the strip.' All the artists tried at various periods to gain Frank time, both to rest and to be able to work normal hours. Whenever they succeeded, and he found himself with a few weeks in hand, they were quickly eaten up as he decided to completely re-draw a page that to most people's eyes was perfectly good already, or crammed more and more detail into frames. At one stage, before the fracas with the rival publisher, Greta Tomlinson was shocked to find Frank drawing all his characters with jagged, craggy strokes. Thinking that this was tiredness, Greta did her best to smooth out the roughest lines, only to be told that Frank wanted the jagged effect; it was his way of experimenting with techniques and making changes in his style (he also toyed for a bit with scraperboard, but it took too long to be adopted as the only way of drawing).

Although Desmond Walduck was not part of Frank's team at Epsom, he did not escape the gruelling workload. Desmond first became involved with Dan Dare when he illustrated one of the Eagle 'Spacebooks'; Frank apparently preferred his work to that done by a couple of other contributors and made a note to use Desmond more often. The next opportunity arose with the publication of a Dan Dare 'pop-up' book, then, in September 1953, Desmond was asked to take over the full strip. Frank had over-done it again, and utterly exhausted, was ordered to leave the comic alone, and retire to his bed. He was in the middle of 'Operation Saturn' and the scamps were taken over by Donald Harley, who drew out the two pages in pencil from scripts sent through the mail via the Hulton main office. His scamps were then sent to Desmond, who continued to do finished artwork on the comic, without a break, until the end of the 'Prisoners of Space' story. He worked alone, despite Frank's original stipulation that an artist should be asked to complete only one colour page per week, and he had no access to the models or reference sheets in the Epsom studio. Today, as Desmond says, 'I am free of the rat-race of commercial art to paint the pictures I want to paint'.

'The Dan Dare strip used to take me all week, working into the small hours; trying to get away from the deadline to enjoy Christmas, Easter or a Summer break, was hell. I had to take the work with me when I took my young family for a holiday. It was non-stop work. Finally, in the very last episode of 'Prisoners of Space' I drew a portrait of myself, as a press cameraman. That's me in the green hat. After the weekly strip, my work with Hulton continued. I filled-in when artists were ill, or on holiday I also did work in the Dan Dare Annuals, and for Swift. But it's hard to remember, it was all so long ago." Don Harley remembers the period working with Walduck. Yes, it is true Desmond had to do two pages and complained about the pressure, but Harley believes Walduck was also doing other work besides that for Eagle, and he could have put more effort into Dan Dare had it not been for that. Harley opines that his pencil sketches were better than the final pages that appeared.

While Frank fought through each day in his studio, up in London, Marcus was going from strength to strength. It is well known that he launched three more red-masted prestige comics,

Scottish Scientist Galileo McHoo, from the 1959 story 'Safari in Space', was based directly on Ronald Graham who sometimes posed for the studio.

each appealing to different age groups; what is less well known is that in addition to his responsibilities for the juvenile publications, Marcus was also made Editor-in-Chief of Hulton's magazine for women, *Housewife*.

In 1955 Edward Hulton was knighted and his company moved into the newly-built Hulton House, which was then, and remained for some years, the most impressive office-block in Fleet Street. In 1956 Sir Edward announced his most remarkable scheme to date, a plan to introduce the first national newspaper able to offer its readers (and advertisers) full colour on the front, back and middle pages. *The Sunday Star* was to be tabloid, price four (old) pence and printed in Manchester. The aspect of this news that mattered to Frank was that the designated Editor-in-Chief was Marcus Morris.

In addition to his duties at Hulton, Marcus also kept up his involvement in the church. He had resigned the living in St James in Birkdale when it became clear that his job as Editor of Eagle was going to be a permanent one, but still had permission from the Bishop of London to officiate, and was licenced as assistant vicar at St Brides, Fleet Street. He also let it be known he was available to preach, or take services anywhere in the country that cared to invite him, and did so, he says, on most Sundays. How he could effectively oversee *The Sunday Star*, then preach from a distant pulpit just hours after his fourpenny coloured had rolled off the Mancunian presses was a question that never had to be answered, for *The Sunday Star* never rose.

Frank's 'Man from Nowhere' trilogy ended in April 1958, followed by 'The Phantom Fleet' (not a success in most people's eyes, Marcus gave him instructions to cut it short) and, in the first week in January 1959, by 'Safari in Space'. This was to be the first of a new series in which Dan was to journey from planet to planet in search of his father who had been one of Earth's first space-pilots. But a little before 'Safari in Space', a safari in Russia signalled a train of events which led to Marcus quitting Eagle and his other Hulton posts for ever, most of Frank's studio resigning, his headquarters in Epsom virtually being shut down, and Frank himself leaving, under a cloud, for Israel. The leading participants in these events are Cecil Harmsworth King, proprietor of the Mirror Group of Newspapers, Hugh Cudlipp, editorial director of the *Daily Mirror* and, in the early stages, the Honourable Michael Berry and Family, who owned the controlling interest in Amalgamated Press, probably the leading Fleet Street publishing house.

January 1959 saw Hugh Cudlipp and his wife in Russia, observing (as he puts it in his book *At Your Peril*) 'Khruchschev and his henchmen at Kremlin parties' when into the USSR his boss Cecil King shot a telegram. It was cryptically worded since the news it conveyed was not for public consumption but Cudlipp quickly divined it meant that King wanted to buy a controlling interest in Amalgamated Press, and wanted his editorial director's comments. In the event, however, he hardly waited for comment but offered to buy the Berry family's 1,573,442 shares. Amalgamated Press was no small beer, controlling as it did 42 weeklies, 23 monthlies and 20 annuals. Fleet Street observers described it as 'publishers of the largest range of periodicals and specialist magazines in the world'. In fact the outfit was left alone by the Berry Family, being run for them by a group of Amalgamated directors; these directors (who had not been consulted about the sale) were very upset. Michael Berry, however, let it be understood that he could sell his shares if he so decided, and the best thing the Amalgamated directors could do about it was to advise the remaining shareholders on their best course of action. And since Cecil King had been careful to buy a controlling interest, the best course of action was to sell their shares to King too, which a number of them duly did.

At first glance this take-over battle seems to have nothing to do with Frank or Marcus, who

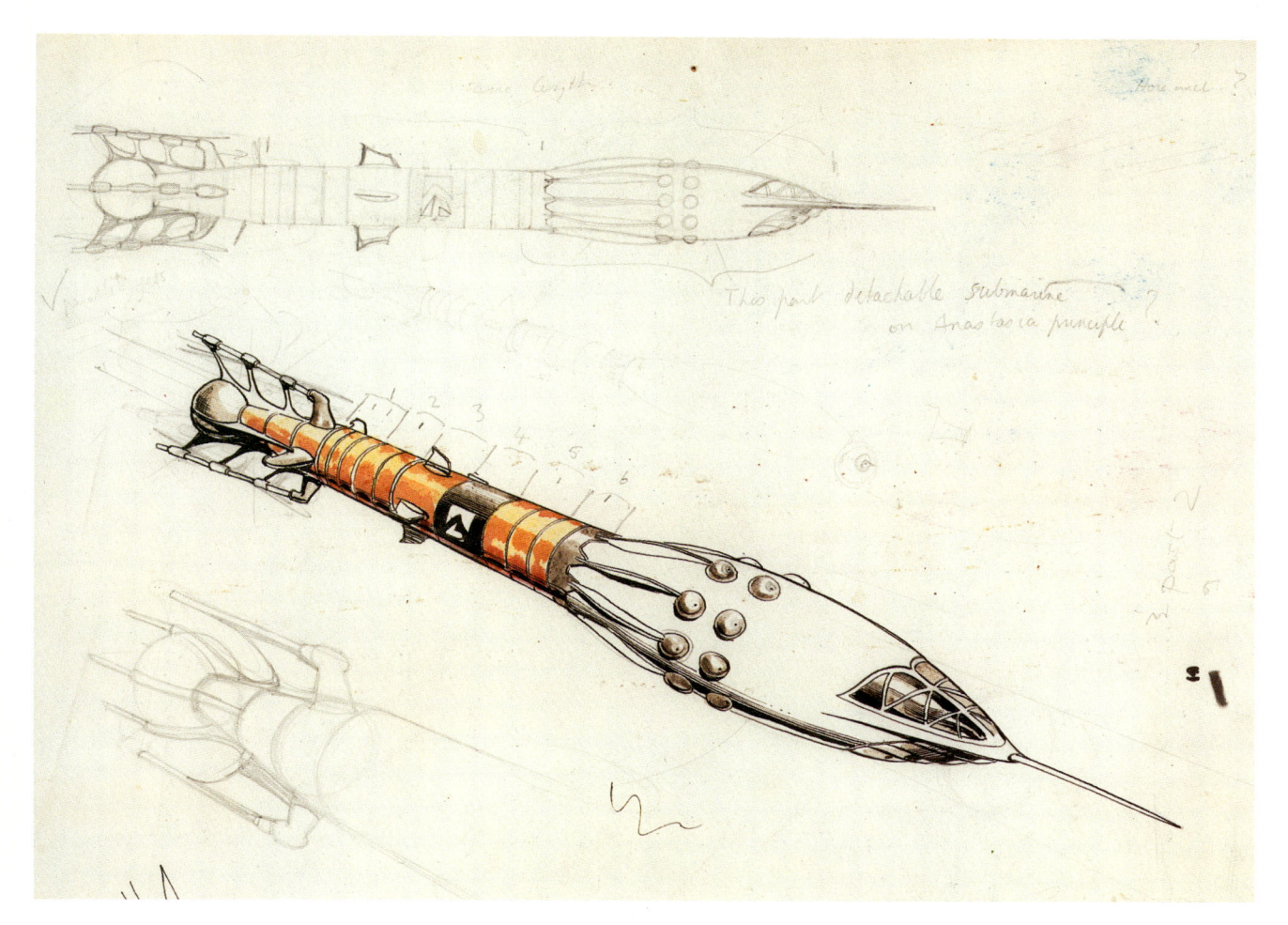

This concept sketch for an alien spacecraft, a Pescod ship from 'Phantom Fleet' (1958) demonstrates the detailed work that went into such inventions. This drawing is probably by Eric Eden produced after consultations with Hampson. The frame shows the spacecraft as they appeared in the story itself.

Visual and finished artwork for an episode from 'The Ship that Lived' (1958). This visual is unusual, being by Eric Eden, with comments by Hampson. It shows the development of the 'Space Shark' insignia, some thoughts as to the pilot position and even a check on the speed, converting Venusian Units to mph!

These pages, as nearly all the post-1954 work, were drawn 12¼″×9½″ the same size as printed in Eagle, making tremendous demands on the artists.

EARTHMEN – ONLY THE GREAT MEKONTAN VETEO - CRANES CAN DO THIS STUPENDOUS TASK.
COME! WE WILL SHOW YOU!
NTERCEPTORS
U.N.P.F.
ALLIED
ALERT
THERON
RAMPS
INDIA
PERU
W.CHINA
PLOTS
HOSTILES
WE MEET AGAIN, COLONEL DARE!
THIS IS YOUR MASTER – THE MIGHTY MEKON OF MEKONTA! HERE IS MY FINAL COMMAND – *ANY FURTHER ORDER IS TO BE IGNORED!*
DESTROY THAT SHIP!
DESTROY...
FRANK HAMPSON.

worked neither for Amalgamated or the Mirror Group. But the event caused considerable rumblings at a third publishing House, Odhams Press, who felt that they could not allow Cecil King to grow so big, without bolstering their own position in the market. The quickest way to do that, of course, was to take-over someone themselves, so a bare two months after the Mirror took over Amalgamated, Odhams and Hulton Press issued a joint statement that Odhams were making a £1,800,000 offer for the entire capital of Hulton. The Hulton family and directors held fifty-nine percent of the share capital. They announced they would accept the Odhams offer and the deal was done. So from there being five top publishing houses on that cold day in January 1959, when the Cudlipps left for the Kremlin, there were now, a brief four months later, only three; The Mirror Group, Odhams Press and George Newnes. Soon there were to be only two, and a short while after that only one, but these two takeovers still lay in the future.

Why did Sir Edward Hulton make no effort to keep his business; what made him sell out so easily? Hulton Press it seems had been tottering between profit and loss since early 1957 – just two years after the group had felt rich enough to build its own Fleet Street office block. Television had arrived, in particular the burgeoning Independent Companies and the whole magazine world was feeling the pinch. The general-interest magazines in particular were fighting a losing battle and these included *John Bull, Illustrated,* and two of Hulton's top money-spinners, *Picture Post* and *Lilliput*. Sir Thomas Hopkinson argues in his book that it was bad editorial direction that killed *Picture Post* and not BBC and ITV. But since he had been ordered by Sir Edward Hulton to relinquish his editorial command to the worried peer, this stance is hardly surprising; independent observers agree that there was little any of the publishing houses could do in the face of the many news and current affairs programmes.

In their last financial year the Hulton Press had not paid their shareholders a penny in dividends. The Hulton family decided the fight against television was lost and they'd better get out while the going was good, and at £1,800,000 the going was quite good enough. Frank and Marcus however couldn't get out, and were soon to discover that Odhams women's magazines were also feeling the competition. Dan Dare's creator in Epsom and Eagle's Editor in London both began to wonder how the going would be for them.

From 'Reign of the Robots' and 'The Ship that Lived' 1957/1958 reproduced from original artwork.

Top left *Two lizard faced Treens demonstrate the importance Hampson gave to the lighting within each frame.*

Top right and Middle *The Mekon – cold merciless ruler of the Treens of Northern Venus.*

Left *Two Treen Fighters taking off from Mekonta, capital of Treenland. Reproduced the same size as it was drawn, it displays the fine line work and depth that went into each frame.*

BEWARE TREENS

On his good days Frank could turn a pretty phrase and once, at work in the Bakery, he heard the footsteps of Marcus and Chad Varah at the door. 'Ey-oop', he said turning to the others, "Ware Treens!' It felt like that to him when Odhams took over Hulton and Eagle for the new owners had little sympathy for the philosophy behind the comic; Marcus believes they neither understood it nor wished to understand it. They had their own ideas about how juvenile publications were produced and the ex-Hulton papers would soon fall in line. One of the points of difference was the Odhams men believed in action, pace and variety, energetic layouts – for energetic read messy says Eric Eden – and plenty of wham, bam, powie. However, they were astute enough to know they had a good thing in Dan Dare, though, says Keith Watson, they had little idea why. 'They couldn't see the difference between a page of Frank's artwork and artwork for any other Eagle strip but they could see Frank's pages cost a lot more and decided it wouldn't stay that way for long.'

Then suddenly it seemed this expensive strip was going to pay them handsomely when they were approached by a film company who wanted to bring Dan Dare to the screen. I am told the plan was to make a cinemascope movie to be directed by Lindsay Anderson, a brave project since these were days long before the blockbusters like *Star Wars*.

In 1958 the moguls believed no-one could make a successful space film for it was impossible to get the hardware authentic and the aliens and monsters looked exactly what they were, models and actors dressed in nasty costumes and grotesquely made-up. Even Kubrick's renowned 2001 space odyssey never made money, no matter what cult following it picked up, indeed cinemagoers put out-of-this-world films a long way down their list of movies they must see.

Today the film rights to Dan Dare are owned by Phenomenal Films who have registered offices in Portland Place and have issued 100 shares, 55 of which are owned by Mr Paul de Savary, the other 45 by Societe Cinematographique de Financement et d'Inventissement with registered offices in Panama. There are two directors, Mr de Savary himself and Mrs A de Savary who is also company secretary. Paul de Savary has tried several times to film Dan Dare promising big-name stars and even bigger budgets but these films have never come to fruition. The nearest he got was in 1980, when together with Lew Grade of ATV and production company Lee Lacy he began work on a thirteen-part TV series. Shooting was due to begin at Elstree the third week in January 1981 and there was talk of using big names, especially to write the music. You may think the music in Dan Dare is hardly important but the kind of series producer Leon Clifton had in mind made it very important. There were even plans at one stage to produce rough storylines and not write dialogue until the music had been composed and recorded. But Lew Grade, who'd just burned his fingers on several disastrous films, including *Raise the Titanic* which lost £26.4 millions, pulled out and the TV Dare was postponed. The single common factor to these attempts, aside from the fact that none of them has come off, is that Frank has never been offered the chance to make money out of them, the nearest he has been involved is as a 'technical consultant' who may or may not get his name somewhere in the credits. This is despite the fact that Phenomenal Films not only want to use his characters but was even prepared to use part of his scripts, altering them only where they might have dated, or could include love interest. One name bandied about as writer of Dan Dare films is Phil Redmond creator of the TV series *Grange Hill*.

Keith Watson in 1959.

Robert 'Pop' Hampson, Don Harley and Frank Hampson.

"DAN & DONANZA" — WORKING ROUGH FOR ALTERNATIVE VIEW OF ROTORSHIP I CONTROL ROOM — TAKE OFF SEQUENCE

A detailed preparatory pencil drawing by Eric Eden, produced for a strip that was published in the 1953 Dan Dare Spacebook.

It seems that there was some care taken to see that stories of this 1958 film attempt were kept away from Frank, certainly Don Harley never heard of them. However the subterfuge failed and it takes little imagination to picture Frank's reaction especially, as we shall see, since Frank had harboured plans to film Dan Dare himself and had a number of other schemes at the back of his mind to turn Dan into an even greater money-spinner. He now says it was partly to expedite the commercial exploitation of his hero that he set up his studio system in the first place. When stories of the film project filtered back to him he began to bombard Odhams with his own ideas. He emphasised the immense potential of Dare and the many ways he could be used not just to pay for the studio but also to be a fresh source of income to the publishers. He also left them in no doubt about the unfairness of the way he, as originator and developer was now being treated. The point is, of course, that Odhams were under no compulsion to pay heed to Frank at all, in law they could do with Dare what they liked and what they liked was to let the film company worry about whether Frank was to make anything.

It ought to be said that as publishers Odhams had no experience of and no interest in film making, decided it was a risky business (which everyone around was assuring them it was) and all they wanted to do was sign the necessary contracts and be done with it.

Frank was in a miserable dilemma. He had lost all his authority over Eagle, he no longer had Marcus as friend and spokesman in the boardroom since the whole Hulton board had disappeared. Moreover Marcus was fighting to keep Eagle intact, and keep his job as editor and looked unlikely to win either battle. It is something of a mystery as to why Odhams thought the Hulton comics had to change for they were by far the strongest papers left in the Hulton empire but there was a general feeling about that they had been run by amateurs and it was time for the professionals to show how things should be done. First and foremost Odhams were looking for economies and Frank's studio was clearly one place to find them. No matter that it had been running for nine years and had served Hulton well, Hulton no longer existed so past services counted for nothing. It is ironic that in the very early days some Hulton staffers actually believed things would improve since, they whispered, they'd got rid of Hulton's wife and her maurauding ways. In fact the opposite happened and from being editor-in-chief of so many publications Marcus now found himself being given less and less to do. To the professional comic-makers he was still regarded as a vicar and vicars have no place in Fleet Street, Odhams were convinced that they could produce better material for children than he and his men had ever devised.

The Dan Dare film looked certain to go ahead, and Frank was to get nothing. It had a bad effect on his health. At last, feeling friendless, helpless and hopeless, miserable that others were to harvest the profits of his work and depressed at the injustice of the thing, he decided to give up the comic strip. If he couldn't have Dare completely, he didn't want him at all, and had no intention of continuing to work the way he had been, while others enjoyed the rewards. To avoid the inevitable suffering the film must bring, he decided to cut himself completely free.

But Dan Dare had to continue, even if Frank wouldn't draw him and the artist had to recommend a successor. If justice had been done, care of the strip would have passed to Donald Harley who had done years of sterling work with Frank, taken control of the strip on many occasions, especially when, for a number of reasons, Frank had been forced to rest, and was the man Frank acknowledged to be 'the second best Dan Dare artist in the world'. It may be that Don didn't want the job; it's more likely that Frank thought if the strip was to leave his hands then it would be seen to have left his hands and Don Harley's work was too similar to Frank's own for that to be immediately obvious. Whatever the reason, Don Harley was passed over in favour of another Eagle artist who Frank admired, although the man had never tried his hand at the Dare pages. This was Frank Bellamy, who for some time had produced striking and distinctive artwork for the lives-of-famous-men series on Eagle's back cover. Frank recommended to Marcus and Clifford Makins (assistant editor) that Bellamy should take over where he left off. Bellamy agreed, and it was further decided that some of the artists currently working in Bayford Lodge, in particular Harley and Keith Watson, should move to premises in London, taking as much of the reference material as they thought they required. As far as I can tell, Frank believed that his slow and expensive (but effective) way of working, from preliminary sketches and posed photographs, was to be continued, but Bellamy had no use for such production methods; not that he was against them, he simply couldn't see why they were necessary.

With Frank Bellamy in charge, but working for the most part in his studio at home, Harley and Watson were more-or-less dumped in a disused canteen in an Odhams owned building. Don and Keith tried for a time to work Frank's way, but got no support from the bosses. It seems they couldn't wait to disband the Dan Dare studio and alter the strip as completely as they could whilst still keeping the characters (barely) recognisable. Everything was to be changed; the uniforms, hardware, weapons, the style of drawing and the pace of the story. Some of this may have been to give Frank Bellamy a free hand, but there were certainly men at Odhams who believed Hampson's stories were slow, his artwork 'cardboard', his characters beginning to date and that a general dullness had come over the work which readers were beginning to notice and would come to reject. Anyway, it was these 'defects' Bellamy was expected to put right, and would he please produce his first week's work as quickly as possible so the editors could see how this would be brought about. (Just for the record, this change-over took place during a long printing strike, so the last page of Dan Dare Frank Hampson ever drew, appeared in an Eagle without a date.) Bellamy got to work, and to everyone's consternation, presented his first front page in which the leading character in the main frame (Dan) was virtually unrecognisable. When Bellamy left the meeting, his work was passed quickly to Don Harley who was asked to re-draw the frame to make the space colonel himself again. So the artwork Bellamy had spent painful hours producing to the brief he thought he had been given was altered back to something approaching Hampson's style; when Bellamy saw the changes he was devastated.

Working this way left everyone dissatisfied. Bellamy wasn't being allowed to do his thing, Don and Keith weren't doing Frank's thing and the editors weren't getting what they thought they wanted. There was distress all round. Keith Watson went back to Frank in Bayford Lodge to explain the situation and see whether he could bring any influence to bear. In particular, Keith was dismayed that the studio method of working was being so quickly and completely dismantled. Frank was upset but also determined to distance himself from what was happening; if Odhams wanted to destroy the Hampson Dare then they could do it without his help. He had asked to come off the project to take a rest from the treadmill, be free of the chagrin of the film farce, of the alien ideas Odhams wanted to bring into the strip, indeed of the whole Odhams philosophy of comics. The idea of writing and drawing to the highest level of intelligence and expecting the readers to rise to that, instead of settling for some lower common denominator, made no sense to them.

Finally, Bellamy settled into drawing Dan Dare his way, and it has to be said, that some thought it was a very good way. In the *World Encyclopedia of Comics* for example, the piece of artwork that shows the intrepid space-pilot is from Bellamy's hand, not Frank Hampson's. It

OUCH! LEGGO!

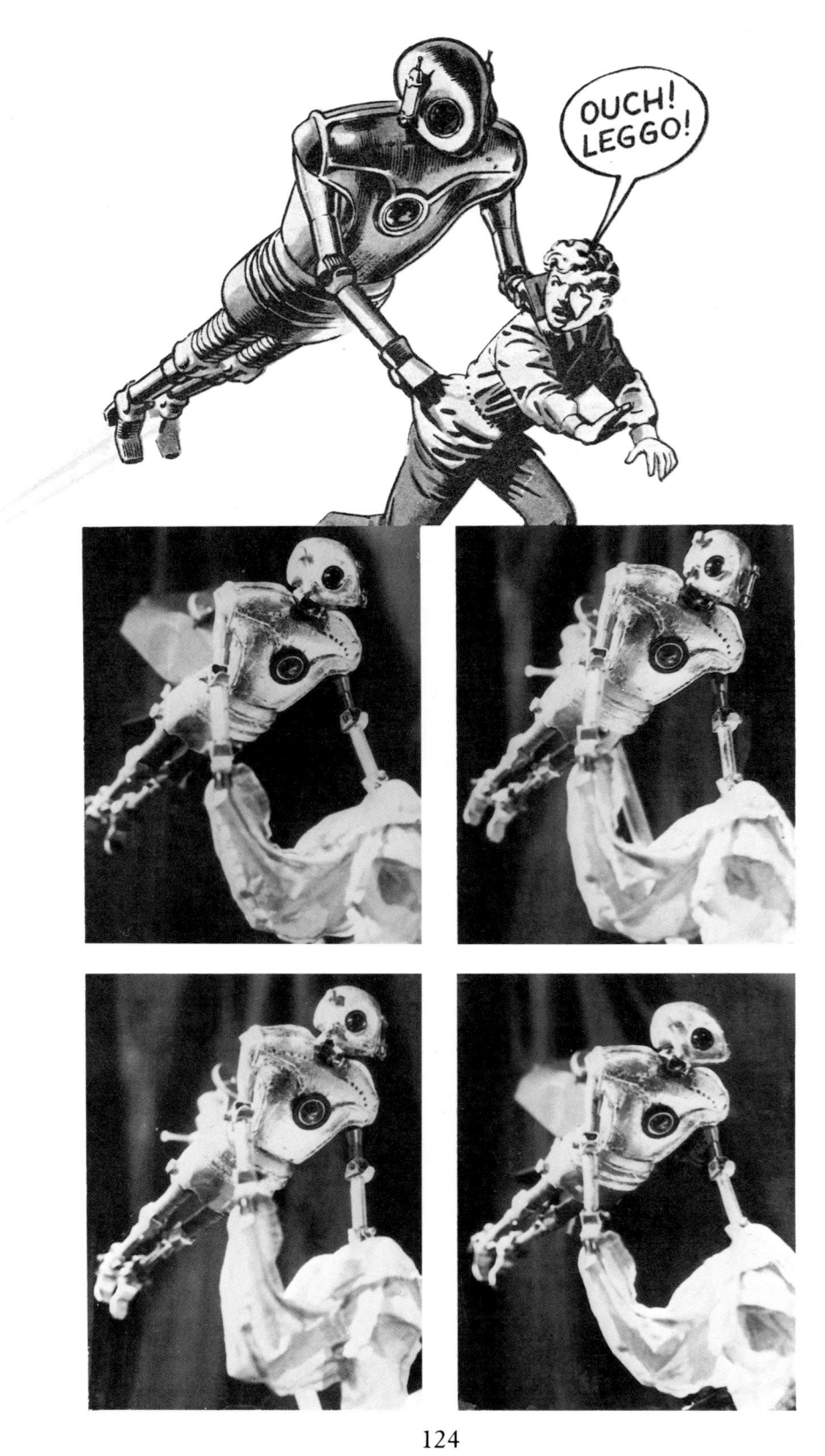

seems a strange choice since it was Frank who created the strip and it was an Englishman, Denis Gifford who compiled the British entries for the *World Encyclopedia* (although the book is published by a Frenchman) and Gifford could not offer the excuse that he didn't know of Frank Hampson. It is misrepresentations like this (however unintentional) that have made Frank believe there are many ways in which he has been denied recognition for his work; not that he doesn't have a fulsome entry in the *World Encyclopedia* under his own name; shame though that they couldn't have been sure to use his pictures. It's also true that Bellamy artwork, not only for Dare, but many of the other strips he produced (Frazer of Africa, The Happy Warrior, Marco Polo) sells very nicely thankyou in the little side shops in London where you can procure such things, and the price has gone up since the artist died. His wife was advertising it in *Exchange & Mart* at the end of 1984 for £250 a page.

Frank (Hampson) did not much like what Ballamy did to his heroes, although there were artists to follow who did worse – and, according to the purists, better – because Bellamy threw away Frank's ideas about the importance of continuity, character definition and pictorial sub-plot. Of his time drawing Dan Dare Frank Bellamy has said 'I only agreed to draw Dan Dare for one year. I didn't like revamping Frank Hampson's characters, his creations, but had the directive from upstairs – that's what they wanted, and you can only give the client what he wants, so that was it'. There was nothing Frank Hampson could do about it, and he probably waged a hard inner fight to remain indifferent to the changes that were quickly but inexorably coming about.

Having finally cut himself free, Frank's pressing problem was to decide what he should do next. He is quite adamant that he will not speak of this time since it brings back memories too unpleasant – and possibly even disturbing – to contemplate. There is an idea that any rehearsing of this part of his past may result in a recurrence of the black dog depression that has haunted him for many years, leading to the need for medicine to regain his equilibrium. Keith Watson, who called on Frank on several occasions, remembers that he set to producing a series of new strips, one or more of which he hoped would be developed into a full length story. They included one based on a first world war ace, the opening episode of which showed a dog-fight between the hero and a Red-Baron-type character, which is witnessed by two observers in a balloon. Every piece of the wicker basket under the balloon was drawn-in, complete with all the correct shadows. 'The work was incredible' says Keith, 'Frank at his best. If only someone would use him now there would be great strip cartoons still to come.' Another of Frank's ideas was to have as hero, a boy who worked in a travel agency, which meant Frank could use the whole world as his venue and create stories in any place, featuring any race of people, and building into the plot wonders like the pyramids, the Taj Mahal, wild beasts, rain forests, electric storms where planes were in danger of being felled by lightning, hurricanes at sea, the lot. It allowed so much more scope than, say, a cowboy strip, or a historical piece where travel is limited and the action becomes predictable. How many of these new strips Frank began is not certain; rumours vary from two to half a dozen (although that many is unlikely). But, so the tale goes, all of them had rough storylines and highly finished pages of the first instalment.

Whether Odhams wouldn't accept these stories, whether Frank was unhappy with them or whether he insisted on assistance before agreeing to go ahead, I haven't been able to discover, but Frank then embarked on what he was later to say was his life-time's ambition, a strip cartoon version of the life of Christ. To prepare himself for this, he asked his employers to

Left *Model of an 'Elektrobot' in flight. 'Reign of the Robots', (1958).*

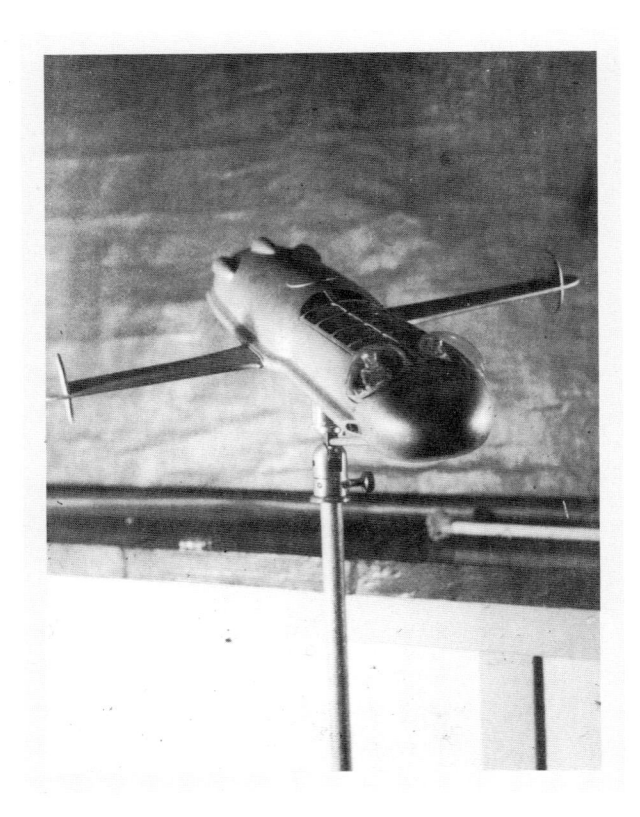

A model of Dan Dare's personal spacecraft 'Anastasia' set on a tripod for a series of reference photographs, shown here with an illustration of 'Annie' from the strip.

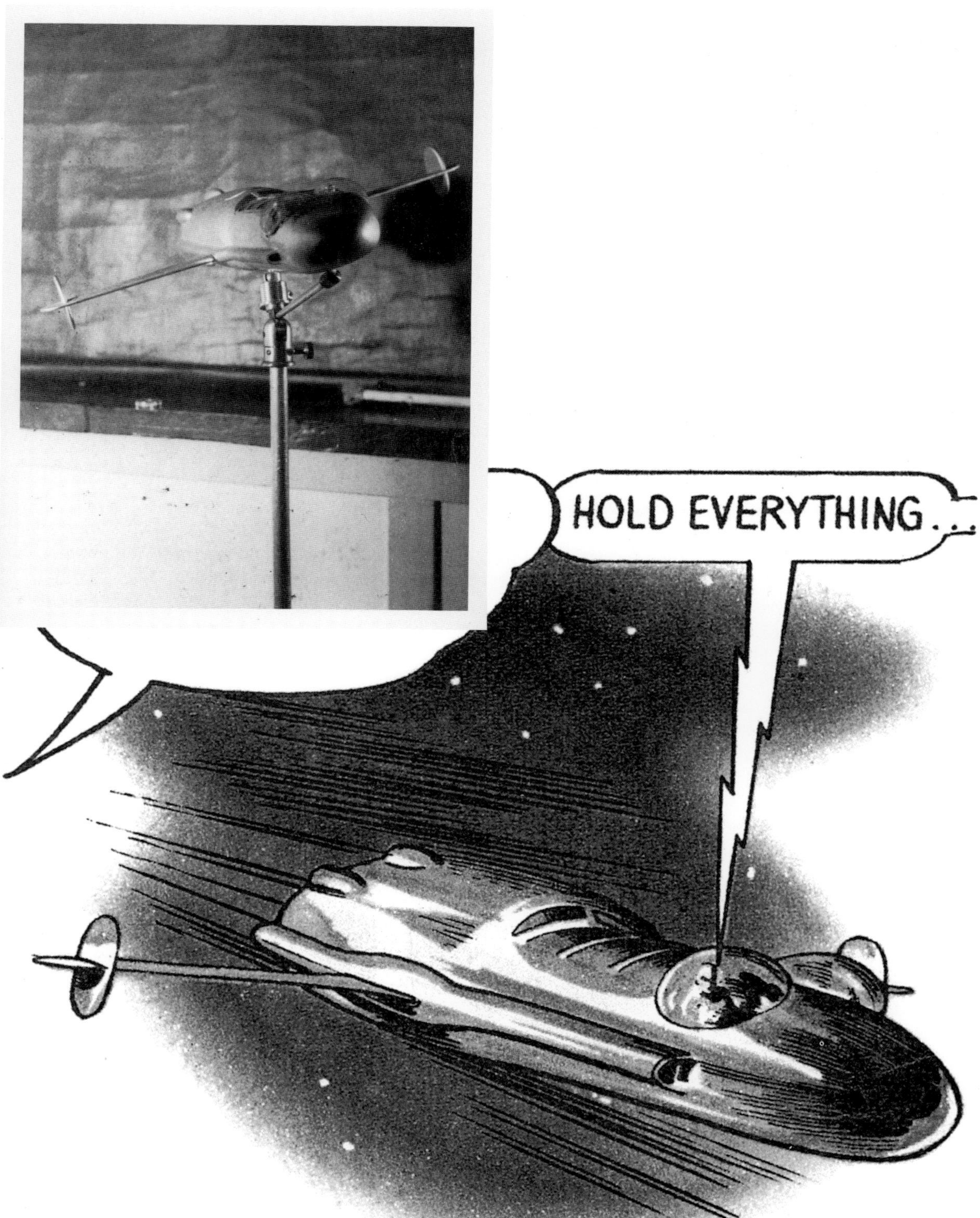
HOLD EVERYTHING...

send him on a trip to the holy land, a request which they granted, agreeing also to pay his expenses. It's been reported that Clifford Makins was overheard in a lift saying that, as far as he was concerned, Frank needn't bother to come back. Frank wasn't the only one to be facing problems; Marcus too was unhappy and in the mood to call it a day. He, however, was to have one of those strokes of good fortune which, it seems, he has enjoyed through much of his life. Here is how he tells the story.

'Towards the end of the fifties was the time of the great press take-overs and Hulton, having closed *Picture Post*, decided they would sell out. And they sold to what was then Odhams Press, who became our new masters. I felt they didn't really understand what we were trying to do. But it so happened that out of the blue at that time, I was approached by the man who was my predecessor at the National Magazine Company, and asked whether I would join him with a view to taking over as managing director. He was looking for a successor. So, as I say, quite out of the blue – I wasn't looking around, or thinking of going anywhere else at all – I had this very good offer. I decided to take it. I had been running Eagle for ten years and thought perhaps it was time for a change. And since I had the opportunity, I left at the end of 1959.'

In 1964, Marcus became managing director and editor-in-chief at the National Magazine Company, which produces publications like *Cosmopolitan* and *She*, all of them hugely successful and long-running. In fact, National Magazine is the single example of William Randolph Hearst's excursion into British publishing, and there's little of the yellow press about it. From this point on, Marcus had little to do with Frank Hampson, although if the credits are to be believed, he and Marcus collaborated on Frank's *chef d'oueuvre*, the 'Road of Courage'. This appeared on the back page of Eagle after Marcus had left so it's plain that Odhams were happy enough to cash in on the fact that 'The Vicar' still appeared to be working for the company.

Keith Watson, too, had had enough of working for Odhams, under conditions wildly different from the days when he first joined the studio; saddened at the new way of producing Dan Dare and the lack of understanding as to what constituted a well-drawn page, he went to the new editor, Clifford Makins and handed in his resignation. His leaving, far from being treated with any show of disappointment, was accepted almost with contempt, Makins suggesting that the goodbye letter was timely enough and had it not arrived when it did Keith would shortly have been dismissed anyway. Makins, says Keith, told the Eagle staffers after the takeover, that now Odhams were masters, there would be no 'sentiment'; more to the point, there was considerable resentment and bad feeling generated and scant respect for the artists who had worked loyally for the comics for years. One of them, who asked to be taken off his current strip, and had found two other artists, equally capable, and willing to take his place, was told when he asked for this transfer, to leave, and expect no more work from any of the Odhams publications, ever again. Eric Eden and Don Harley also left the company, believing (wrongly as it happened) that they had seen the last of their days on Dan Dare.

Odhams' take-over of Hulton was only the first of their moves to expand. They intervened in a bid made by the *News of the World*, to buy George Newnes and Company. The *News of the World* bid did not come as a pleasant one to Newnes and through a tip on the 'old boy network', Newnes told Odhams that they would be interested in a deal. Odhams, after some short negotiations, offered a total of £13 millions for the rival publisher, and the shareholders were delighted although there were a few City-watchers who believed the offer to be too high. In the event, they were proved wrong, Odhams had made a shrewd calculation of what Newnes were worth and the deal was wrapped up in May 1959. The five major firms which

> THE VENUSIANS, WHO CALL THEMSELVES 'TREENS,' HAVE PROMISED THAT THE SURVIVORS OF THE DARE EXPEDITION — SIR HUBERT GUEST, PROFESSOR PEABODY AND SPACEMAN DIGBY, WILL BE RETURNED AS SOON AS THEY RECOVER FROM THE INJURIES THEY RECEIVED WHEN THEY LANDED ON VENUS.

> REASSURING MESSAGES RECORDED IN THEIR OWN VOICES BY THESE SURVIVORS WERE BROUGHT BY THE TREENS. NOW HERE IS A TELEREEL OF THE TREEN ENVOY ARRIVING AT THE SPACE FLEET H.Q. IN LONDON AN IMPORTANT STATEMENT IS EXPECTED LATE TONIGHT OR EARLY TOMORROW

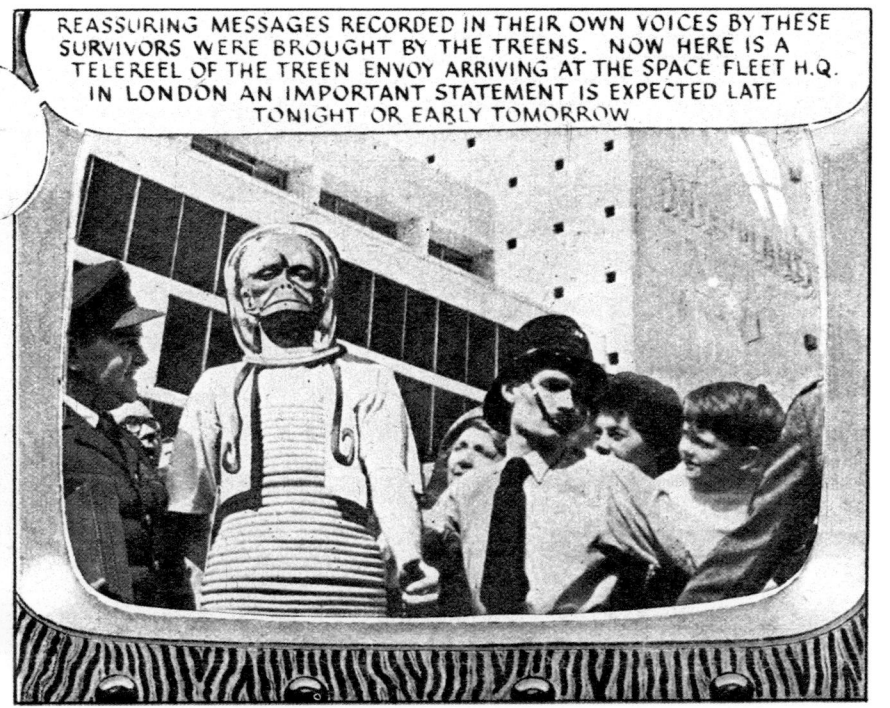

Another 'first' for Hampson – the use of photographs in the strip. Greta Tomlinson posing as the newsreader (Dan Dare had it first even with female TV newsreaders!)

To ensure accuracy and continuity in the strip a full scale model of Space Fleet Headquarters was built which was then photographed, retouched and numbered to identify the locations.

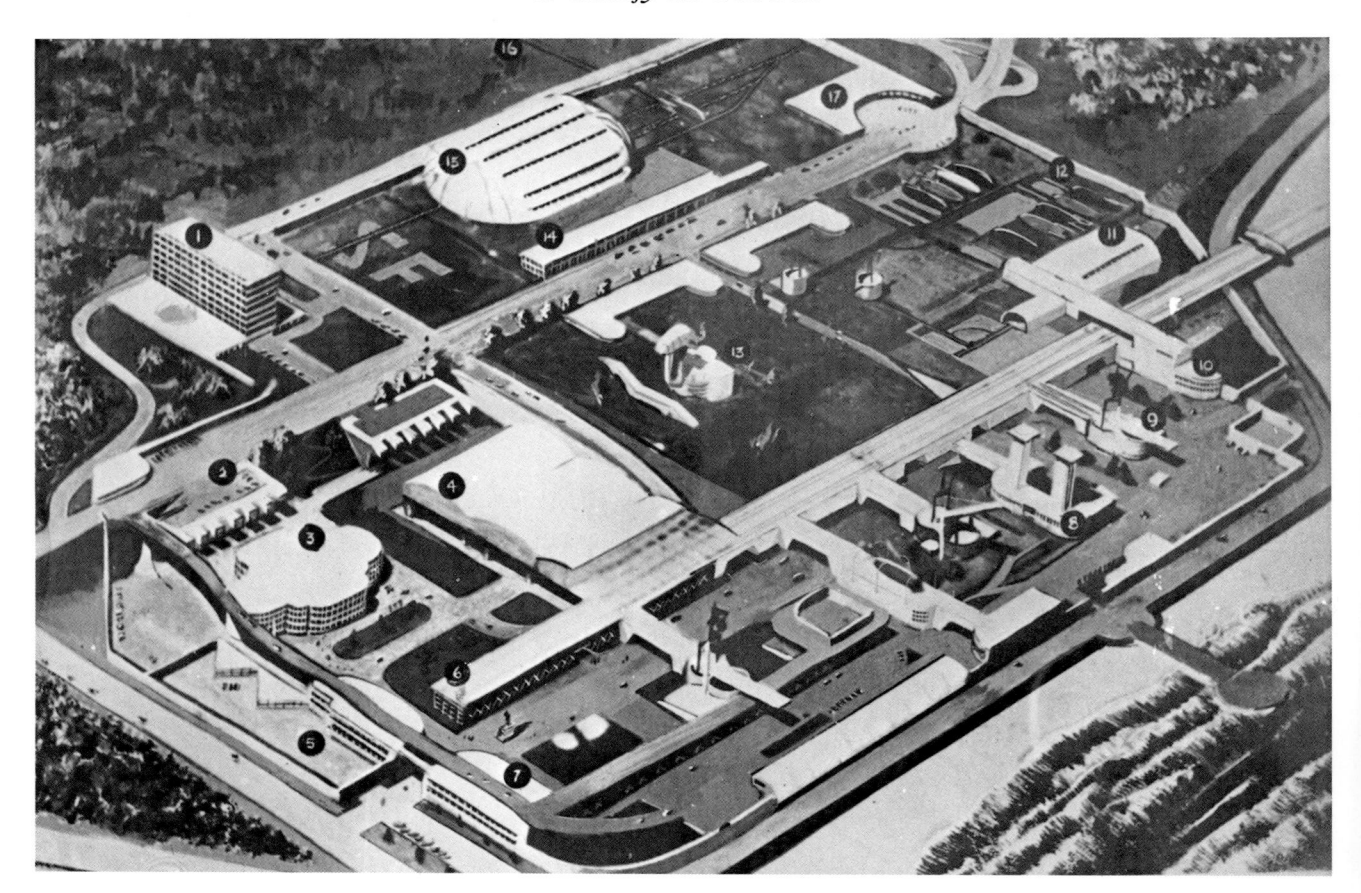

had previously divided magazine publishing between them were now reduced to two in number, all as a result of the Mirror's bid for Amalgamated Press.

In his Bayford Lodge studio, Frank was now virtually on his own, his one remaining helper, Joan Porter the only artist not to leave with Dan Dare. He busied himself with preparations for the trip to Israel. The script for the Road of Courage, which Frank had intended to put together with Marcus, was not finished when Frank left. Undeterred, he toured the holy land, taking photographs, researching in the libraries and museums, and even buying some clothing to help him get the costumes of the area accurate. In the early days, when Frank was drawing the life of St Paul, he had sent Eric Eden to London (from Southport, not Epsom, a much longer journey) to visit the Science Museum in South Kensington and find out what kind of boat St Paul was likely to travel in when he left Palestine on his trip to Rome. Eden spent the whole day there making sketches and notes of reference so Frank could get the ship authentic even though it was only to appear in a few frames. Now that this new story was to be based in Palestine during the Roman occupation, Frank was determined to get every detail right. He followed up his overseas research with more research back home, checking the Roman legion uniforms and weapons of the time, and getting the geography and time scale of the story fixed in his mind. He took special care searching out faces; photographs and paintings of people whose features were almost definitive of a type. For the Road of Courage, he decided he would draw the same size as the comic reproduced; this helped to save time with the colouring and Frank now had only one helper to do that. Finally, with the story mapped out, and all the material he needed on his desk, in his head, hung on tailors dummies or arranged on his bookshelves, and with Joan Porter to assist with the colour work, organise the photography, make the costumes and do the additional research that would be needed, Frank began to draw the last great strip he was to produce for Eagle, or for any other comic or publisher he would ever work for.

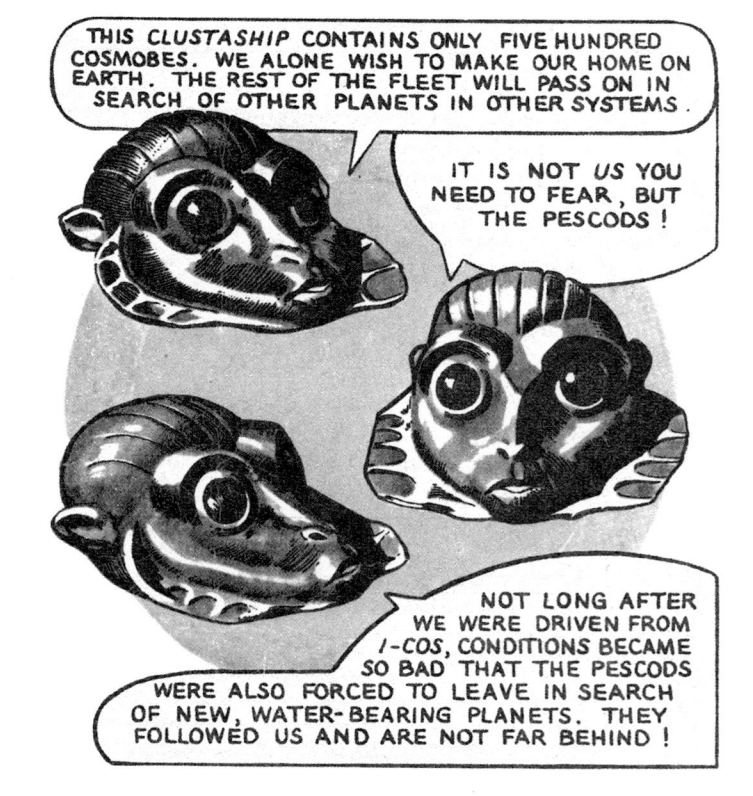

> THIS *CLUSTASHIP* CONTAINS ONLY FIVE HUNDRED COSMOBES. WE ALONE WISH TO MAKE OUR HOME ON EARTH. THE REST OF THE FLEET WILL PASS ON IN SEARCH OF OTHER PLANETS IN OTHER SYSTEMS.

> IT IS NOT *US* YOU NEED TO FEAR, BUT THE PESCODS!

> NOT LONG AFTER WE WERE DRIVEN FROM *I-COS*, CONDITIONS BECAME SO BAD THAT THE PESCODS WERE ALSO FORCED TO LEAVE IN SEARCH OF NEW, WATER-BEARING PLANETS. THEY FOLLOWED US AND ARE NOT FAR BEHIND!

THE LAST GREAT STRIP AND THE LAST GOOD OFFER

The crimson-cloaked centurion urges his white charger through the market place and a gold-earringed Ethiopian slave reels away from the hooves. A Greek drinking wine at the roadside turns and scowls at the shouted command: 'In the name of Caesar, make way!' Shoppers round the grape-hung stalls look up in resentment, a hawker with fresh-killed hares slung on a pole over his shoulders sneers at overweening authority and running ahead of the legionary, a rascally ten year old chuckles at the furore. Altogether there are twenty-six people crammed into the frame, the very first in Frank's version of the life of Christ, titled 'The Road of Courage', a title that might well have something to do with the road the artist thought *he* had travelled.

The strip, all fifty-six episodes of it, is an enthralling study of *types*. Jesus himself is one of the beautiful people, blonde haired, blonde bearded and with an (almost) permanent half smile on his face; to my mind the least successful of Frank's creations. But powerful faces confront you out of the pages; Herod with every black and angry eyebrow meticulously inked in; curly-headed John the Baptist with his heavily furrowed forehead and Lex O'Malley-type beard; Varus, the Syrian Governor, with aquiline nose and golden locks, popping a grape into his thin-lipped mouth as he promises the Jews a lesson they'll never forget. Frank made Caiaphas bony and sensual, with burnt-sienna eyes, coiffeured hair and beard, and caught the cunning and intelligence of the man, feeling his way on the political tightrope between Jew and Roman and quite clearly up to the job. Not once did Frank strike any note of anti-semitism; there are no evil men on the road of courage, just anxious ones buffeted by the stresses of the time, doing their best as they saw it.

This is the strip where Frank takes the opportunity to do his own versions of some of the great classical paintings, the last supper, throwing the money-lenders out of the temple, Christ entering Jerusalem on an ass, the agony in the garden, and Jesus carrying his cross to calvary. There are only two big events he hasn't painted, the nativity and the resurrection, and the former he tackled and had printed in a Christmas issue of one of the early Eagles. What comes over, especially in the de-luxe edition* of this strip is the great variety of the personalities shown, the energy of the battle scenes between the legions and the zealots and Frank's blazing colours and immense attention to detail. In one frame, the young Jesus has to say 'Doesn't the temple look wonderful?' And indeed it does; when the editors of this edition lay emphasis on the draughtsmanship, inventiveness and almost documentary authenticity that permeates the story, it isn't simply publisher's blurb.

It's not surprising that an artist with Frank's skill was approached on a number of occasions with offers of work elsewhere. For better or worse, he refused them all, and told me that the reason for his loyalty was not because he didn't like money, or wasn't flattered by the attentions of other publishers, but because of the pension deal that Sir Edward Hulton had arranged for him. It was after one of these approaches that Frank consulted the Hulton chief above a move, and was assured, hand on heart, that whatever happened, both to the knight

Left Model head of a 'Cosmobe' together with artwork from the 'Phantom Fleet' story (1958).

---

* A de-luxe edition of 'The Road of Courage' was printed, using original artwork, by Dragon's Dream in 1981. Although the page size is slightly smaller than the work appeared in Eagle, the reproduction is excellent, and readers who would like a memento of Frank's *chef d'oeuvre* are recommended to the book. Fifty-six colour pages and available in hard and soft back.

and his publishing group, Frank would be well looked after. Frank Hampson's generation is the very last to believe that men will spend the major part of their lives with just one company, and legislation has now recognised that ambitious people will move to advance themselves and their pensions should not suffer because of it. It is ironic that the most spectacular of these offers should be made to Frank at a time when he was disillusioned with his present job, and all the more surprising, therefore, that he turned it down.

The approach came after Odhams had taken over Hulton, and was in the process of taking over George Newnes, and it came from the only rival left in the field, the Mirror Group. They had a hankering to publish the kind of comic papers that proved so successful with Hulton, and to this end, produced a dummy of a new paper for boys, called *Bulldog*. An eagle, so the argument went, was in fact the symbol of the United States, whilst a bulldog was definitively British so the paper had the glowering face of the hound, grimacing, Churchill-like from the masthead. The *Bulldog* was based very much on the early 'Eagle', it was printed photogravure (or, at least, that was the intent) and the first two pages were to carry a strip as innovative and powerful as Frank's Dan Dare. There was, of course, only one artist who could create such a strip, and that was Frank himself, so the Mirror group set out to poach him. This decision had the backing of high authority at the Mirror, Hugh Cudlipp knew of Frank and his work, had an idea of the money he was being paid, and the kind of money the Mirror would have to find if they were to lure him away. There was talk too, that money might not be enough, and an account at Harrods, or a prestige car or company-bought-holiday may have to be part of the deal. (Rumour had it that Marcus had been given an account at Harrods when his stock ran high at Hulton).

The approach was made by Leonard Matthews, energetic boss of the Mirror's juvenile publications, the man who produced *Princess*, *Harold Hare* and *Buster*, and who understood better than Marcus that a young girl's heart is reached more quickly with stories of ponies and graceful ballerinas than the adventures of airline pilots like Kitty Hawke (that was Frank's view too). Frank came to London to hear the deal and there is no doubt he was willing to listen. Frank says today that his understanding with Odhams was that he should hand over his Dan Dare strip to Frank Bellamy for as long as it took to finish 'The Road of Courage' and then take the space-adventure back again. In view of what we know about the film deal, this version hardly rings true, but it is immaterial since there was no way that Odhams were going to rebuild Frank's Dan Dare group, having taken so much trouble to see it dismantled.

The idea of *Bulldog* was explained to Frank and he had a chance to inspect the dummy, which had been prepared by artists in Leonard Matthews' department. He was assured that the Mirror was serious in its intent to launch, and was invited to take artistic charge of the paper, on the promise that he would be given virtually a free hand. Getting round to the salary they were prepared to offer was a delicate business. 'If we'd told Frank he could write his own cheque who knows what he – or anyone in that position – would have asked for. And at the same time, he would probably have become suspicious; was this danger-money, or what? But Hugh Cudlipp wanted him and was prepared to be generous, so it was decided to take his existing salary of £3,500, and double it.' It must be said that part of this generosity was in anticipation of the press reports that would appear about how the creator of Eagle, at present, the leading Odhams comic, was now to head up a totally new – and better – Mirror comic.

Frank explained to the Mirror that he would like time to think but since he was not definitely against the idea, Cudlipp was led to understand that Frank was interested. Meanwhile, the news of Frank's proposed £7,000 a year, reached the higher echelons of The Mirror. It was a heck of a salary just for taking charge of a comic; more to the point, it was a

Eric Eden, Harold Johns and Robert Hampson take aim to save Dan Dare from the Treens in the first Dan Dare story, 1950.

AMBROSE

PETER ROCK.

FRANK HAMPSON

higher salary than many directors were getting themselves, for looking after magazines with higher circulations, and earning greater profits than *Bulldog* was ever likely to pull in. Leonard Matthews was under pressure, even though the salary had been approved by Cudlipp. 'And,' says Matthews, 'if it was more than my directors were getting, how much more do you think it was than *I* was getting?' When it became clear Frank was dragging his heels, Hugh Cudlipp demanded to speak to the artist face to face. 'What is it you want?' asked the editorial director; 'You name it and you can have it.' It was an invitation for Frank to write his own cheque. Frank wanted the money, the recognition and the prestige the job would undoubtedly bring. *But he didn't want to draw*. If he was to be in charge of *Bulldog*, he would supervise overall policy and set and maintain standards and direction but he wanted to leave the penmanship to the artists he would recruit under him. Understandably, Hugh Cudlipp would not agree; for £7,000 and as many facilities as Frank could dream up, the Mirror must have Frank's unique artwork.

On that understanding, the interview closed, and Frank retired to Epsom to think the deal over. On the one hand, he was in the middle of 'The Road of Courage', the strip he'd wanted to do all his life, and into which he had put so much effort and time. Also there was a chance that he would be able to get Dan Dare back into his charge, and once more develop the strip along lines that were already forming in his head, whether he could re-build his studio team or not. Then there was the precious pension scheme, although Leonard Matthews thinks that if Frank had brought that matter up, he could certainly have been accommodated. Then there was the devil – you – know syndrome; things hadn't got too bad at Odhams and the Mirror directors had the reputation of being a no-holds-barred operating team. Finally, there was his own state of health; could he stand ten more years working for *Bulldog* at the same pace and under the same pressures that he had worked for 'Eagle'?

Frank took his time to mull the quandary over, and his silence was of no help to Matthews. He was being ground between the millstones of Hugh Cudlipp, wanting a 'yes' decision, and the Mirror directors hoping for a 'no' decision (damn the idea of employing someone more highly paid than you are!) and his own people who had worked hard to produce the *Bulldog* dummy and didn't want to see it die. In the end, Matthews thinks, it was the ruling that Frank must draw for *Bulldog* that made him write a brief but adamant letter turning the offer down. He gave no reason, but said simply that he wanted to stay where he was, and that was his last word. Now someone had to tell Hugh Cudlipp that he couldn't have a front-page story as innovative and powerful as Dan Dare. The tricky task was done by turning *Bulldog* into a vehicle specially created for Frank Hampson, and since Frank refused to drive it, then the vehicle couldn't go. Cudlipp, by this time, had other fish to fry and let the matter rest, much to chagrin of the artists and writers who had put the original together. The strange and ironic twist to this story is, that if the Mirror men had waited slightly less than a year, they would have had Frank anyway, and had him for his existing £3,500 a year.

For in January 1961, while Frank was about two-thirds of the way through 'The Road of Courage', the Chairman of Odhams Press and Cecil King of the Mirror Group began talks of a merger. It was a sound move economically for both groups had magazines competing against each other and losing money. In the early, tentative stages, these subtle negotiations seemed to be going well, but then the Odhams people got cold feet and started to run for cover, fearing if a merger were to take place, the Odhams Board would be the poorer for it. Odhams re-opened negotiations with Roy Thomson (talks with him had begun many months ago but been allowed to peter out) and jointly they announced on television that *they* were to merge. A formal offer of a merger between the Mirror Group and Odhams was made by letter on

'Peter Rock' – *the opening episode.*

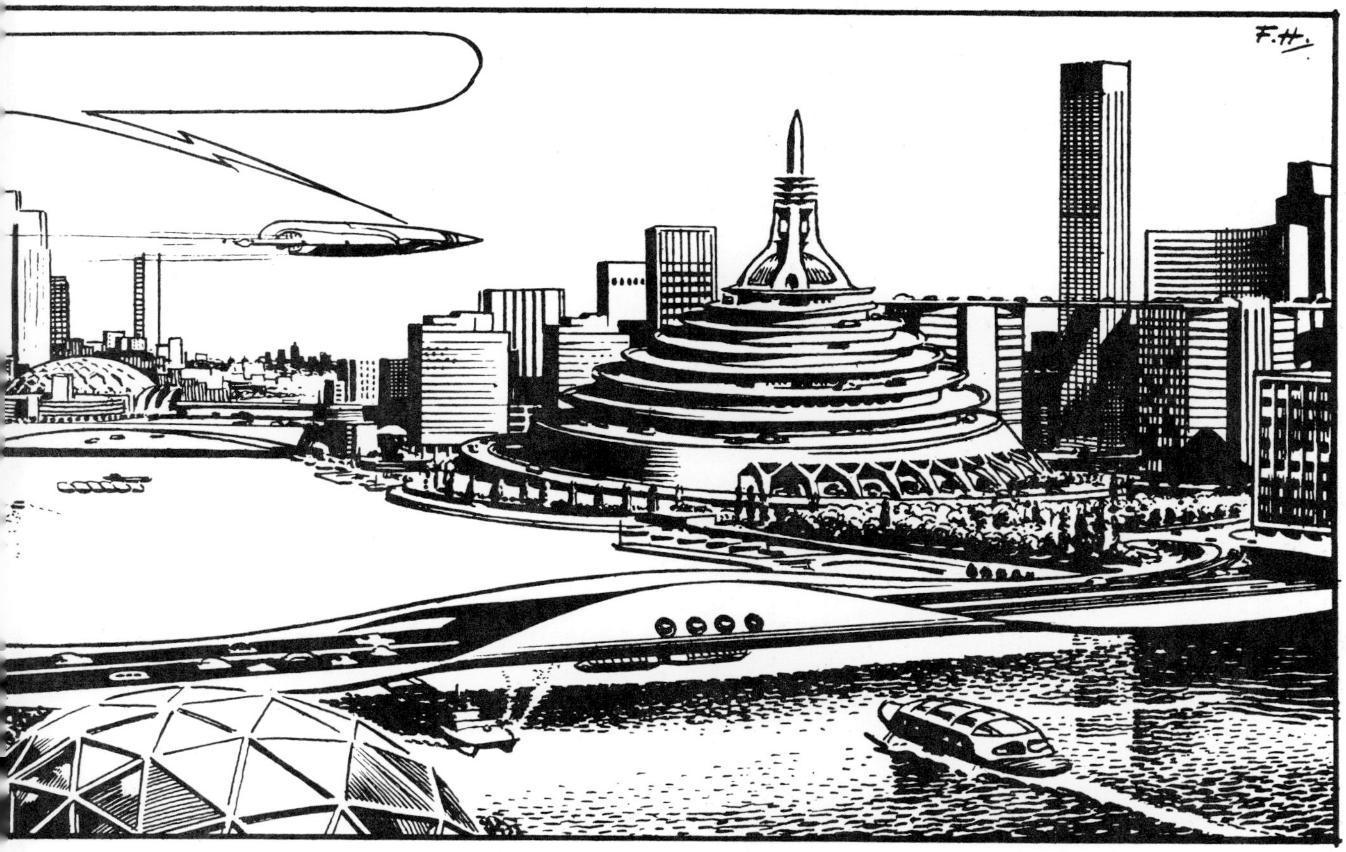
F.H.

January 27th. It was turned down by letter the following day, on the pretence that such an idea had only been glanced at and that there was really nothing serious about it. This formal, calculated snub made Cecil King declare war. As Odhams and Thomson battled to put their deal together, King began systematically, to take them both apart. It was a bloody fight, from which Roy Thomson retired and returned to Canada, leaving Odhams at the Mirror Group's mercy. King marched on regardless, cutting down the ranks of Odhams directors and shareholders mustered against him, and on 22nd March 1961, emerged victorious, announcing that over 90 per cent of the Odhams shareholders had finally accepted the Mirror offer. The Battle of Longacre was a resounding triumph for the men in Fleetway House. Frank was now owned by the Mirror Group and his 'Road of Courage' strip had three episodes left to run.

It would be quite wrong to assume that as soon as Eagle came under the Mirror umbrella, they set about altering it, or even bothered to get in touch with Frank. With his bible story now finished (and he had worked through Christmas, Easter and the Summer without a break) what he needed was a rest. Once, while he was still working on Dan Dare, he confided to Eric Eden that what he would really like to do was to create a black and white strip on his own, and Eden believes if he had taken this course, he would have finished up with a national newspaper strip 'on a level with Rip Kirby, which was the best at the time. Admittedly, we would have lost out on Dan Dare but Frank might have found the going easier, and be in better health today'. The fact is, that with the Mirror Group's bid for Odhams completed, the conglomerate owned a number of national papers, including the *Daily Mirror, Daily Record* (in Scotland), *Daily Herald,* and *Sunday Pictorial,* and it may have been with one of these papers in mind that Frank began the next step in his career.

He set about creating 'Peter Rock', which he described as a 'strip cartoon of the most superior and luxurious kind'. Translated, that meant that Frank drew it beautifully and to a purpose, and although it might contain echoes of Dan Dare, a young, handsome and intelligent hero with a bolshy and amusing assistant, together with a similarity in some of the futuristic inventions (three dimensional TV, herbal pipes and flying chairs, for example) there was a social awareness in the story which gave it a genuinely adult interest. 'Peter Rock' is in black and white, and produced in daily episodes of three-frames-a-day; to sell it to his bosses, Frank produced about three weeks' episodes and wrote the following rationale:

'The sociological aim behind this strip is to attack the colour bar by ignoring it. We present a future state in which a person's colour is immaterial. Thus, Rock's boss, Laura, is a negress, but no-one refers to the fact. It is, by implication, accepted that she is of exactly the same social standing as a white girl doing the same job. It is, by implication, also accepted that Rock should find nothing unusual about working under someone who is both coloured and female. The same thing applies, of course, to all the other characters in the story. The action takes place in the future (Frank dated the opening episode in the year 2,000 AD) but on Earth. It is not concerned with space ships and planetary monsters but with daily life. Ambrose, Rock's friend, and assistant, is in a constant ferment against status-seekers. He should reflect the factory-floor attitude.

'Laura, Rock and Ambrose all work for a UN Department of scientific investigation and "trouble-shooters". (Alternatively, it could be a private firm in the same capacity.) As a suggested opening situation, it is assumed that at this period, the Earth's weather has been brought under control, and that agriculture of all kinds is therefore based on a rigid schedule of weather, arranged to suit intensive cultivation of various products, all over the world. Deliberate and malignant interference with these schedules could cause untold havoc to

One of the 'Bovril' advertisement strips drawn by Frank Hampson in 1962.

agriculture, and, if pursued on a larger scale, result in the artificial creation of "natural" disasters. First indications of such interference are the cause of Rock and Ambrose being hastily summoned to HQ in the specimen opening drawings.'

Several points can be made: first the venue was world-wide, so, as with the boy-in-the-travel-agency idea, Frank had the globe in which to set his tales; the adventures took place on Earth and were about 'every-day life', much more interesting from a sociological viewpoint than flitting about the galaxy; the strip dealt with natural disasters, a sure-fire way (as every editor knows) of attracting readership; and it featured Ambrose, a working class chap, which is what the readers of the newspapers in the Mirror stable undoubtedly were. As we know, 'Peter Rock' never appeared. In fact, after Frank sent the strip to his bosses, he did not see the artwork again for twenty years. It was actually rescued by an ex-Odhams employee, who passed it to a friend who was a Frank Hampson addict, who returned it to the artist at a meeting they had in 1980.

The question is, why? It was the kind of work-load Frank could easily have coped with. It was very well drawn and there was nothing like it appearing anywhere else. Frank had a track record which would have ensured him a following in any newspaper, comic strips are an important part of a paper's way of boosting and holding circulation. The strip had a 'message' and the *Daily Mirror*, the most vivid and the largest circulation daily of the time clearly had the option of running it, as did the *Sunday Pictorial*, which under Cudlipp's editorship (although Cudlipp was now Chairman of Odhams) was always happy to run a crusade, especially if it was sugar-coated in comic strip form. Frank had already met Cudlipp (although in circumstances which would not have made a second meeting easy) and he may well have considered contacting the Chairman again. Instead, it appears he had to deal with minions, and boorish, unsympathetic minions at that. He spoke to me of telephone calls between himself and head office when he was told that parts of his artwork were unacceptable and would have to be re-drawn. This kind of treatment, from people who had probably never illustrated anything in their lives, was more than Frank, never a patient soul, would tolerate.

Eric Eden says Frank was never able to negotiate his way through Fleet Street; he was up against people who may have been less intelligent but had a great deal more guile and ruthlessness, and despite a decade of outstanding creativity, he could not find anyone who was now willing to use him. Leonard Matthews says that it must never be assumed that editors didn't want to use Frank, and implies that rather the boot was on the other foot, and that Frank made it very difficult to allow himself to be used. It depends, I suppose, *how* people want to use you! There is a daunting aspect to Frank's character which, when he decides he doesn't like something, makes him impossible to deal with. Moreover, he no longer had a champion in the boardrooms, and there was no reason why any of the Odhams chiefs should take up his cause. After all, what was in it for them?

In earlier times, when Frank had his studio around him to admire what he was doing, and confirm to him his effort was worthwhile, it wasn't hard to keep up his morale. Contempt was an attitude he had never had to contend with, or, for that matter, ever deserved. While he was thinking, writing, researching and drawing he was fixed in his own firmament and able to believe in himself. While his work appeared, he could see the effect it had, on readers, fellow artists and rivals. But now he was on his own, with only Joan Porter as his loyal and unshakeable supporter helping him, and Dorothy in the background, always on hand when he needed her, going about her business as wife and mother, producing meals at ungodly hours and taking him to bed when he fell asleep over his easel.

In London there was the chaos and uncertainty which must follow any take-over on the

Mirror/Odhams scale; it was so major that it brought about a Royal Commission to report on the health of the Press. In Epsom there was doubt, mystification, at the way Frank was being treated and, probably, depression. The last straw was a telephone call from Fleet Street when someone told Frank that his work had been rejected. The tone was dictatorial and he replaced the receiver in despair. He walked unsteadily through the house to his bedroom, lay back on his bed and closing his eyes with a mighty sigh, tried to stop thinking. It was time to go; to forget about pushing the boulder up the hill and make his final goodbye. Around the mid-summer of 1961, in a wasteland created by three years of inter-company wars, Frank Hampson put himself out of a job.

Frank Hampson in 1965 with some of the many models produced for the Dan Dare strip.

NIGHT AND FOG

The series of Fleet Street takeovers, from 1958 to 1961 left the government and the media-watchers quite seriously shaken up, and eventually Parliament called for (another) Royal Commission on the Press. The commission invited (amongst many other persons) submissions from the Mirror Group, and in their written reply, Cecil King and Hugh Cudlipp produced a commendable number of reasons why this diminution of ownership, culminating in one gigantic corporation controlling virtually all the magazines, periodicals, juvenile publications, annuals and encyclopedias coming out of England, was a 'good thing'. The thrust of the argument was two-fold. The bigger the company owning the papers, it was said, the better chance the weaker ones had of surviving, for they could be supported by the strong. But if – the Mirror's reply continued – certain publications still went to the wall, this was because they were either weakly edited, poorly written and unimaginatively promoted, or the great British public simply didn't want them. Moreover, one only had to use ones eyes to see that there was a journal to suit every taste, cover every interest, cater for every political colour and serve every trade and industry, and when new interests, trades or political parties arose, then the right new publication would arrive for their followers to read.

So far, so good. As we should expect, the argument was economically sound, politically chaste and based on the purest business principles. It said, in so many words, big is beautiful, and when Hulton Press, smallest of the publishers, lost control of Eagle, the comic and all its sister papers fell into a decline, resulting in their slow, but quite inevitable death. The more you reduce the quality and content of a paper, the more readers stop buying it, and it is worth recording here, the lifespan of these comics: they are as follows.

Eagle was published for 991 issues, from between 14th April 1950 and 26th April 1969, just missing its 1,000th edition. *Girl* was launched on 2nd November 1951 and continued until it was incorporated with *Princess* on 3rd October, 1964 (in other words, once Hulton sold it, it continued for only half the number of years as when Hulton controlled it). *Robin* began on 28th March, 1953 and continued until May 1967 when it became '*New Robin* and *Story Time*', and *Swift*, birth-date 20th March 1954, was incorporated with Eagle on 3rd March, 1963. After 1959, the circulations of all the comics began to fall, and when Eagle finally died (or was killed off) the current editor was able to boast that he received only six letters of protest. He conveniently forgot to mention the thousands of letters of protest that arrived during the slow murder.

We also know, for it is part of what this book is about, the effect the press take-overs had on individuals employed on the comics. Are we expected to believe that Frank, Don Harley, Keith Watson, Eric Eden, Frank Bellamy, Frank Humphris and Norman Williams were the only artists whose work was considered dispensable? Were there no writers who suffered? No photographers whose work, however fresh, innovative and exciting, could not be 'afforded'? Did no typographer suffer? No layout man get forced into producing worse layouts, because they were more 'exciting'? Was it only the 750,000 schoolboys who read the original Eagle who were disappointed when its quality crumbled? Of course not. It would be foolish to suppose that around Fleet Street, bad writers, artists and photographers didn't lose their livelihoods too, but that, I suppose, is their own lookout; the bad sink and the good swim. But, alas, in this instance, some of the good sank too and some of the bad continued to swim, with greater and greater vigour, until there wasn't a quality comic of the like of Eagle to be

From a 'Lady Penelope' strip drawn by Hampson in the mid-60s for TV21 comic.

seen. Not anywhere. And not since.

It was the philosopher, H. D. Thoreau who said: 'greater than the power of mighty armies is the force of an idea whose time has come.' Eagle burst into the publishing world with a force that overcame all the inertia and all the objections against it; it was still travelling like an unstoppable train when it arrived at the newsagents and its power swept its readers along. The force continued, albeit it with diminishing strength as long as there were people who understood it and were willing to serve it. Eagle was travelling from left-to-right. It was struck by an even greater force travelling from right-to-left. In the collision, Frank and his colleagues were the casualties.

Modern publishers say that the original Eagle would be a laughing-stock today, old-fashioned and out of its time. I think the claim is nonsense, but be that as it may. The reason there isn't a publication for kids of the same calibre today, is because there aren't the men to create it. The Society of Strip Illustrators will tell you they can *find* the men to create it. But they don't. And they don't because they can't. And they can't, not because (as they believe) modern-day publishers are massed against them, but because they aren't clever enough. That's not a criticism; who can blame them for not being the best in the world? But they must understand the forces massed against the creation of a new comic today are no greater – and no smaller – than the forces massed against Eagle in 1950. As proof that breakthroughs can be made today, you need only look to *Star Wars*. That film and its successors broke through the massed ranks of Hollywood moguls who 'knew', without question, that space-films were losers. Then George Lucas had an *idea*. What's missing in the world of illustrators is the man to have the idea.

So what happened when Frank went into the wilderness? One of the things that happened is that all over the country, little groups of fans got together and produced, albeit amateurishly (and naively, forlornly and gradually) fanzines lamenting his disappearance, and trying vainly to re-create the excitement he created with his illustrations. They retold his stories, reprinted his pictures, their hearts leapt when they heard rumours of yet another Dan Dare film on the stocks. They wrote to each other whenever they came across anything new Frank drew. They formed societies and pen-pal clubs, collected his artwork, wrote to him asking for a sign that he might one day come back, begged for interviews, bombarded him with their literature, telephoned his wife asking after his health, what he was doing, where he was working and how they could find more examples of his drawings.

In fact, these were few and far between. From 1961 to 1964, Frank produced some illustrations for *Reveille*, some advertising strips for Bovril and the National Coal Board (these based on a real family, who were delighted to recognise themselves in the national newspapers) some cigarette advertisements which appeared in Africa, the odd illustration for the *Radio Times*, and a few weeks of a strip called 'Gun Law' which belonged to Harry Bishop, who asked Frank to take over when he fell ill. Frank was also asked to submit some samples for Modesty Blaise but the publishers didn't like his style; not racy or sexy enough.

He was approached to do a strip of some importance, accepted the job and went off to do the research he always insisted on. But as the copy date drew near, he became afraid he couldn't do it by himself and asked for an assistant. He was told he could have any assistant he liked as long as he was prepared to pay him out of the fee they agreed, for there was no extra money forthcoming to produce the strip. Frank rejected the job.

In 1964, he struck up a relationship with Ladybird Books and since the book trade is much gentler with its artists than Fleet Street, and to all intents and purposes, Frank didn't really have a deadline at all, he found them good people to work with. He illustrated seven of their books at the rate of about one a year, carrying out all the research himself. Drawing the Battle of Hastings he could not discover whether King Harold of England really died from an arrow in the eye, or, as some historians have it, a spear in the chest. There is, it seems, no definitive answer, so Frank shows the dying king pierced by both weapons. His last book for Ladybird was about the life of Winston Churchill and once more, he delved into the libraries, searching out the uniforms Churchill wore, with the correct insignia, the places he fought his battles, spoke to his constituents, won his elections. But illness struck again during the production of these illustrations, much to the regret of Douglas Keen, Editorial Director of Ladybird, and the Churchill book was never finished. Later, when Frank was made an honorary life member of the Association of Illustrators, he asked the Director of that association to help him get back some of his original artwork. But Ladybird, who store all their originals at their Loughborough offices, were loathe to give back what they had already paid for, lest their printing plates should be damaged and have to be remade when they wanted to issue new editions of their books.

The overall tenor of this time in the wilderness is summed up in a letter Frank wrote to the editor of one of the Hampson fanzines, called '*Astral*'. The editor had sent Frank copies of his hero-worshipping, typewritten magazine for years, without so much as receiving an acknowledgement; perhaps Frank knew that anything he did with his pen would be published so he forbore even to write. But finally, with the fanzine closing down, its editor presumably having exorcised Frank Hampson from his system, the artist sent him this one letter of thanks and congratulation. It is dated 20th June, 1964. "Dear Mr. Skilleter, I have always been in a quandary about you, your colleagues and "*Astral*". On the one hand, your enthusiasm and very real achievement were enough to make any creator proud of his creation. You deserve the utmost respect and encouragement. On the other, Dare has been, for me, a long and bitter personal tragedy. I will not go into details, which would take pages of explanation and could only express the frustration and anger which have been my chief enemy for many years.

'Bitterness is a corrosive poison and the worst quality in the world for stultifying creativity. I have no wish to transmit it to anyone, and regard with abhorrence the infection of the young by it. Therefore, I have stayed silent. Recently, however, I saw that you are publishing your

The Birth of the Phant Nation

'Rogue Planet' saw Frank Hampson at his most inventive since the first 'Venus' story. He devised Phantos, its terrain, the terrifying warrior race of the Phants, their architecture, costumes, hardware and weaponry, all thought through to the last detail. It was consistent, convincing and above all original and very good to look at. It is not too much to claim that Hampson's abilities as a conceptual artist have been unsurpassed, even by artists contributing to the most expensive screen extravaganzas of the last two decades.

Top left *Super-Phants of the High Command of varying rank.*

Top right *Three Super-Phants of the High Command, from left to right, Military, Scientific, Air and Space.*

Right *Gogol, the dread High Phant of Phantos, together with a continuity sketch.*

"LET THEM GORGE THEMSELVES! BY 'LOS-RISE' THEY WILL BE FIGHTING MAD..."

"THEN WE WILL ATTACK CHAKRA AND DESTROY THE CENTRE OF CRYPT CIVILIZATION!"

"SUPER-PHANT ▲ REPORTING!"
"SUPER-PHANT ● REPORTING!"
"SUPER-PHANT ■ REPORTING!"

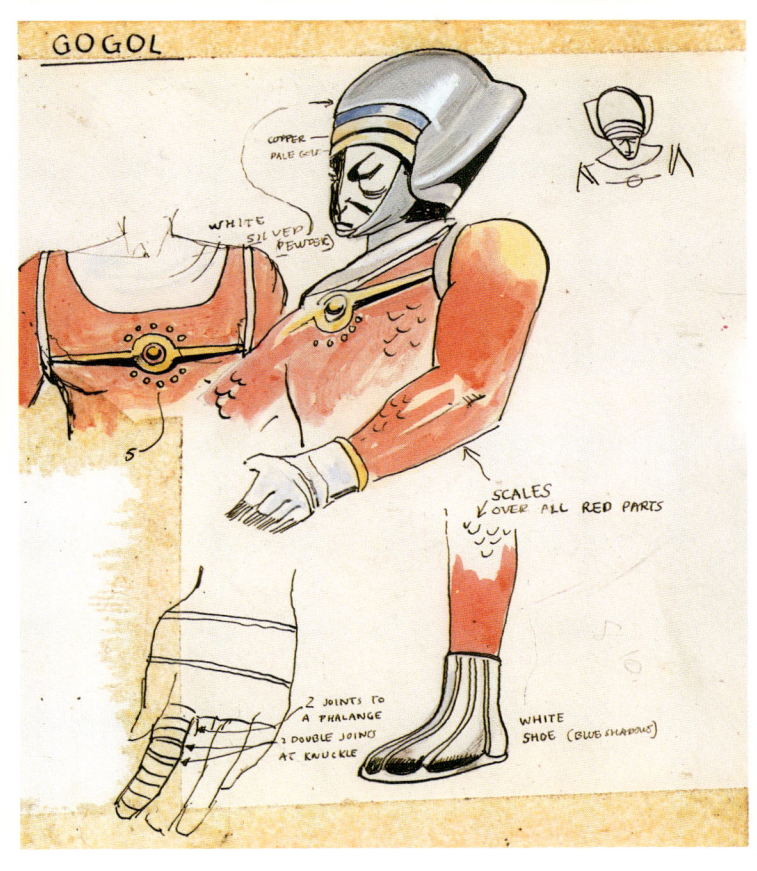

GOGOL

COPPER PALE GOLD
WHITE SILVER PEWTER
SCALES OVER ALL RED PARTS
2 JOINTS TO A PHALANGE, DOUBLE JOINTS AT KNUCKLE
WHITE SHOE (BLUE SHADOWS)

"WHAT IS THIS CREATURE? HE IS NOT ONE OF US!"

"NOR IS HE A CRYPT, O GOGOL!"

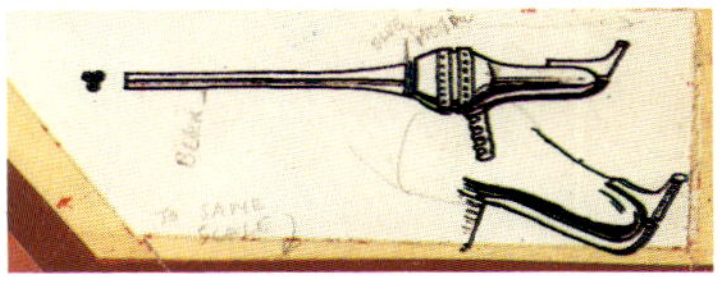

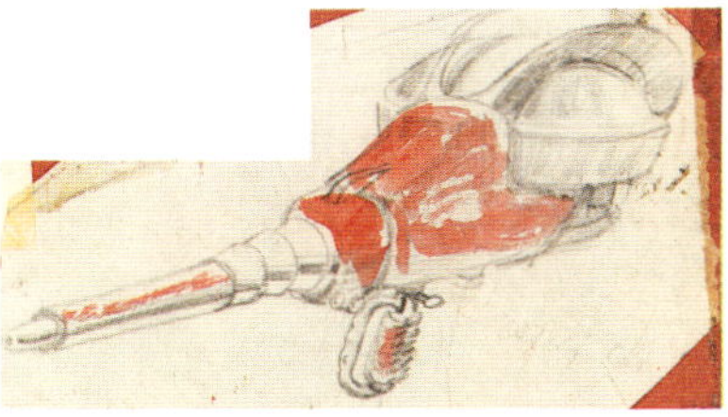

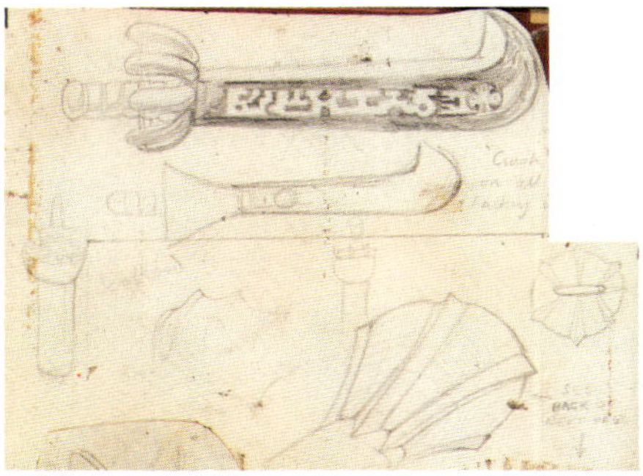

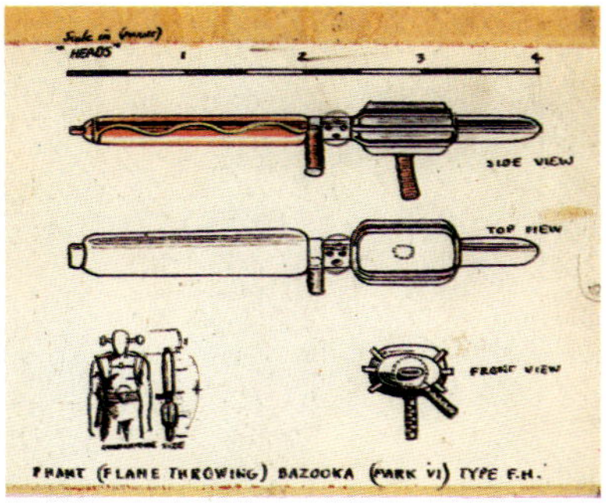
"HEADS"
1
2
3
4
SIDE VIEW
TOP VIEW
FRONT VIEW
PHANT (FLAME THROWING) BAZOOKA (MARK VI) TYPE F.H.

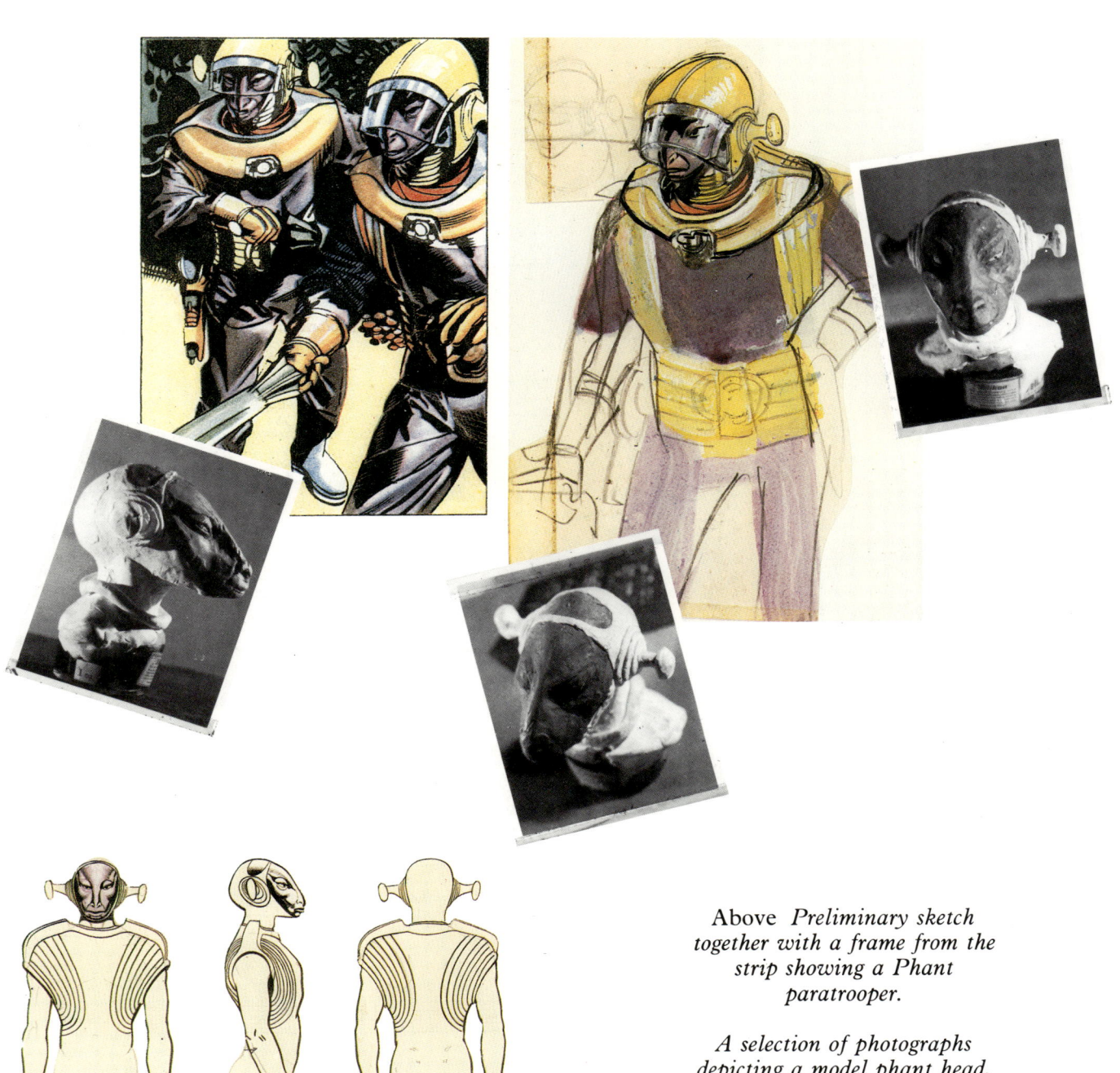

Above *Preliminary sketch together with a frame from the strip showing a Phant paratrooper.*

A selection of photographs depicting a model phant head, shot from varying angles. This model was only a few inches high and built on top of a Pelikan ink bottle.

Left *Proportion diagram of a Phant also showing the personal radio antennae head pieces.*

THE KRUELS!

MAKE WAY FOR THE KRUELS!

FIRST YOU WILL HAVE AUDIENCE WITH US — THE SEVEN KRUELS OF *PHANTOS*...

FRANK HAMPSON

...BIND THE PRISONERS AND BRING THEM TO THE GREAT CAVERN! WE SHALL DECIDE IF YOUR REPORT IS OF SUFFICIENT IMPORTANCE FOR ORAK'S HEARING!

last issue of "*Astral*" and must say "well done" to a splendid effort. In particular, your penetration to the heart of the mental attitude characterised by the strip – a comprehension denied to its publishers. (Sic) Well done indeed. The very best of success to you and your companions. May you have a long and successful career in publishing. Yours sincerely, Frank Hampson'.

There, in one handwritten page to a stranger (albeit a sincere admirer) is all the evidence you need of the inner battle Frank waged with himself. As if this psychological fight wasn't enough, in 1970 he began to suffer pains in his throat, which, after tests, doctors diagnosed as cancer of the traches. It probably came about through years of labouring over his artwork with a pipe almost permanently in his mouth. He picked up the pipe smoking habit from his father, and passed it on to Dan Dare; Greta Tomlinson says he had a pipe and a packet of indigestion tablets beside him always. If one of the tablets wasn't on his tongue then the pipe was clenched between his teeth. The illness made Frank both frightened and determined not to go gently. He withdrew his savings from the bank, cashed in his life policies and planned (and travelled) one last golden journey to Samarkand. But the cancer began to respond to the weekly visits he paid to hospital for radiation treatment and six months later, he was still alive and his throat showing signs that the disease was arrested. The radiation treatment, however, affected his voice box and his clear way of speaking has never returned. Three years later he was virtually cured, though he would not tempt fate by claiming so much, and wrote that the disease was 'now seemingly capable of a cautiously optimistic prognosis.'

But in spirit he was uplifted, for, at last, something had turned out in his favour. He began to take an interest in the fan mail he was still receiving, and towards Christmas of 1973 replied to Alan Vince, an enthusiast who had been writing to him, without any sign that his letters had ever arrived, for years.

'I am sorry that I have not written to you before. The Ostrich tendency to shy away, mentally, from the many painful memories of my last years on Eagle (and the anguish of seeing Dan Dare in alien, clumsy hands) must, I'm afraid, also account for the many inexcusable-seeming rudenesss on my part. However, all things pass. If you are still interested in talking to me about the creation of Eagle and Dan Dare, perhaps you could come here some time over Christmas or in January. I shall be free from the 21st December.'

Frank need have no fear of not being forgiven by his fans. Early in January, 1974, Alan Vince took up that invitation and during the visit, taped some three hours of conversation in which the artist explained some of the history and philosophy behind his work. We must bear in mind that Frank is now talking with the benefit of hindsight, and has had a decade to

Page 150, top *Hampson took the time to sketch a Phant head imposed on their emblem for the cover of a studio folder holding photographs of a model Phant head.*

Middle *Examples of Phant weaponry.*

Lower left *Sketch of a Phant trooper detailing the pistol and its positioning in the holster.*

Right *Concept sketch of a Phant Officer.*

This page, left *The Seven Kruels – merciless Warrior Priests of Orak (the mystic Master-Brain of Phantos) – together with two of the reference photographs.*

A Ladybird 'Easy-Reading' Book
'Through the Ages'
FOOD
5b Out in the sun
The Ladybird Key Words Reading Scheme
A LADYBIRD B
'Lives of the Great
Madam

ists'
CURIE
A LADYBIRD BOOK
Kings and Queens
Book 2
A FIRST LADYBIRD BOOK OF
Nursery Rhymes

WHO'S WHO

DIG
SPACEMAN (CL.1). ALBERT FITZWILLIAM DIGBY, DAN'S BATMAN AND FAITHFUL COMPANION BORN 1960 IN WIGAN LANCS, MARRIED, 4 CHILDREN (3 GIRLS, 1 BOY). HOBBIES: FOOTBALL, JIGSAW, SLEEPING.

PROF
PROFESSOR JOCELYN MABEL PEABODY, EXPERT ON NUTRITION AGRICULTURE AND BOTANY. ATTACHED TO VENUS EXPEDITION IN SEARCH FOOD IN 1996 AND SINCE APPOINTED PERMANENT SPECIAL ADVISER TO FLEET EXPLORATION AND RESEARCH DEPARTMENT WITH HONORARY RANK OF PILOT/CAPTAIN. BORN IN MORETON GLOS. HOBBIES: SKIING, RIDING, NETBALL.

DAN
COLONEL DAN DARE O.U.N. INTERPLANET SPACE FLEET AWARDED THE ORDER OF THE UNITED NATIONS FOR LEADERSHIP IN THE VENUS EXPEDITION 1996. BORN 1967 IN MANCHESTER, ENGLAND. HOBBIES: CRICKET, FENCING, RIDING, PAINTING, MODEL MAKING.

HANK
PILOT CAPTAIN HENRY BRENNAN HOGAN. PIERRE'S PARTICULAR BUDDY. A VERY EFFICIENT PILOT WITH A HATRED OF RED TAPE. BORN IN HOUSTON TEXAS OF AN IRISH FAMILY. HOBBIES: BOXING, CAR RACING, PHOTOGRAPHY, BASEBALL

PIERRE
PILOT/MAJOR PIERRE AUGUST LAFAYETTE. HANK'S 'COPAIN' OR PAL, SHREWD, ANALYTICAL MATHEMATICAL FRENCH OFFICER FROM DIJON. HOBBIES: GASTRONOMY, THREE DIMENSIONAL CHESS, FISHING.

SIR HUBERT (SOMETIMES KNOWN AS 'ORRIBLE 'UBERT)
MARSHAL OF SPACE SIR HUBERT GASCOIGNE GUEST, K.C.B., O.M., O.U.N., D.S.O., D.F.C., BORN 1943. EX-R.A.F. CONTROLLER OF THE INTERPLANET SPACE FLEET, A PIONEER OF SPACE TRAVEL, HE WAS IN THE CREW OF THE FIRST MANNED ROCKET TO THE MOON AND COMMANDED A SHIP IN ADMIRAL GROSVENOR'S FIRST EXPEDITION TO MARS.
ALTHOUGH LONG OVER AGE FOR ACTIVE SERVICE HE ALSO ACCOMPANIED THE 1996 EXPEDITION TO VENUS. HOBBIES: SWIMMING, RIDING, CHESS, WRITING, TECHNICAL HISTORY OF FLEET ORGANISATION AND STRUCTURE.

FRANK HAMPSON

reflect on the first ten years of Eagle. The conversation was lucid and fascinating, and here are some brief parts of it.

'I was determined to produce a real character, and a consistant character in Dan Dare. I loved inventing things, it was great fun. My favourite character was Sir Hubert Guest, based on my father; he became the most lifelike of my creations as it was just a question of drawing a series of pictures of a real person. Dan, Digby, Hank and Pierre were basically pure cartoon, although Dan and Dig each had a little of me in them. Some of Dan's features were mine; I had a series of pictures taken of my hair-style which did, in fact, become Dan's and I also gave him my nose. Dig was a combination of myself and a batman I had in the army, a chap called Thornton. He wasn't Dig's build but he had that kind of outlook and attitude to life.

'I was keen the strip should have an international flavour as I was a great champion of the United Nations. Trouble is, it doesn't seem to work. It did in Dan Dare though. I found that once I began to think along certain lines, all kinds of ideas would come to me. It was the same if I was designing a space station or a new alien life form. I tried to show a clean-cut difference between good and evil, but I've always detested stories where the hero has an automatic physical superiority over his opponents. It is not my experience that straight lefts can be relied on for the triumph of virtue any more than bullies can be relied on to be cowards. I preferred Dan to prevail by intelligence, common sense and determination. As regards death, it is, of course, a fact of life. I don't think the strip shirked it – there was the Dapon, "Old Handlebars" in the Venus story – and I remember a lady at Hulton being quite upset about his demise.

'The Mekon was always a great favourite, flying around on his little chair. He was meant to show the depths that a scientifically based society could sink to; a superbrain with no emotions at all. He kept cropping up because we kept running out of villains. And I didn't want to produce a strip without a female, in a way it was a blow struck for women's lib, so we had Professor Peabody, who was there to be rescued. She was also very clever and attractive and it paved the way for a few arguments between her and Sir Hubert. Early on, we were feeling our way. But as we got the experience and saw how things reproduced, we were able to develop away from the American cartoon style. Now and again, I might do a front page single frame. There was the big view of Mekonta in the first story; it took quite a time to draw and I was happy with the way it turned out. I was also very proud of the first frame in the "Safari in Space" story. I would never draw a page and have a word balloon added afterwards. To spend days putting in bags of detail, only to have it covered up by a lettering artist back at the office, that would never suit me.

'I suppose I was lucky that Dan Dare was my strip and I had control over it. We weren't tied down to a strict script, and since some of the stories lasted over many months, I was able to add the odd twist or new character to fill it out. I really had a free hand with this. Marcus got on with editing the paper and I concentrated on Dan. Marcus knew I was happy to be left with this, and – a very few broad suggestions aside – acceded to my wishes as far as he possibly could. The work came fairly easily to me because I enjoyed it so much. Funnily enough, Alan Stranks, who later become my scriptwriter, said I had wasted far too much in the first story. He felt he could have spun it out for at least five years. Someone once told me I could not make a Dare story last for more than three months, but as you know, they lasted much longer than that, and held the reader's interest.

'"Safari in Space", which came much later, I wanted to be the basis of a whole new series of stories. I was planning to have Dan follow a trail to many different planets looking for his father, but it never got that far. By this time, the big-takeovers in Fleet Street had started and it began to look like the end for me. Frank Bellamy took over, then Don and Bruce and finally Keith Watson. I'm not saying that as an artist Bellamy wasn't doing a good job. He was as much a victim of the changing face of Eagle as I was.

'I needed a break. The plan was that I should do something else for a year, and then return to Dare. But the basic trouble was that there was always, for me, a canker in the apple with Dare. From the beginning, I foresaw the commercial exploitation of the strip. Had we been able to retain the profits for the Society for Christian Publicity, as planned, I expected them to be used for the extension of our activities, in particular the studio. At the time we launched Eagle I was confident we could sell an American version, tailored for script and technique to the American Sunday Supplements. Buck Rogers and Flash Gordon had gone out, but there was surely an upsurge of interest in space to come. We would use our expertise and inventions, together with the space fleet set up, our team method of working and our central filing and records system, but, and this was vital, it would have to be scripted very differently. The speed of the story and the general requirements of that market were very different. It is, however, a very lucrative one.

'I set out to train, organise and recruit as many people as I could. Given we could win that source of income, the next step would be the production of a pilot animated film. This would be ideal for science fiction because the realistic but simplified drawings would enable fantasy to be integrated with realism very happily. It was a logical progression of steps to build something really big. Unfortunately for me, the circumstances of Eagle's production made it impossible for me to retain the copyright, and therefore the control. Due to various factors beyond our control, the profits from the strip, from the licencing of the name "Dan Dare" and from the radio show built around it, could not be used in this way. I, doggedly, tried for years to implement these ideas, but it was a losing struggle. Hulton were fighting to save their brilliant *Picture Post* and we were under increasing pressure from competitors. Finally, came the crunch when Hulton's were taken over, and the firm taking over were taken over themselves. It was a very very unhappy time for me; I'd rather not go into details.

'On the subject of Dan Dare, I have to quote Wolf Mankovitz who interviewed me and summed it up this way. "Frank Hampson has created something bigger tham himself." On Eagle, I think it lost its direction. The people who took over from Marcus, didn't have the same feel for it. It wasn't a question of being old fashioned. I have no doubt that Dan Dare could still be going today. The ideas were there, the plans, the team. I wanted the feature to be carried over into films, if you like in the way Walt Disney grew on Mickey Mouse. There was no argument over its success. Oh, I had great plans.'

That conversation (and I have omitted large sections which cover ground already explored) was held on 5th January 1974. In March 1982 a new Eagle was launched and one of the main characters (not the lead story, but subsequently promoted to the lead) was Dan Dare.

Right *Frank Hampson 1950. Sequence of photographs used as references for the Dan Dare face.*

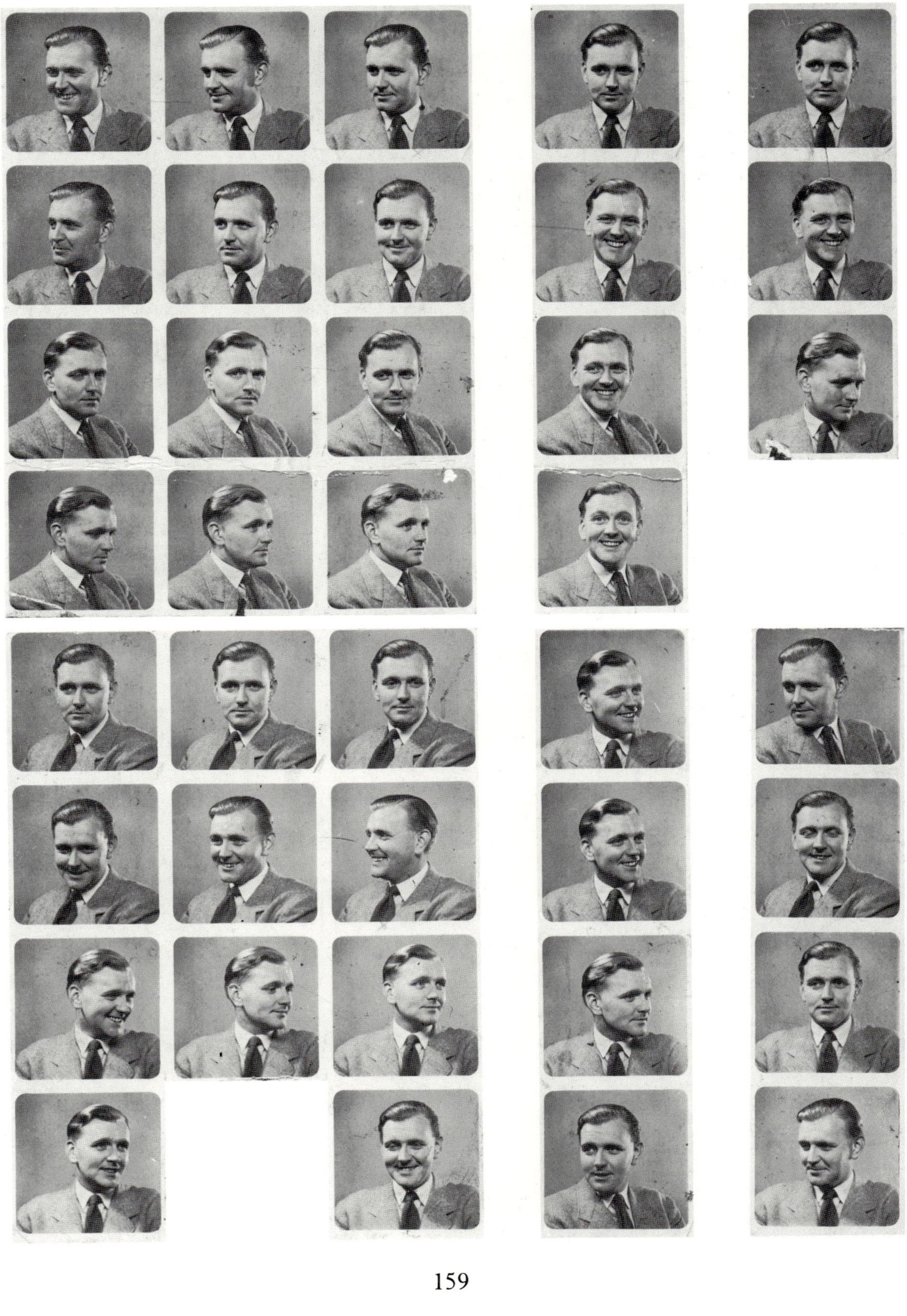

THE BEST IN THE WORLD

If any University were to introduce a chair to advance the study of the history and development of the strip cartoon, one of the best qualified candidates to fill it would be Denis Gifford. Already the author of a number of authoritative books on the subject, and possessing the sense of fun and love of childhood fantasy necessary for such a post, Gifford is a member of the Society of Strip Illustrators and has, at his home in south-east London, a collection of comics numbering some twenty thousand, including the most rare and most humorous of their style and period. His works include *Happy Days*, a history of 100 years of comics, *Victorian Comics*, a compilation of the same, and the *British Comic Catalogue 1874–1974* which, for some reason, is as much in demand in the USA as in this country.

Denis Gifford is also President of the ACE, the Association of Comic Enthusiasts, and writes a regular column in the magazine *Illustrators* under the heading 'Slopers Alley', which, as you will gather, is a play on the name of the first ever comic character Ally Sloper. The comic which Denis says has always been his favourite – the funniest he has ever seen – is *Film Fun*, the standard of which he considers so high that all others may be judged by it. I believe it is also fair to say that in his list of best comics 'Eagle' is unlikely to feature; it's not funny enough.

However Denis is important to us for, from November 1974 he began to feature quite a bit in Frank's life and without him Frank would never have received his award as the best artist and writer of strip cartoons. It was Denis who got Frank to Lucca, who told the festival committee of Frank's life and times, who made Frank take samples of his artwork to put on display, and who got Frank to the awards ceremony, sat by his side and applauded with the rest as he mounted the podium to receive his prize. It was Denis who got Frank home safely when the ceremony was over and who called up the papers to get the good news published. Up until that time, he says, he'd had no contact at all with the publicity machine and no insight into how it worked.

Gifford and Hampson first met face to face after the comic buff had been asked to compile 100 entries for the *World Encyclopedia of Comics*, published by the French enthusiast, Maurice Horn. Horn is also part-author of *A History of the Comic Strip*, first published in France under the title 'Bande Designée et Figuration Narrative' in 1967 and translated and published in America the following year. It contains not a single mention of Frank Hampson and attributes Dan Dare to Keith Watson, who was drawing the strip at the time. Denis, under instructions from Horn to see that his entries were 'authentic and accurate', wrote to Frank asking for biographical details. Frank supplied these, whereupon Denis drove down to Epsom to lunch with the artist and his wife and tape-record his story.

USA, France, Italy and the Eastern European countries are where interest in the strip cartoon is at its highest and all of them organise comic conventions at which the creators and their readers can get together. In the USA these are held in, amongst other cities, San Diego, Chicago and Orlando, but the one which makes all others pale in significance is the bi-annual 'world' convention which takes place in the Commune of Lucca in the region of Tuscany, in Italy, and makes – so one visitor to the affair wrote – 'a comics fan feel like he's dead and gone to heaven'.

The Director of this week-long gathering is the Italian Publisher and comics entrepreneur, Rinaldo Traini, and it was from Traini that Denis received in October 1975 a letter inviting

Frank Hampson with an 'old friend' 1976.

'Safari in Space' 1959

Don Harley as Digby and Frank Hampson's son, Peter, as Flamer Spry.

Panel 1
THE REST OF DAN'S PARTY ARE BROUGHT DOWN INTO THE CHAMBER BENEATH THE TRANSPARENT DOME.

IF MY GUESS IS RIGHT, PROFESSOR, ALL THIS BEGAN BEFORE YOU WERE BORN...

I GUESS THEY'RE KEEPING US APART SO THAT WE CAN'T HATCH UP AN ESCAPE PLAN. WHO DO YOU THINK IS BEHIND THIS, SIR HUBERT?

Panel 2
AND THE MAN WHO PLANNED IT IS DETERMINED TO PROVE SOMETHING WHICH CAN *NEVER* BE PROVED IN OUR LIFE-TIME!

Panel 3
GOOD NIGHT, GENTLEMEN! IN THE MORNING, YOU WILL LEARN WHAT YOU WISH TO KNOW FROM THE LIPS OF OUR CHIEFTAIN HIMSELF.

IT CAN'T BE TOO SOON FOR ME!

NOR ME — I'VE GOT A FEW HOME TRUTHS TO RAM DOWN THE SPALPEEN'S THROAT!

Panel 4
WHITE HEATHER — AND *FRESH*! HOW THE DICKENS DID THAT GET HERE?

THEY SEEM TO HAVE ESTABLISHED PERFECT EARTH CONDITIONS IN THIS SPACE-BUBBLE...

THERE'S A BIG BRAIN BEHIND THIS LARK, LEX!

Panel 5
MEANWHILE, FLAMER IS SHOWN TO *HIS* QUARTERS!

IN HERE, CADET — YOU'LL FIND COMPANY INSIDE.

Panel 6
DIGBY — SIR!

OUCH! DON'T SHOUT — MY HEAD'S *SPLITTING*!

WHERE ARE WE?

Panel 7
DON'T *YOU* KNOW?

ME? ALL I KNOW IS THAT I WAS COOKING DINNER — THEN I CAME TO IN HERE, ABOUT AN HOUR AGO.

Panel 8
RAPIDLY FLAMER EXPLAINS TO THE BEMUSED DIGBY.

...SO YOU SEE, WE'VE ALL BEEN KIDNAPPED AND BROUGHT HERE. WHAT DO YOU THINK ABOUT IT ALL?

Panel 9
NAY, IT'S BEYOND ME, FLAMER LAD! I'M TOO FAGGED OUT TO THINK. LET'S GET SOME SHUT-EYE...

Panel 10
G-GREAT GRIEF! WHAT'S THIS?

Panel 11
WHAT A CARRY ON!

SLEEP ON IT, DANNY BOY.

I CAN'T SLEEP ON AN EMPTY STOMACH. ALL I WANT IS FOOD — *GRUB* — SUMMAT TO FILL MY WIDE, EMPTY SPACES!

I'M CERTAIN I KNOW *WHERE* WE ARE, AND *WHO* BROUGHT US HERE — BUT I WISH I KNEW *WHY*.

IT'LL LOOK CLEARER IN THE MORNING — IF THERE *IS* ANY MORNING UP HERE!

TO BE CONTINUED

him to represent British comics. His fare would be paid (by air) and his hotel expenses met, provided he was willing to give the delegates a half-hour talk, with 'compulsory' slides (the letter was in Italian and it took Denis and his friendly neighbourhood translator some time to work out the details) on the subject Denis had covered so well in one of his books: *100 years of British comics*. Denis admits quite frankly that until he got this letter he had no idea that Lucca existed or what it was about and it's understandable that he was a touch dubious about such a generous offer appearing out of the blue, in exchange for what was really a piece of bread-and-butter lecturing. In the event he had to prepare a large quantity of slides, which set him back a large cheque, but there is no doubt that in financial terms, and remembering the overall outcome of the convention for both himself and Frank, he emerged decidedly on the credit side in this arrangement.

One further aspect of the invitation emphasised the organisers' seriousness and generosity; Denis could, if he so wished, bring with him a leading member of the UK comic fraternity – preferably an artist who could display in the convention hall examples of his artwork. Again, the fare and hotel costs would be met.

Recovering from his surprise at this unsolicited and philanthropic invitation and making one or two enquiries to find out more about the Lucca Comics Convention, Denis then put his mind to whom he might ask to accompany him. As has been said, Eagle is not his favourite comic (perhaps he finds the almost religious fervour of some Frank Hampson fans too much for him) so it was not Frank's name that sprang to his mind at once. He has another hero among modern comic artists, whose style, he believes, is the most imitated in British comics today and who has virtually changed the face of them: ex D. C. Thompson and IPC artist, Leo Baxendale. (It's worth noting as an aside here that Baxendale gave up drawing comics when he found IPC began reprinting on a massive scale a tidal wave of his early work, for which he was not getting paid a penny.) Denis asked Baxendale if a trip to Lucca would interest him but Baxendale couldn't make it. It was then Denis's mind went back to the long talk he had had with Frank earlier in the year and he began to wonder whether Frank, who was not tied to any comic and therefore not up against deadlines which would deny him the chance to take a week off work, would like to come. In fact Frank was employed as a technician at Ewell County Technical College, drawing illustrations to accompany lectures.

The question in Frank's mind was why anyone should pay for an airline ticket and hotel accommodation to take an artist to the Convention, without expecting anything in return. But it seemed the offer was genuine and there really were no strings attached. Frank hadn't had a trip abroad for years, the College were willing after some persuasion to allow him time off and it didn't take Denis a lot of talking to get him to agree. But he must, Denis told him, be sure to bring some of his original artwork. To get this, Frank had to apply to IPC, who currently held most of his work in their vaults in Fleetway House. IPC agreed to release certain boards on the understanding that they were booked out, treated with care and returned to the curator of artwork when the trip to Lucca was over. To anyone who knew just how poorly the artwork was stored, these strict conditions appeared somewhat over-zealous. James Slattery, who was later to rescue much Eagle artwork from these vaults, has told me: 'I'd be telling less than the truth if I said that the drawings were stored with British Museum precision. Between half and three-quarters of Frank's work simply wasn't there; other parts had been cut up for use in posters and re-issued stories. Nobody seemed to realise how much effort it had taken to create, or that it was, literally, irreplaceable.' How important this was, and how disappointing to Frank, will become clear as the Lucca story unfolds. It's worth noting that Slattery, who was a writer for Dragon's Dream, publishers of some of Frank's work, was allowed access to the IPC vaults for four weeks and he and a colleague gathered as many original Eagle boards as they could find and took them to the Dragon's Dream studios to be cleaned up, re-masked, photographed and indexed.

I have never been to a Lucca Comics Convention myself and I understand if you want to go you are best to book your accommodation early in the year, although the festival doesn't open until November. Hotels are hard to find and transport from Pisa is by bus or train. I am indebted to Richard Marschall and *Comics Journal* for the following description of the event.

'Lucca is a quantum jump from the American conventions which are, for the most part, a series of dealers' rooms (for the sale of old and current comics) and a few panels and film shows. I believe the comic strip has come further in Europe than the States and this fair reflects these advances and represents several levels of the art simultaneously. There *are* dealers selling the old and the new, from all over the world, but there are also lectures by – and for – scholars, as well as monographs, panels, erudite papers and slide shows, all being presented at the same time and all the time. If you want to meet artists and writers, at Lucca you'll find the best in the business from places as diverse as South America, Japan and the eastern European nations. If animation is your 'thing' you can sit in on round-the-clock screenings of cartoons from all the major studios, from all the countries that are leaders in producing these, literally, moving pictures.

'If you are a collector, it's here you can pick up the very latest from the publishers, often before they've been released to dealers and newsagents. If you follow the superheroes, they're here too: Superman, Incredible Hulk, Wonderwoman, *et al*, in their tight-fitting, muscle-bulging costumes and capes. Lucca is also a forum for new research, an animation and illustration festival, a grand awards ceremony and a love-in, where fans, scriptwriters, balloon letterers, scholars, artists, agents and dealers meet, talk, exchange papers, try to sell ideas, compare the latest work with what has appeared before and enjoy each other's company both at the formal events and in the local cafes. These conversations are likely to go on until the wee small hours when everyone has talked themselves into a state of happy exhaustion.

'When you arrive, you can get (from the local Chamber of Commerce, whose job it is to oil the festival wheels) a packet several inches thick, with press releases, publicity material, artists' samples, magazines, miniature posters, schedules and the dates, times and places of all the official events, carefully detailed so you know where you should be, and when, to catch a certain person or show. Events are held round most of the centre of the town, in theatres, halls and even tents. The major locales are the Giglio Theatre and a big, air-supported bubble set up in the town square. In the theatre they show the animated films – all kinds of them, including theatrical, puppetry, industrial, commercial and, of course, experimental. The lectures are held here too. What do they talk about? Commercial and technical problems, obviously, and where the money is to come from for their next project. But also how the comic heroes have lately spilled into the movies, the influence of American artists on, say, the British or French, and vice versa, and illustrated examinations of the work of the most respected strip artists.' (As far as artists influencing each other is concerned, fans have recently discovered how Frank's Dan Dare has been pillaged and plagiarised many times over, the copyists stealing not just plots, hardware and dramatic situations, but often using identical layouts of the frames and even repeating sections of the dialogue).

'In the bubble in the town square, you'll find an incredible array of themes, formats and levels of sophistication. There are quality books, some full of the most gorgeous colour-work, alongside kid's stuff, action, adventure, science fiction and real gutsy Westerns. On one side, costumed heroes, on the other, adaptations of the classics. Here, slapstick, pratfalls and bash-

Frank Hampson in the latter half of the 70s.

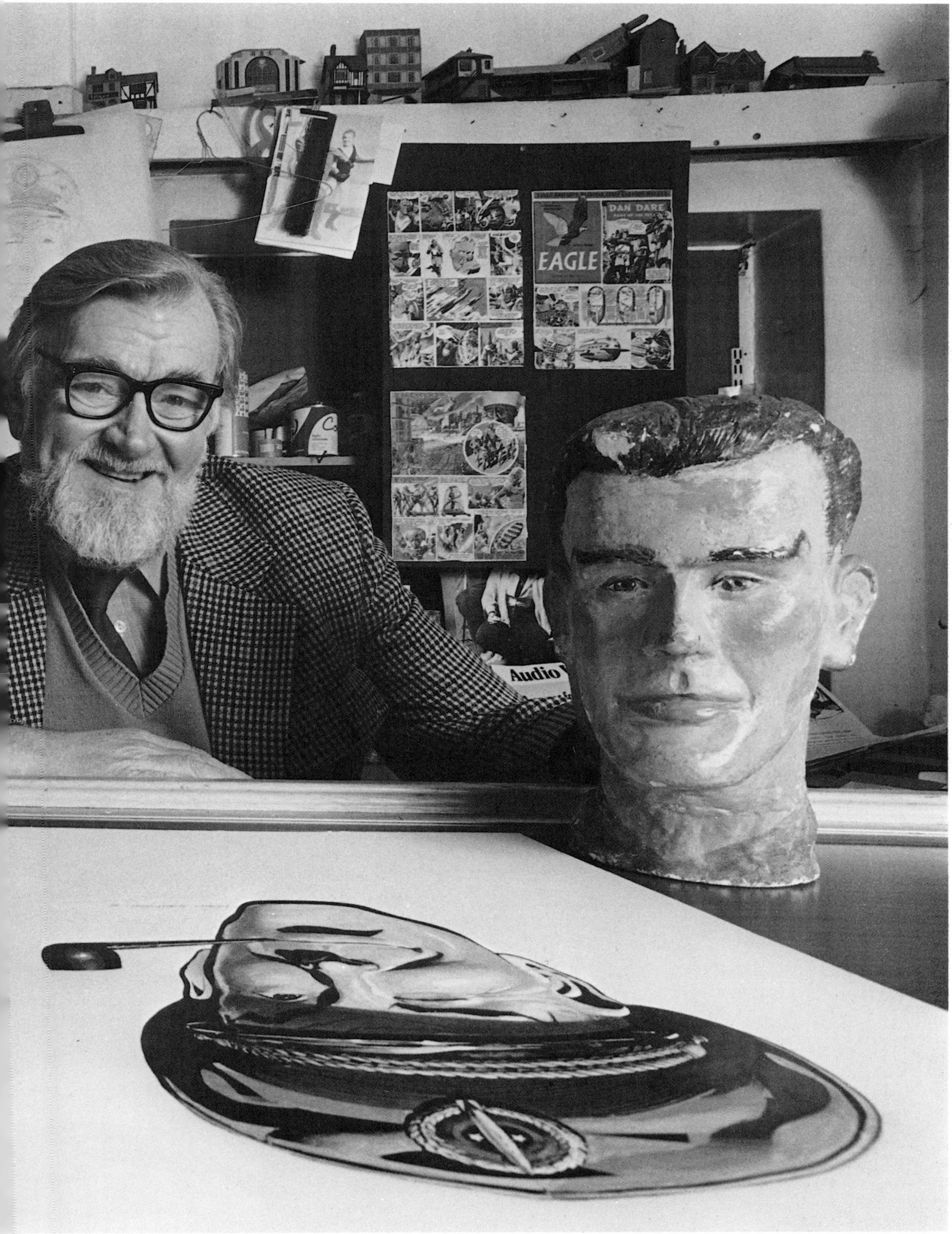
DAN DARE
EAGLE

A full page colour illustration by Frank Hampson for the Radio Times 'Doctor Who Tenth Anniversary Special', 1973.

street humour; there, war stories; Britain versus Germany, US versus Vietnam, not forgetting the Foreign Legion. And, of course, the ubiquitous cheap superhero books in their countless volumes from DC Comics.

'There are four hotels which the habitues prefer and all of them are great '30s Art Deco places. The Napoleon was built as the Hotel Mussolini but was tactfully re-christened after the fall of the dictator. Its lobbies, meeting rooms and bars are filled each day with the creators and their hangers-on. Friendships are renewed, sketches and autographs exchanged, deals negotiated, fine points argued, acquaintances made and addresses exchanged with promises to correspond and meet again two years hence. The festival takes two years to prepare and runs in a smooth, first class, highly professional way and the guest list of speakers (although it probably means little to the uninitiated) reads like a Who's Who in the world of comics and animated films. It's a centre of seriousness in this not over-serious field, everybody makes friends and money and has a great deal of fun.'

Into this comic-fan's Mecca, Frank and Denis arrived on the 1st November 1975. They had met at London's Heathrow and boarded a 'plane for Pisa. At Pisa they were greeted by the driver of a plush limousine and whisked in unaccustomed luxury – and at no charge – to the Napoleon Hotel, where they were treated as expected guests and shown into adjacent rooms. The evening was spent over a pleasant dinner and the following morning the two men made their way to the air-filled balloon, which seemed to be the focal point of the festival and a hive of bustle and activity. Here festival officials greeted them as friends and checked off their names on the list of invited celebrities. Frank was ushered to a large display board where he was invited to show his precious artwork. He spent an hour pinning up his boards and being careful to put his name over the top of his work, despite the fact that much of it was signed anyway. It was to prove an immense draw over the five days it remained on exhibition and caused the delegates to seek Frank out, congratulate him and quiz him on the strip, his time on Eagle and his life in general.

Frank had gone to Lucca quite unaware of what to expect and afraid that in this hub of the comics business he might be regarded as a has-been. What he found was that, far from being seen as an unknown artist in a foreign country, he was a renowned and respected hero-figure whose work was deeply admired. When the delegates found his art-work and learned that the creator of Dan Dare was alive and well and mingling among them, he was beseiged by enthusiasts, young and old, smothered in congratulations (not to say adulation) and begged for his autograph and often a small thumbnail sketch of the head of Dare – or any other of his characters he was willing to draw – which his followers could make a prize part of their collections. (As an aside here, it's interesting to note that under the terms of his contract Frank is not allowed to draw Dan Dare any more; small heads of people is all he is allowed to produce. Anything more is deemed a breach of copyright.) Frank remained at the centre of attention for the first few days he stayed at the convention. The Italians were familiar with the Dare strip which has been printed in their country in the 1950s. That part of the syndication Frank knew about. What he didn't know, but was quick to discover as he walked round the stalls of the dealers, was that Dan Dare was also being syndicated currently and brand new copies of his strip were on sale, both on the streets and inside the air-filled balloon. Neither he nor Denis knew of this latest release, which upset Frank since he was not receiving royalties for it.

Whilst Frank was entertaining his admirers and touring the festival in search of copies of the Italian Dan Dare (both the '50s and '70s versions), Denis was talking to the festival organisers about the man who was causing so much excitement. One in particular was deeply interested in Frank, an Italian artist of great skill and renown, Hugo Pratt, who had spent time working in the UK and was a member of the festival Committee. Pratt was anxious to learn all about Frank, and Denis, who had only recently made a study of his story and taken three hours of tape for his archives, was well placed to fill in the details. Pratt, delighted that Denis had managed to persuade Hampson to come, was astonished, not to say daunted, by his personal history, the tragedy that he was no longer drawing and the sad aspect of his health and financial position after years of prolific work and international syndication. These details were passed on to the full body of the Committee, one of whose duties is to decide who, amongst the artists, scriptwriters, producers and publishers, should be nominated for the annual awards. Strange though it may seem, these awards are not finalised until the festival itself, so no-one can know in advance who is to receive one.

There are three grades of Lucca award – gold, silver and bronze – and the trophies themselves are small replicas of 'The Yellow Kid', a character from the early American comics. 'The Yellow Kid' was conceived and drawn by an artist, Richard Outcault, and appeared in a newspaper, *New York World* which was bought by Joseph Pulitzer in 1883.

As with most successful comic creations, 'The Yellow Kid' evolved slowly through a strip called 'Down Hogan's Alley' which related the generally unsavoury doings of the citizens of a New York slum. One of the principal characters was a bald rascal with enormous ears and simian features, who always wore a huge white shirt. Although the *New York World* had printed colour pages, they hadn't yet managed to reproduce the colour yellow and thought what a good idea it would be to give the rascal a huge yellow shirt. They kept their experiments inside the printing house until February 16th 1896, when they launched an issue full of the blazing colour. It was a complete success, the brilliant shirt attracted the eye at once and the character quickly came to be christened 'The Yellow Kid'.

Whilst the festival Committee was locked in conclave mulling over who to honour, Frank began to spend more and more time in Lucca and the surrounding countryside, away from the convention itself. Denis duly gave his half-hour lecture on 100 years of British comics which received acclaim for its insight, research and erudition and, since Frank was polite enough to put in an appearance at his talk, Denis took the opportunity to introduce him formally to the delegates. The awards ceremony is held on the last full day of the convention and the evening before, Hugo Pratt took Denis aside and, noting that Frank was not always around, asked him to be sure that the artist was present at the awards ceremony and in a seat fairly near the front of the meeting. Denis agreed, saying nothing of this to Frank although it must now have been clear to him that the Committee had some award in mind. The problem was, Lucca Awards are meant to be for *current* work; the citations are made by judges from the US, Europe and South America, all of whom are actively at work and skilled and successful practitioners in their field. The judges decided however that the presence of Frank at Lucca and the outstanding quality of the original artwork he had brought to show – to which the printed versions had scarcely done justice – called for a bending of the rules. They agreed to create, especially for him, a unique award: he was to be declared the 'prestigioso maestro' and acknowledged as the best writer and illustrator of strip cartoons since the end of World War Two.

Frank accepted the trophy amid tumultuous applause. 'It was a staggering moment,' Denis said later, 'both for him and for me. An international acknowledgement by his peers, people who themselves create and understand what creation entails. I think that's what mattered

Right *Frank Hampson with his Yellow Kid Award, 1975.*

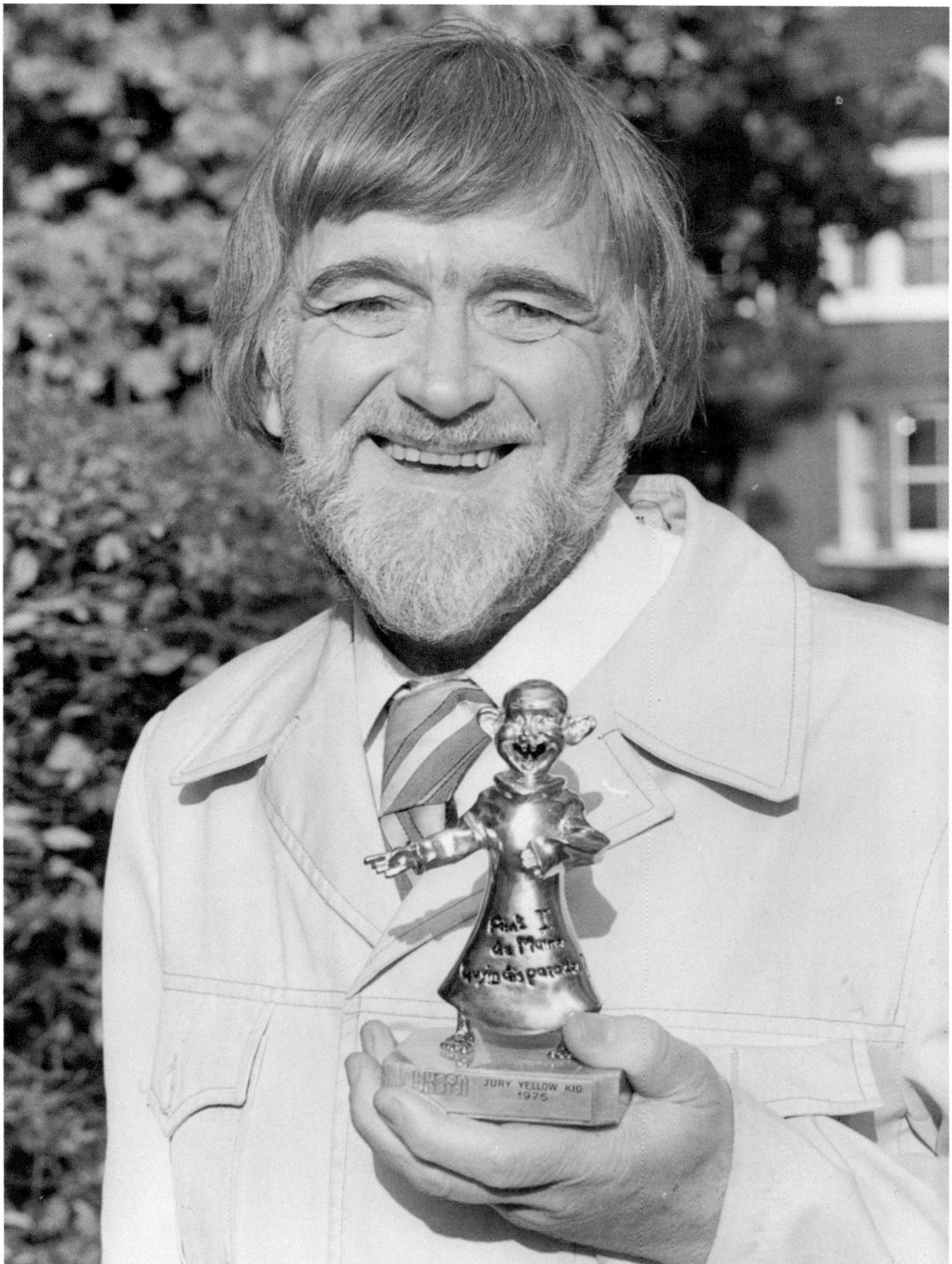
JURY YELLOW KID
1975

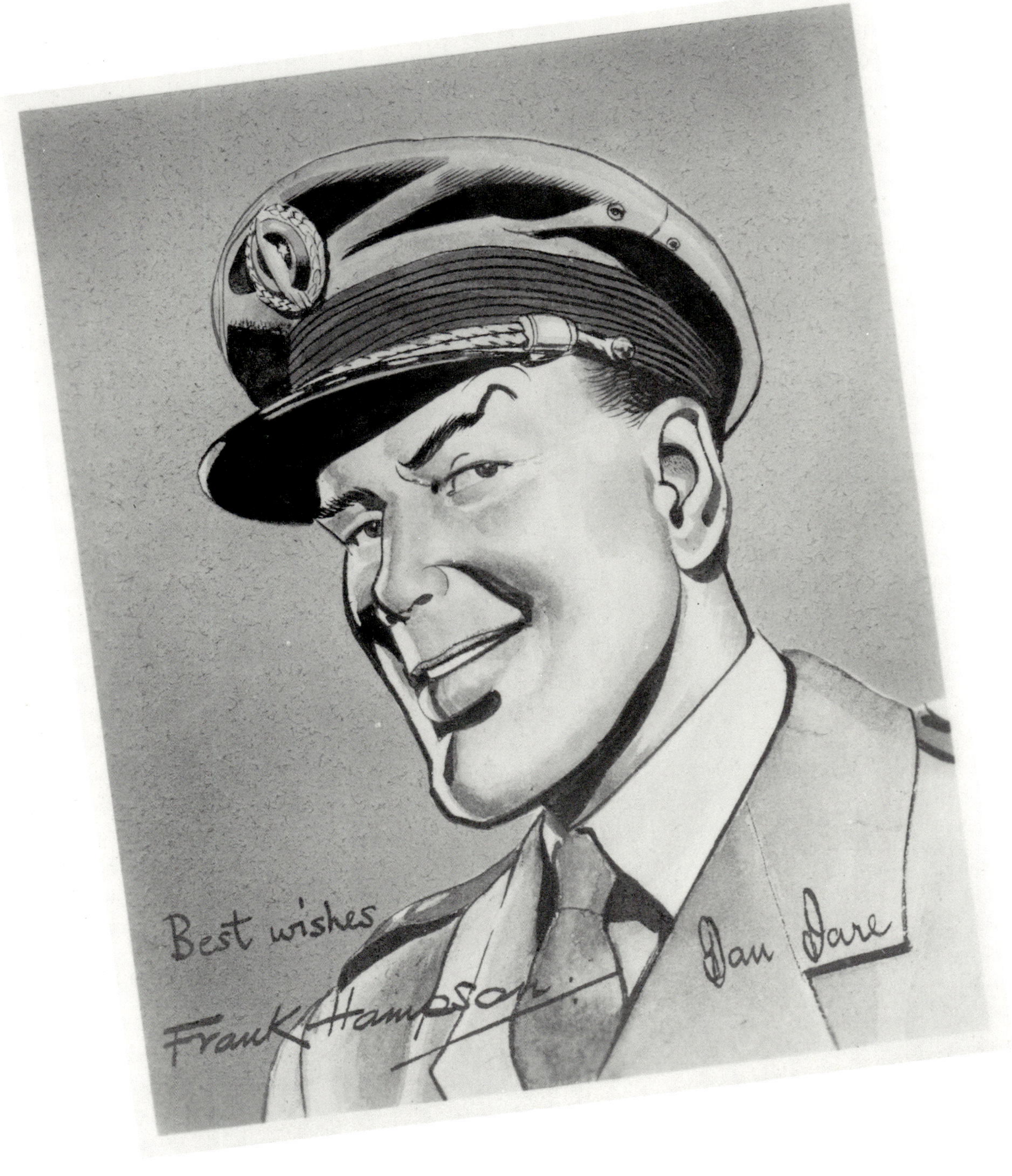
Best wishes
Frank Hampson
Dan Dare

most to Frank.' The Italian publishing company who were running Dan Dare approached Frank and asked if he would prevail on IPC to send them the original artwork for the whole of the Venus story, since they were eager to reprint it in a de-luxe edition. Bound in hardback, it was to be a genuine collector's item. The publishers were delighted that as Frank's agents (so they thought) their house had shared in the 'Yellow Kid' award which is valued very highly and, in Italy at least, has a commercial value too; before Frank's appearance they had been trying to win one for years.

But, as James Slattery reported, the original artwork for the Venus story no longer existed in the form of a coherent collection. It had been dispersed among souvenir hunters, collectors and fellow artists; indeed it seems at one stage anyone in the vaults of Fleetway House could, with comparative ease, help themselves to a piece. On writing to IPC, Frank got a reply confirming that the company no longer held any of his original boards. This statement was repeated in a letter to the Curator of a Northern museum who wrote to the company asking if he could put some of Frank's work on display. There have been various other tales over the years about how Dan Dare was burned to death in a fire in the Corporation archives, drowned when their vaults were flooded, and that while he was being transferred to a new store – presumably for safer keeping – he uncharacteristically went AWOL. All of which makes life very hard for any publisher wishing to revive him. It *is* possible to reprint Dan Dare by photographing old copies of Eagle but it is not possible to reprint him in perfect register and capture all the detail and brilliant colour. This isn't just disappointing for publishers and Dan Dare fans, it's also money out of Frank's pocket.

Elated as Frank undoubtedly was at the acclaim and recognition, there was a jarring side to the Lucca convention. Frank says that not only did he find current editions of Dan Dare in Italian but also in Yugoslavian. The news angered Frank since, as with the 1975 Italian syndication, he had received no money for the Yugoslavian Dan Dare either.

After a few words of thanks to the judges and the audience and raising the trophy above his head in elation, Frank returned to his seat. He left the meeting shortly after the ceremony closed and no-one was to see him for the rest of the evening, nor the whole of the next day when he and Denis were due to return home. Frank was still 'missing' when Denis arrived at Pisa airport and only appeared shortly before the 'plane was due to take off. Outwardly settled, Denis says he sensed that Frank was inwardly much disturbed and believes the bitterness of being denied the financial rewards of his work was the problem. His condition worried Denis not a little and he was anxious to deliver Frank back home safely, since it was at his invitation and his urging that the artist had come to Italy in the first place. The two men said goodbye at Heathrow, Frank to make his own way back to Epsom (not a straightforward journey from London Airport) and Denis to contact the London papers and spread the good news. They had arrived late in the afternoon and he was keen to catch the night editors in order to make the street the following morning.

UP LIKE A ROCKET, DOWN LIKE A STICK

Denis was lucky when he rang his first newspaper (The Guardian) to get through to John Ezard. He could have spoken to any number of reporters who would have gone back through their clippings and produced a minced-up piece along the lines of, 'Great news! Dan Dare, Pilot of the Future, may soon be on the launching pads again'. (Don't laugh, that kind of thing was appearing in follow-up features ten days later.) Instead, he found someone with a personal as well as professional interest in the story, well informed about Eagle and Frank and able to ask pertinent questions. Denis and Ezard got along so well that when he rang off, Denis decided he'd spread enough good news for one night, which meant that the next day's *Guardian* had a scoop. Ezard called Frank as soon as the artist got home and the paper printed the news as lead story on the arts page, across eight columns and with frames from the Venus story as illustrations. To reprint all of the piece here would be to repeat most of what you've read already but here's an abbreviated version, with some new facts Ezard dug out.

'Frank Hampson, cartoonist of the past, and father of Dan Dare, Pilot of the Future, said shakily down the 'phone yesterday: "I have to be very careful these days not to raise my blood pressure by getting excited." The health risk is real, but so, this week, is the temptation to get excited. After fifteen years of almost total obscurity he has just been voted the best post-war comic illustrator in the world, by 200 delegates and judges at this year's International Exhibition of Comics and Animated Films at Lucca. The judges decided that the work he did, up to more than twenty-five years ago, was not only better than anyone else's current work, but better than anything else produced since the war. He did not know it still commanded any respect or value. He had thought the only respect or promotion he could command now, would come from getting educational qualifications. So today, the man who is – although he did not know it until this week – one of the most fervently collected of pop artists, sits for the first-year exam in an Open University Course in the History of Art.

'When his examinations are over, he plans to dig out his old IPC contract to see if he is owed any royalties. With their son grown up and their mortgage paid from Frank's Eagle earnings, he and his wife can live on his pay. But more money would be welcome. More important, he is again daring to think of a return to comics, although his interest in graphic education persists. "I'm not supposed to get excited talking about this kind of thing", he said, "but I must admit I'm tempted to."'

And, of course, he was excited. He scribbled a note to his friend, Alan Vince: 'Have just got back from the International Salon at Lucca (Italy) where Dan and I won an Oscar: the Yellow Kid award for 1975. This is very important and exciting. There may be a whole new life for Dan Dare ahead. I can't explain more at the moment (I have to sit a University Exam on Thursday) but it could be that your old copies of Eagle, especially Volume I, may be invaluable. Please don't do or say anything about them until I get in touch with you.'

Having got their scoop, the *Guardian* didn't let the matter go. Next day there were another seven column inches following up the story.

'Massive response to the *Guardian*'s rediscovery of Frank Hampson, the man who drew Dan Dare in the Eagle comics of our youth. Ezard's 'phone has been ringing constantly.

Readers asking after Hampson, follow-up specialists from other papers doing likewise, a publisher who always wanted to commission greetings cards from the man who drew the green-headed Mekon and the rest, but didn't know where to find him. And from Paul de Savary, Managing Director of Phenomenal Films, who wants Hampson to work on a ten million dollar "James Bond style" space opera with Cornell Wilde directing and probably Roger Moore as a highly permissive Dan Dare.

'The oddity of the story is that IPC (which own the rights of the original works) can find no record of the (widespread) use of Hampson's work abroad over the last decade. The company is urgently investigating the theory that versions of Hampson's comics circulating at this year's International Exhibition of Comics at Lucca were pirated. IPC, like Hampson, could use the money just now.'

Having seen the effect Ezard's piece had, Denis was also determined not to let things go. He was in touch with Atticus of the *Sunday Times* who, on 9th November 1975, wrote:

'The learned jury responsible for the annual award for the best comics illustrator (who have just selected Britain's Frank Hampson, creator of Dan Dare) are going to have to think again about the name. At the moment it is called the Yellow Kid award after what has always been supposed to be the first cartoon character (American). Denis Gifford who, as the nation's custodian of all things nostalgic, is a comics enthusiast, has now shown it was the British who got in first and the award – if it is to commemorate the first cartoon character – will have to become the Ally Sloper.'

After getting in a plug for his latest work, another comic catalogue, Denis let it be known that he too was thinking of getting into comics for real. 'Gifford now feels himself compelled to do a book on Eagle and Dan Dare and he has been tempting Hampson. Hampson says he'll never be tempted back to working to a deadline (which may account for my own three-foot grey beard) but the signs are distinctly hopeful.'

As soon as he'd cleared his exam, Frank made a search for hopeful signs in his contract with IPC. He discovered he was guaranteed 25% of syndication profits and applied to the Corporation for the same. Eventually they paid him £199 and, a couple of years later, followed this with a further £30. But he got nothing for the Yugoslavian reprints, of which IPC insisted they had no knowledge whatever. Gifford believes that at this stage Frank should have found himself a good copyright lawyer and is sure that, with proper legal help, he could have got more. Frank's attitude is that it's notoriously difficult to prove when a strip has been pirated and he had neither the energy nor the inclination to argue. Myself, if I could produce copies of a Yugoslavian comic carrying Dan Dare I would deem this as proof the strip was running and that *someone* ought to pay. Denis thinks Frank took the money he was offered and probably signed a piece of paper saying he was satisfied and would press the matter no more. He was fifty-seven, far from fit and probably balanced the certain effects a legal battle would have on his health against the possible effect it would have on his bank balance.

But Epsom and Fleet Street weren't the only places where adrenalin was running. There is a generation of programme planners at the BBC who were raised on Dan Dare and they are usually happy to have Frank on a show. Their radio programmes put out the news of the Lucca award the same day as it appeared in the *Guardian,* and a few days later their television side sent a team to interview Frank. He appeared on Nationwide (not for the first – or last – time) full of joy about the trophy. It was the BBC, in fact, who gave Frank his first commendation ever. As far back as November 1950, in an educational programme to the British Forces, they picked out his work and chose it as one of the two best strips currently appearing. What the other one was the *Southport Visiter* does not record.

Copyright ©1976 Marvel Comics Group. Used with permission.

176

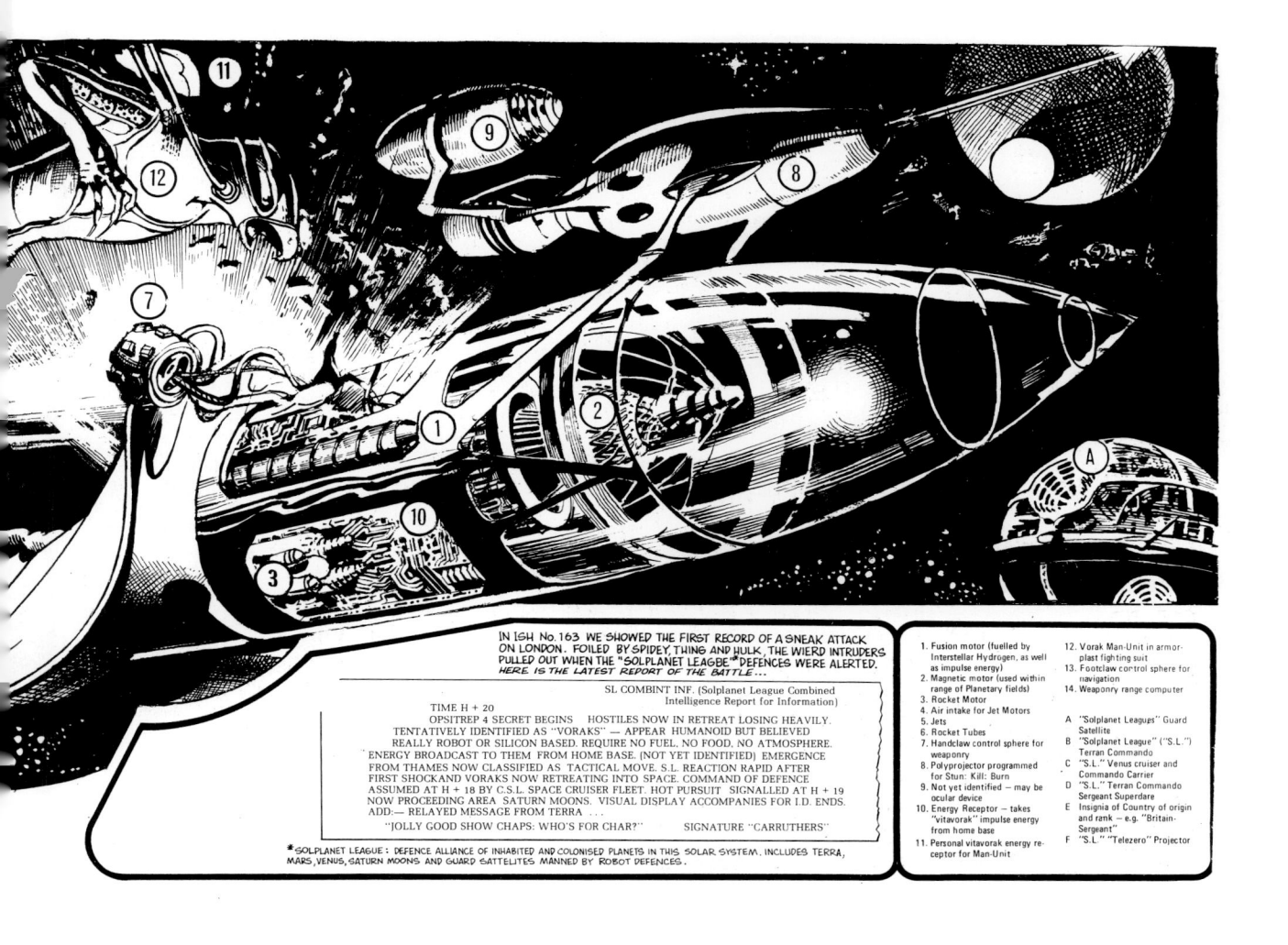

IN ISH No. 163 WE SHOWED THE FIRST RECORD OF A SNEAK ATTACK ON LONDON. FOILED BY SPIDEY, THING AND HULK, THE WIERD INTRUDERS PULLED OUT WHEN THE "SOLPLANET LEAGBE" DEFENCES WERE ALERTED. HERE IS THE LATEST REPORT OF THE BATTLE...

SL COMBINT INF. (Solplanet League Combined Intelligence Report for Information)

TIME H + 20
OPSITREP 4 SECRET BEGINS   HOSTILES NOW IN RETREAT LOSING HEAVILY. TENTATIVELY IDENTIFIED AS "VORAKS" — APPEAR HUMANOID BUT BELIEVED REALLY ROBOT OR SILICON BASED. REQUIRE NO FUEL, NO FOOD, NO ATMOSPHERE. ENERGY BROADCAST TO THEM FROM HOME BASE. (NOT YET IDENTIFIED) EMERGENCE FROM THAMES NOW CLASSIFIED AS TACTICAL MOVE. S.L. REACTION RAPID AFTER FIRST SHOCK AND VORAKS NOW RETREATING INTO SPACE. COMMAND OF DEFENCE ASSUMED AT H + 18 BY C.S.L. SPACE CRUISER FLEET. HOT PURSUIT SIGNALLED AT H + 19 NOW PROCEEDING AREA SATURN MOONS. VISUAL DISPLAY ACCOMPANIES FOR I.D. ENDS. ADD:— RELAYED MESSAGE FROM TERRA ...
"JOLLY GOOD SHOW CHAPS: WHO'S FOR CHAR?"   SIGNATURE "CARRUTHERS"

*SOLPLANET LEAGUE : DEFENCE ALLIANCE OF INHABITED AND COLONISED PLANETS IN THIS SOLAR SYSTEM. INCLUDES TERRA, MARS, VENUS, SATURN MOONS AND GUARD SATTELITES MANNED BY ROBOT DEFENCES.

1. Fusion motor (fuelled by Interstellar Hydrogen, as well as impulse energy)
2. Magnetic motor (used within range of Planetary fields)
3. Rocket Motor
4. Air intake for Jet Motors
5. Jets
6. Rocket Tubes
7. Handclaw control sphere for weaponry
8. Polyprojector programmed for Stun: Kill: Burn
9. Not yet identified — may be ocular device
10. Energy Receptor – takes "vitavorak" impulse energy from home base
11. Personal vitavorak energy receptor for Man-Unit
12. Vorak Man-Unit in armor-plast fighting suit
13. Footclaw control sphere for navigation
14. Weaponry range computer

A "Solplanet Leagues" Guard Satellite
B "Solplanet League" ("S.L.") Terran Commando
C "S.L." Venus cruiser and Commando Carrier
D "S.L." Terran Commando Sergeant Superdare
E Insignia of Country of origin and rank – e.g. Britain-Sergeant
F "S.L." "Telezero" Projector

'Counter Attack' which appeared in the centre spread of 'Spiderman'. One of two spreads Frank Hampson produced for Marvel Comics in 1976.

There was talk of reviving Dan Dare on the shop floor of IPC but the general view taken was that he would have to be more abrasive and shorn of the 'rather prissy, head prefect mannerisms' he displayed when he first appeared. He needed a 'leaner jaw, more piercing eyes and a disposition rather less blandly goody-goody' (the descriptions come by courtesy of IPC). In another neck of the woods a writer, Angus P. Alan, had the notion to turn Frank's Venus story into a full narrative. This he did, and sold the manuscript to the New English Library who brought the tale out in paperback. Just so you get a taste of Mr Alan's style, here's the opening paragraph:

'Melted beyond endurance, the permanon-steel lattice-work of the launch gantry tumbled away like so much spaghetti as "Kingfisher", like a giant aluminium cucumber, lifted slowly away on its blazing tail-jets, the glaring fire from its belly dazzlingly white, even through the polarised glass of the stressed windows in the command observation bunker. The concrete of the apron shimmered in the backlash of the huge engines, and Sir Hubert Guest felt the harsh edges of the control console vibrate beneath his clutching fingers, cutting so sharply into his hands that he had to let go, and, assuming his customary pose of calm and quiet, fold his arms.'

The New English Library book used Frank's artwork for its front cover (in colour) and black and white frames from his Venus story on virtually every page. His name appears bigger than Angus P. Alan's and students at Ewell Technical College brought him copies and asked him if he'd written it. No, the writing wasn't Frank's, although the story was the same. The story about royalties was the same too – Frank got nothing.

A number of other publishers had similar wheezes. Ernest Hecht of Souvenir Press, an old fan of Dan's, and a friend of Denis Gifford's, was happy to publish anything Denis wanted to write about Frank and Eagle. Quite independently Michael Joseph picked up the vibes; their idea was to ask Marcus, as Eagle's first editor, whether he would like to write a book. In the offices of *Astral* (this fanzine, although given up by one enthusiast, quickly found a home and a duplicating machine elsewhere) pens were already scribbling; their greatest hero had been officially *crowned* the greatest; all their admiration and effort in keeping Frank's name alive had come to fruition! In London's Vintage Magazine Shop old copies of the comic were marked up in price, the sudden surge in demand made Eagle hard to come by. Complete volumes began to be advertised in *Exchange and Mart* for £50 a piece (that's nearly a quid a copy – not bad considering they originally sold for three old pence). Serious collectors began to think about getting some original artwork; it could be had for £30 a sheet, but you'd be lucky to get any of the early work and even luckier to get any with Frank's name on it.

Gradually the dust began to settle and it became clear that either Marcus could do a book or Denis could do a book, but they couldn't both do one. Neither publisher would take the risk, knowing the other might pip him to the post. Marcus won the race because he had access to two of IPC's senior directors and, through them, obtained permission to reproduce the original Eagle pages in glorious technicolour. Denis, who thought at first that he too had permission to use old Eagle pictures, was soon disabused. Then, out of the blue, he got a call from Marcus, as a result of which they agreed to work together. Denis would choose the strips to be featured, Marcus would write a lengthy and authoritative introduction, Michael Joseph were happy because they'd got the editor and the top authority on comics collaborating, and neither 'author' had to give up his project. So they went ahead and Denis claims it was he who put together most of *The Best of Eagle*, a compilation which appeared in hardback in August 1977. What Denis hadn't done was put together a written contract. His name was removed from the book's front cover (Marcus insisted that at no stage was it ever intended to be there in the first place) and his credit relegated to an inside page alongside Clifford Makins' name.

Frank Hampson receiving his Alley Sloper award from Denis Gifford and Bob Monkhouse.

Makins, says Denis ruefully, only came in for a few days 'to help out'. The anthology contains forty pages of Frank's colour artwork, nearly half the colour pages in the whole book. It also contains a six thousand word introduction by Marcus, written in the first person, in which he tells of the background to the launch of Eagle. Marcus, of course, received royalties and had his name in big print on the cover. Denis got money but no big credits. Frank got nothing.

What is conspicuous to the outside observer is that what the characters in Frank's life say is quite different from what they do. Marcus speaks of Frank with quiet respect. He is, in the words of the commissionaire who stands guard in the National Magazine Company's building, 'the perfect gentleman'. The directors of IPC have made a special point of creating an award of their own and, at a comics conference held in London, presenting it to Frank in recognition of all he has done for cartooning. The conference, titled Comics 101 – and held to commemorate 101 years of British comics – was originated and organised by Denis. He thought that Lucca was such a good idea that every country should have one, so he booked an hotel and put his show on the road. Taking the hint from Atticus (or maybe it was Denis who gave Atticus the hint in the first place) he had Ally Sloper awards made for this conference. Frank qualified for one of these, accepted the invitation to be one of the guests of honour, and was duly honoured.

Comics 101 was a merry affair. There was a reception, drinks and a hearty meal before the artists received their Ally Slopers which were lined up on the President's table in all their glistening china clay glory. Then came the speeches and more drinks and one of the delegates rose to move to another place. In passing the row of statuettes he accidentally gave the table a hefty knock. The Ally Slopers fell like dominoes and, to a man, their china heads snapped off. A waiter was despatched for superglue and repairs were made while the audience talked among themselves. Frank was not honoured this time as the world's greatest but as the creator of the best *adventure* strip. You might think somebody should have made special mention of his work on 'The Road of Courage' but nobody, it seemed, thought religious strips deserved an Oscar.

A strange little piece appeared in the *Guardian* in March 1976 about how Denis had persuaded the editor of *Reveille* to run a strip titled 'Dan Dare and Son'. But, you protest, the intrepid colonel was never married. In this story it was held that he did take a wife, Professor Jocelyn Peabody (who else?), and there was a sprightly lad who joined his Dad in further space adventures. The strip was to be drawn by artist John Burns and Denis had hopes that Frank would lend a hand; certainly he would get a credit as originator of the main character. This idea, like so many others in which Frank has been involved, died a death (IPC killed it) much to the relief of the purists.

In February 1977, IPC prepared the newsagents for the launch of their comic *2000 AD*, which was finally and definitely to feature Dan Dare. They printed a full colour poster about the spaceman's history and introduced their own version of Dan, who (shades of Buck Rogers) gets frozen in suspended animation and comes back to life centuries later. It was needful for Dan to go through these traumas since, in *2000 AD*, he looked nothing like his old self. In the IPC poster Frank rates just half a sentence.

2000 AD arrived in March 1977 and in July the *Daily Mirror* and Nationwide picked up a puritan campaign by some Welsh miners, disgruntled at the impoverished dialogue and gratuitous violence. Denis was invited to provide copies of the original Eagle, so the old and new Dan Dares could be compared on television. It was a case of the media creating a case for the media to investigate.

In September 1977 Frank wrote again to Alan Vince:

'I have left the technical college where the woman who was my boss has made life unbearable for me. At the moment I'm concentrating on my Open University Courses (final exams in October) but a man named Roger Dean has been in touch with me. Do you know him? He is young and has made a considerable reputation designing record sleeves.

'He and some colleagues, or rather partners of his, have bought the book rights in Dan Dare and plan to produce a trilogy: *The Man from Nowhere*, *Rogue Planet* and *The Reign of the Robots*, in three separate books. They have asked me to co-operate on this by writing a foreword and designing a cover and to this I have agreed. They are also, of course, thinking hard about how to fill the space the Eagle masthead took on each cover.

'I almost forgot to mention! I'm working at the moment on a commission for the Science Museum, South Kensington, for two panels of my characters and machines for a new children's Space Exhibition Gallery they're opening soon. The job has got to be complete by November 14th, so I'm going to be quite busy. The panels are about 8 foot by 4 foot.'

Roger Dean is a science fiction artist who started his small publishing company, with offices in London and Brighton, in 1975. He began his career with three years at the Royal College of Art, studying architecture and furniture design. It's he you have to blame for the decor at Ronnie Scott's Upstairs Club. His skill in draughtsmanship took him into record sleeve design (he showed a promoter his sketchbook) and there followed some remarkable work. Two groups in particular used it: one called 'Yes', big noises (literally) in the USA, and the second, 'Osibisa', who play Nigerian-style funk (honest!).

These sleeves had such visual impact they were reprinted as posters and by 1974 were selling to the tune of half a million a year worldwide. Dean became convinced there was a market for a definitive collection. He'd been careful to keep the copyrights so just needed a publisher to help. But no-one was interested and there followed a frustrating twelve months, during which he knew a market existed but couldn't fill it. Then Roger Dean decided to publish himself.

At the same time as he became a publisher, Dean was producing skilled and imaginative science fiction pictures, so it was natural that he should attract other futuristic artists to his fold. Time travellers, space heroes and BEMs (bug-eyed monsters) are Dragon's Dream's stock in trade and when Dean asked his illustrators how they first became interested in the genre, the most usual answer was Dan Dare. 'There's no work like that around today; why doesn't someone resurrect him?'

So that's what they did. But in order to publish the strip as an unbroken story meant losing the continuously repeated Eagle masthead. Simply to omit it would have left a hole in the artwork; the options were to omit the large picture opposite as well (thus levelling up the frames) or re-draw to fill the extra space. They decided to re-draw and Frank began to develop the first frame of every episode to lose the title panel and the summary for new readers. Open University only left him time to do pencil sketches, but these were passed to Don Harley, who completed the finished artwork – it took him eleven months.

There was a query on how the books should be produced: as a colour broadsheet, distributed through newsagents, or a bookshop publication, on art paper, with a spine, quality printing and a properly researched introduction.

A Dutch printer was awarded the job and the first forty-five episodes of '*The Man from Nowhere*' were reissued as a 116 page art book.

The Dragon's Dream books were meat and drink to the 'Astral Club': Frank's most loyal fans decided it was time for them to have their say and they said it at another convention, this time to mark the thirtieth anniversary of the birth of Eagle. The press plugged the event a

DAN DARE
PILOT OF THE FUTURE
IN
THE MAN FROM NOWHERE
VOLUME ONE

183

EAGLE
CONVENTION 1980

OFFICIAL SOUVENIR BROCHURE

A CONVENTION
TO MARK THE 30th ANNIVERSARY
OF THE 'EAGLE' MAGAZINE

week before it was due but, despite their support and the undoubtedly hard work of the organisers, it was a drably attended affair. Launched at the Y Hotel in London, it stretched over two days, the high spot being an hour-long lecture by Frank on the inside story of his strip. After forty minutes, in a conference room that could have held 250 but was only a third full, I crept away. The sadness of the occasion had seeped into me. There we were, in our early forties, trying to recapture our teens; what we found was a poorly attended event, pitifully short both on the personalities involved and how the whole miracle of Eagle came about. The organisers' hearts were in the right place – the affair had taken two years to organise and, as they said, they needed every minute. But, to succeed with a two-day event like this, you need imagination, experience and money – most of all money. You could buy a one-day pass into Eaglecon '80 for £4.50. And it showed.

At the end of 1980, the papers began to carry reports of a Dan Dare television series. It never happened, which was probably just as well for Frank's blood pressure, but I had the chance to talk to the producer, Leon Clifton, at his headquarters in Mayfair. Clifton is charming and sincere in his wish to produce an excellent television series but, behind the four million dollars set aside for the project, was an astute business organisation. Clifton was generous with his time and by the end of the meeting I thought I had a better idea what these programmes, and indeed most of the television series aimed at kids, had going for them.

Over the back of Clifton's chair hung a brown anorak of material that looked like satin; very smart and very rich. On the back of the anorak was blazoned the familiar flying Eagle from the comic's front page. Encircling the bird, in cartoon bold typeface, were the words, 'Dan Dare, Pilot of the Future', and embroidered in green on the right upper sleeve was the Mekon on his magnetic chair. The anorak was clearly a one-off, for Leon had his own name matched-in on a pocket on the front, but multiply it by a million, then add LPs, cassettes, toys, games and model kits of all descriptions, the script done over as a novel, the *Dan Dare Annual*, jigsaws, T-shirts and maybe even a television game you can play when the show's over: now isn't that what it's all about?

This is not to say that the show itself might have been below par. The actors said to be signed up for the deal included James Fox as Dan, making a return to full-time professional acting after ten years working for an evangelical organisation called 'The Navigators', and Rodney Bewes – a member, incidentally, of the 'Astral Club' – playing Albert Fitzwilliam Digby.

There are a few interesting points to be made about this television series, which had been pre-sold, I was led to believe, to television companies worldwide. The project was 'postponed' scarcely a fortnight before the videotape was due to roll. Videotape is cheaper to use than film and Clifton was confident that, with the advances that have been made in the medium, it can now achieve virtually the same kind of special effects. Cause of the postponement was money. I picked up a titbit that most of de Savary's money was, in fact, coming from his brother, who decided the extravaganza was too risky to commit a large sum into the production. I do

Left Despite its failings, the 1980 Eagle Convention was a happy event for some. There was a comprehensive display of Eagle artwork, examples of merchandise together with artifacts from the Dan Dare studio, and above all there was the chance to talk with a good number of the ex-Eagle people attending such as Marcus Morris, Frank Humphris, Charles Chilton, Macdonald Hastings, Greta Tomlinson (now Edwards), Keith Watson and of course Frank Hampson himself who professed to having enjoyed the event.

CALLING COLONEL DARE!

understand there was a close link-up between the television Dare and the *2000 AD* Dare. Scraps of the storyboards from the production were printed in the comics, as were designs for some of the aliens, particularly the Atlantines or blue-skins (which, incidentally, were turned into green-skins). The television Atlantines didn't look at all like Frank's ancient earthmen who had been shipped to Venus when the Treens landed on Earth 100,000 years ago.

Professor Peabody was decidedly more sexy than the simple girl who appeared in Eagle but, since thirty years have elapsed, that, I suppose, is par for the course. The television series also planned to feature a Russian, a woman with a mind like a knife and a grip like a vice. When I mentioned this to Frank, he divulged that he too wanted to have a Russian in his space fleet to stand alongside the Frenchman and the Yank, but the cold war was bitter in 1950 and he was dissuaded from introducing Boris, despite his faith in the United Nations. He did however manage to squeeze in a negro, who was put in command of the Earth forces dropped on Venus to break the technological deadlock between the two hemispheres of the planet.

2000 AD was urging the kids to look forward to the television Dare and advised them not to lose hope, even when the programmes were put on ice, so it's pretty clear the marketing tie-up between the publishers, ATV, and Phenomenal Films was well established and it's likely that, having come so far, the consortium will try to get Dan on the box again. Part of the programme was in animation and Keith Watson was signed on as an adviser, the main illustrating to be done by two young artists, raised on Frank's work, and a number of freelancers to be commissioned independently. Admittedly the budget was only four million dollars to pay the stars and the pop artists (among whom was numbered Gary Osborne, lyricist to Elton John) and stretch across thirteen instalments. Maybe this was a reason why Frank was to be paid nothing.

However, there were a few bright spots during the five years after fame at Lucca. In October 1978 Frank sat for his Open University Degree and on 26th January 1979 he was formally declared a Batchelor of Arts, alongside Geoff Nulty and ten other people who were presented to the then Prime Minister, James Callaghan, at the University of Milton Keynes. It was Geoff Nulty who stole the headlines in the popular press however, as the £20,000 a year mid-field player for Everton; the football star, already laden with 'O' and 'A' levels, joked about his academic prowess; Frank continued to insist that, prior to the BA, he had no exams to his name at all. In all a total of 5,000 students won honours in the OU that year; the adult education scheme was ten years old; Frank had just turned sixty.

The muse flashed for a brief instant and, as a special treat for *Astral* readers (the fanzine was still going strong and had a paid-up readership of about 120), Frank drew a new Dan Dare strip. In it our hero in his space-fleet uniform, chats to the PM and the University Vice-Chancellor – who Frank also met – as to where the OU should go from here. With some consternation the Vice-Chancellor announces he has had an application from mighty-brain himself; next year the course will be joined by the Mekon!

Before he fell into the doldrums again and declared the reason he studied for his course was to have the initials 'BA' on his gravestone, Frank made one last try for glory. He created Dawn O'Dare, pioneer lady journalist from the *last* century (when you've done the future, go into the past). For how she met and loved the Admiral Crashman, read on.

Left Harold Johns posing as a Treen in a flying war chariot from the Dan Dare story, 1950.

dawn o'dare

REVEALED AT LAST! DISCOVERED IN THE ARCHIVES AT O'DARE CASTLE, Co. MAYO, THIS IS THE STORY OF A SENSATIONAL 19TH CENTURY ANGLO-IRISH VENTURE INTO ---- **HYPERSPACE!** DRAWN BY FRANK HAMPSON, THE STORY OPENS AS **DAWN O'DARE**, PIONEER GIRL REPORTER, IS ON HER FIRST BIG ASSIGNMENT —

"CAN YOU TELL OUR READERS WHERE YOU'RE BOUND FOR ON THIS MISSION, ADMIRAL CRASHMAN?"

© 1976 FRANK HAMPSON

"YES, ME DEAR DAWN, — I'M TAKIN' OVER OUR FAR EAST SQUADRON IN HONG KONG..."

"TOMORROW!"

"TOMORROW? HONG-KONG?"

"BUT THAT'S IMPOSSIBLE ADMIRAL! ...IT'S A THREE MONTH JOURNEY!"

"**NOT** IN OUR **NEW** SHIP, DAWN!"

"LIKE TO SEE?"

"NEW SHIP! **SCHMOO SHIP!** IT'LL ONLY MEAN MORE TROUBLE FOR ARNOLD, THE ADMIRAL'S DEVOTED STEWARD..."

"I'M ARNOLD"

"FOLLOW ME... TO THE BIGGEST THING SINCE NELSON!"

THE LONG GOODBYE

You will remember that at Lucca, one of the Committee members most interested in Frank, and partly instrumental in securing his award, was the powerful, much travelled and prolific Italian artist, Hugo Pratt. One of Hugo's many creations is a nineteenth century sea captain, whose ocean-roving exploits have thrilled many a young comic reader. When Denis Gifford's efforts on Dan Dare and Son were grounded by an embargo from IPC, Denis approached Frank with the idea of producing an entirely new strip, which he was willing to help the artist conceive. And part of the concept included a nineteenth century sea captain. The scheme was: Denis and Frank would collaborate on a script, Frank would do the drawings and the result would be published, for starters, in Gifford's fanzine *Ally Sloper*. You would think that, with Frank's track record, if he produced a new strip he would be able to get it published in a rather more auspicious magazine, with a bigger circulation than the possible 1,000 readers *Ally Sloper* could command. But the thinking was, take one step at a time. Persuade Frank he could start a new strip. Help him conceive it. Wait till he drew it. Publish it in a small-time way to start with. And, if things went well and Frank was able to keep up production, they try and sell the results to one of the big boys.

Frank took the nineteenth century sea captain idea but was not convinced that his main hero should be confined to the seven oceans. Life aboard ship leaves little scope for an artist to expand his venues. So Frank added a pork-pie-hatted, bustle-skirted pioneer lady journalist named Dawn O'Dare, who starred in, and I quote: 'a sensational nineteenth century Anglo-Irish venture into hyperspace.' The story opens as Dawn is on her first big assignment, interviewing Admiral Crashman at the dockside so she can tell her readers where he is bound on his next mission. And surprise, surprise, Admiral Crashman has a side-kick called Arnold, and Arnold the devoted steward, is none other than Batman Digby in a pith helmet. Dawn has a side-kick too, a lanky and dapper photographer, whose job is to snap the pictures on his plate camera and not be heard.

Frank drew a page of impeccable artwork in black and white in which we meet these four characters and in which Admiral Crashman declares he is leaving Liverpool in his sailing ship to take over Britain's far east squadron in Hong Kong. And he will arrive there *tomorrow*! That was the curtain, and the strip was to have woven a tale of time machines and quantum jumps because Admiral Crashman's new ship was nothing less than a time-and-space ship. Dawn O'Dare, was published in the Christmas issue of *Ally Sloper*, 1976, and the readers could hardly wait for the second instalment. Incidentally, Denis spared no trouble announcing that Frank was finally drawing again. He gave the artist the full works, including front cover headlines, an editorial write-up by Peter Hampson (Memoirs of a space cadet) and the best lead page in his fanzine. So what happened in the second episode?

There wasn't one. Alas, Dawn lived and died in the six frames you see here. One or two of the faithful tapped their noses at the time and hint today that perhaps more of the saga lies in the files at Frank's home. Somewhere too, James Dean lives. The truth is Dawn O'Dare was born in the flush of enthusiasm after Lucca and she is living proof that Frank could still do it and that he couldn't do it. What's interesting is that Dawn O'Dare contains none of the visual obfuscation and miserable dialogue that infects comics today. And Frank, at first determined

Left *'Dawn O'Dare'* 1976.

that he was on the road again, made certain he would retain the copyright, and wrote as much on the artwork. But the truth is, he couldn't keep the story up. Of course there were other things to do. Peter Hampson wrote in his editorial that Dad was back in the limelight and 'demands on his time were, and are, very heavy'. But Denis's fanzine only appeared every quarter and one page of artwork every three months shouldn't have been beyond Frank's capacity. It was. There wasn't much – possibly not any – money in Dawn O'Dare and certainly very little kudos; maybe Frank was hoping that one of the national papers would pick her up and he would get an offer.

I think he finally realised that, after so long out of the saddle, he simply could not ride again. For a brief week his creative muse came to him as she had come in the early days. But he was old, tired and not very well.

While Frank was finally acknowledging to himself that he couldn't do it, others up in London were girding their loins in an effort to convince themselves they could. John Sanders, Deputy Managing Director of IPC and the man who has the final say on the kid's stuff, happily admits he's been plagued for years by people asking him to revive the old Eagle. Equally, he had plagued them by telling them not to be so infantile and that all this namby-pamby stuff about Battle of Britain pilots in spaceships, stories of do-gooders on the back page and, indeed, any kid's paper reflecting the Christian ethic, is pie in the sky, propagated by people who simply won't grow up. This is the television and video age and, in his comics, it takes the kids all their time to look at the pictures, never mind work out scientific data in a convoluted story which spends more time developing characters than getting anywhere. The IPC view in 1980 was best expressed by Chris Lowder, the man who boasted he finally killed the original Eagle:

'It was dead anyway; all we did was chuck earth on the coffin. When *Lion* gobbled up the paper, circulation was down to 25,000.'

His answer to the revivalists was:

'Looked at with a cold unprejudiced eye, Eagle was merely a symbol of its time, and no more. Certainly it has about as much relevance to the 1980s as the *Gem* or *Magnet*, or, to dive deeper into the realm of antiquarian study, Deadwood Dick and Jack Harkaway.'

In 1980 it may be that Lowder's bosses were happy to read that view, publicly expressed. But there were people in the company who thought otherwise – David Hunt for one, who is now editor of the new Eagle, and Barrie Tomlinson, head of Boys' Adventure Publications, who over a lunch-time finally persuaded John Sanders it was possible to get a new bird off the ground. There was a long gestation period in the nest however, during which IPC secretly tested new strips in existing comics to find out what the kinds wanted. Tomlinson also analysed hundreds of letters from readers of his other comics and the IPC Market Research Department added their findings (for what they are worth, for I believe with this kind of Market Research, garbage in produces garbage out). On 17th March 1982 they finally launched a brand new Eagle.

Scene: London's Waldorf Hotel in the Aldwych. Time: just before lunch. The journalists, media watchers, BBC cameramen, Denis Gifford, Paul de Savary and script-writer Phil Redmond are scoffing the canapes, sipping green Mekon cocktails and fiddling with the video consoles. Suddenly the trumpets sound (real trumpeters hired from the army) and through a paper screen bursts television wrestler big Big Daddy, sitting astride the bonnet of a white minivan, waving comics in a mighty fist, crying, 'Eagle has landed. Eagle has landed!' He jumps off the bonnet and thrusts a copy into every outstretched hand. The driver of the mini, dressed and made up to look like Dan Dare (yes, even down to the kinky eyebrows) hurries

DAN DARE'S SPACE SUIT

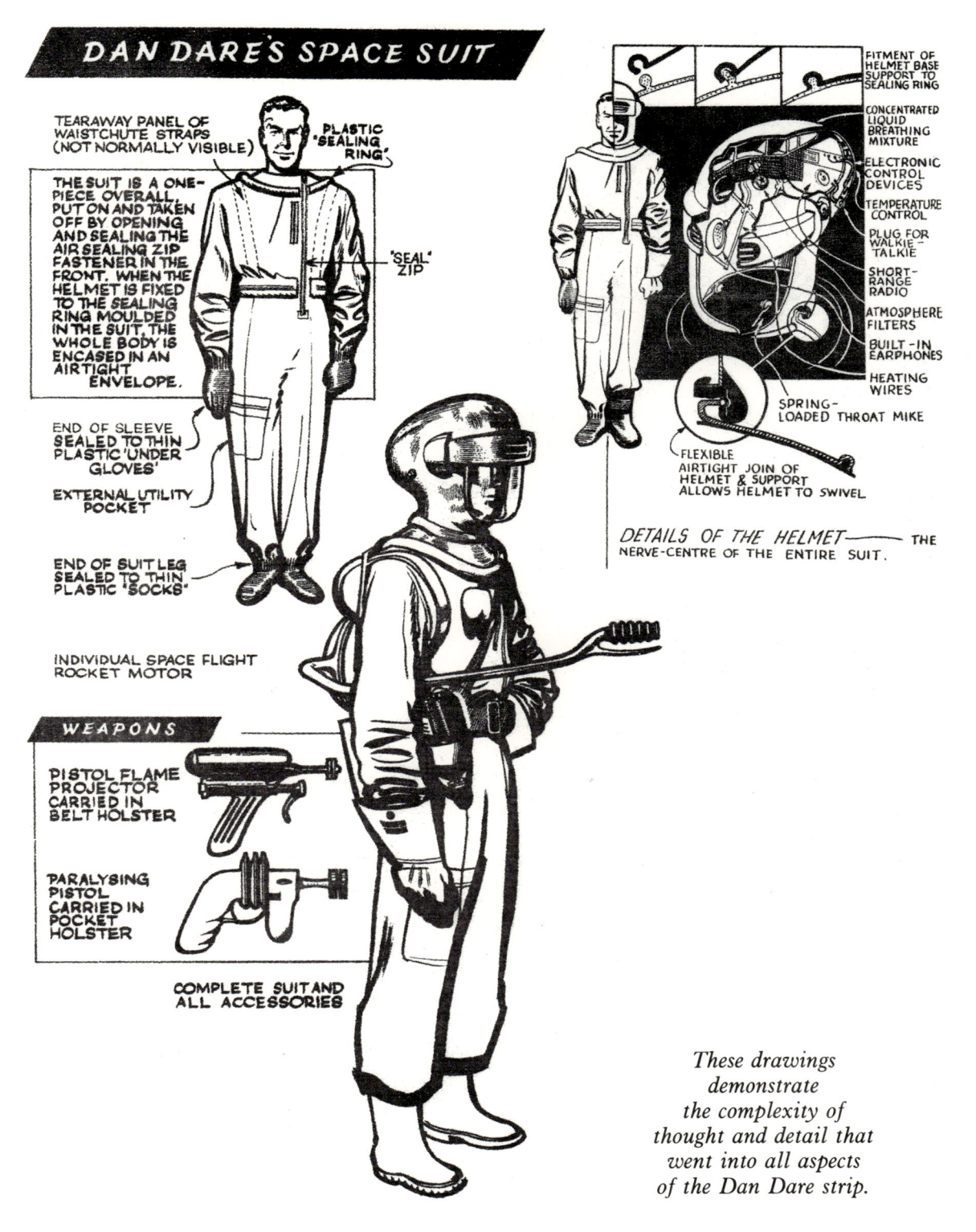

TEARAWAY PANEL OF WAISTCHUTE STRAPS (NOT NORMALLY VISIBLE)

PLASTIC 'SEALING RING'

THE SUIT IS A ONE-PIECE OVERALL, PUT ON AND TAKEN OFF BY OPENING AND SEALING THE AIR SEALING ZIP FASTENER IN THE FRONT. WHEN THE HELMET IS FIXED TO THE SEALING RING MOULDED IN THE SUIT, THE WHOLE BODY IS ENCASED IN AN AIRTIGHT ENVELOPE.

'SEAL' ZIP

END OF SLEEVE SEALED TO THIN PLASTIC 'UNDER GLOVES'

EXTERNAL UTILITY POCKET

END OF SUIT LEG SEALED TO THIN PLASTIC 'SOCKS'

INDIVIDUAL SPACE FLIGHT ROCKET MOTOR

WEAPONS

PISTOL FLAME PROJECTOR CARRIED IN BELT HOLSTER

PARALYSING PISTOL CARRIED IN POCKET HOLSTER

COMPLETE SUIT AND ALL ACCESSORIES

FITMENT OF HELMET BASE SUPPORT TO SEALING RING

CONCENTRATED LIQUID BREATHING MIXTURE

ELECTRONIC CONTROL DEVICES

TEMPERATURE CONTROL

PLUG FOR WALKIE-TALKIE

SHORT-RANGE RADIO

ATMOSPHERE FILTERS

BUILT-IN EARPHONES

HEATING WIRES

SPRING-LOADED THROAT MIKE

FLEXIBLE AIRTIGHT JOIN OF HELMET & SUPPORT ALLOWS HELMET TO SWIVEL

DETAILS OF THE HELMET — THE NERVE-CENTRE OF THE ENTIRE SUIT.

These drawings demonstrate the complexity of thought and detail that went into all aspects of the Dan Dare strip.

to the front of the van with an anguished howl. The weight of the wrestler has left a dent in the bonnet which Dan-the-hire-car-driver has to explain to his company.

But the impatient newsmen have no time for him. We all want to see this phoenix risen from the ashes. And it has some good things going for it, including a coloured hero called Smokey Beckles; Smokey, because he weaves like smoke through opposing football teams before winging the ball to Thunderbolt who (you've guessed) thunders it into the net. But the new comic is barely recognisable, stacked against the old; the page size has shrunk to a standard A4, the brilliant inks are gone, the sweet-smelling paper too. Plodding PC49 is replaced by Sgt Streetwise, who dresses as a dosser and a punk to get his man and although, as Barrie Tomlinson says, 'There's nothing to upset even Mary Whitehouse', there's certainly nothing to woo the schoolmarms, or suspicious parents either.

But Dan Dare is back. He's been banished from the front to the inside pages, with a turn-on to the back. And Eagle, once internationally famous for its pioneering artwork, now consists almost entirely of posed photostrip stories. The big hero is Doomlord, a tall, masked alien come to Earth and Doomlord is a photostrip because photographs, says IPC, look more authentic and appeal more to children raised on television. The initial print run is 340,000 (standard for any new IPC comic). They figure it'll settle down at 250,000 when the Dads have stopped buying it. Neither Frank nor Marcus are among the invited audience, lest they should be regarded as spectres at a costly feast.

The most dismal side of the affair was a headline carried by Frank's local paper, the *Epsom and Ewell Guardian* (91,000 copies weekly) which appeared when IPC broke the news that their eighties version of the comic was coming. 'Comic strip creator forgotten as Eagle waits to swoop' was its front page lead story. You can almost hear the sigh as once again Frank sits with a reporter in the lounge of his home, where sheets of original artwork hang on the walls, and says: 'I feel a bit annoyed that they are using the name again and it makes me feel sad. A younger man will be drawing him and I cannot forecast the assumptions a younger man will have, but Dan will not be the same. It would be difficult for anyone to capture the essential Britishness. My wife is upset too and wonders why they can't invent their own heroes.' But there was no question that Frank could have taken on the job, even if he had been approached (which he wasn't). The new Dan Dare spread across three pages of the paper; Frank could scarcely have produced three frames. And there was no question about recapturing 'that essential Britishness'. It was about the last thing IPC were looking for.

There is a parallel with Frank's story and what happened to two American artists – Joe Shuster and Gerry Siegel – the creators of the three-times filmed Superman. They too relinquished the copyright of their creation, then fell foul of their publishers (there was a

Right These photographs show the complete Dan Dare spacesuit, including the 'individual space flight propulsion unit' that was made for reference use in the studio. Hampson would first conceive and draw the basic figure positions and then use the photographs to check feasibility and lighting. The best would be taken from the photographs and visual to produce the final page.

Over What was to be the start of a new epic journey for Dan Dare in search of his father was sadly the end of Dan Dare for Frank Hampson. A concept sketch with last Hampson page for Dan Dare, fascinating for the absence of balloons and captions. Max Dunlop models the alien's costume, ('Terra Nova' 1959)

EAGLE 6 June 1954
TAKE OVER, DIG – I'LL FIX MAGNETIC GRAPPLES AS WE DRAW ALONGSIDE.
AYE – AYE, SIR!
I WISH YOU'D LET ME COM
YOU, SIR!
NO, DIG – THIS
TIME WHEN I'D RA
BE ALONE
THE AIRLOCK DOOR'S OPEN – I DON'T LIKE THE LOOK OF THIS . . .
THERE'S BEEN SOME SORT OF EXPLOSION HERE . . .
WELL, HERE GOES – I'VE GOT TO FIND OUT . . .
THAT MUST BE – THE PILOT . . .
COSM
SO HE NEVER TOUCHED DOWN ON TERRA NOVA AFTER ALL!
HAS DAN'S JOURNEY TO TERRA NOVA BEEN IN VAIN? READ NEXT WEEK'S EPISODE!
2
All copyright of Dan Dare Pilot
Future is vested in Hulton Pres

TERRA NOVA
projected NATIVE TYPE FIRST ENCOUNTERED.

Saw toothed Animal horns

7 pronged Ceremonial Spear (Tribal Standard)
Normal Spear 5 pronged.

Basketwork Ammunition Carrier (stones or other missiles)

CESTA →

Small wicker shield

"Stand up" Saddle type support.

"Criss-Cross" Interleaved Kilt of naturally elasticated material. Varied Colours + patterns.

"Eagle headed" Riding lizard. Used for hunting and Battle. Max Speed. 45 mph

By pushing "lever" at base of ammunition carrier with end of Cesta, one stone or other missile is released into Cesta, ready to be thrown.

By Frank Hampson

DAN DARE
PILOT OF THE FUTURE
TERRA NOVA

FRANK HAMPSON

THE STORY SO FAR: Dan Dare, Digby and Sir Hubert Guest leave Jocelyn Peabody, Galileo McHoo, 'Flamer' Spry and Lex O'Malley aboard the *Galactic Galleon* and complete their journey to *Terra Nova* – a new world – in *Anastasia*. The three friends, make a successful landing. They are unaware, however, that their arrival has been seen – and reported!

ROME

"MAKE WAY—MAKE WAY THERE!"

"IN THE NAME OF CAESAR, MAKE WAY!"

"I DEMAND PASSAGE, IN THE NAME OF GREAT CAESAR!"

"THERE'S YOUR DESTINATION—JOPPA, PORT FOR JUDAEA."

"TAKE ME TO HEROD, KING OF JUDAEA!"

"GREETINGS, YOUR MAJESTY..."

"I BRING ORDERS FROM THE EMPEROR—GREAT CAESAR."

FRANK HAMPSON

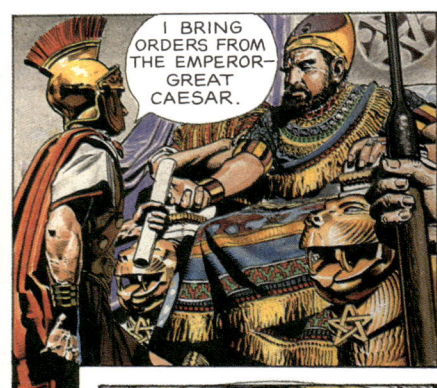

"H'M SO CAESAR WANTS A CENSUS, DOES HE?"

"GUARD COMMANDER! SEND PATROLS INTO THE CITY, AND DOUBLE THE GUARD ON THE PALACE..."

"YES, SIR!"

CAESAR HAS ORDERED A CENSUS—*IN JUDAEA, THAT MEANS BLOODSHED!*

'The Road of Courage': The opening episode was drawn half-up – subsequent pages of artwork were the same size as they appeared on the Eagle page.

This strip gave Hampson the opportunity to display his skill at characterisation to the full, whether the twisted features of pharisees or the sensitive countenance of Mary. The attack of the Zealots is the page Hampson was most satisfied with.

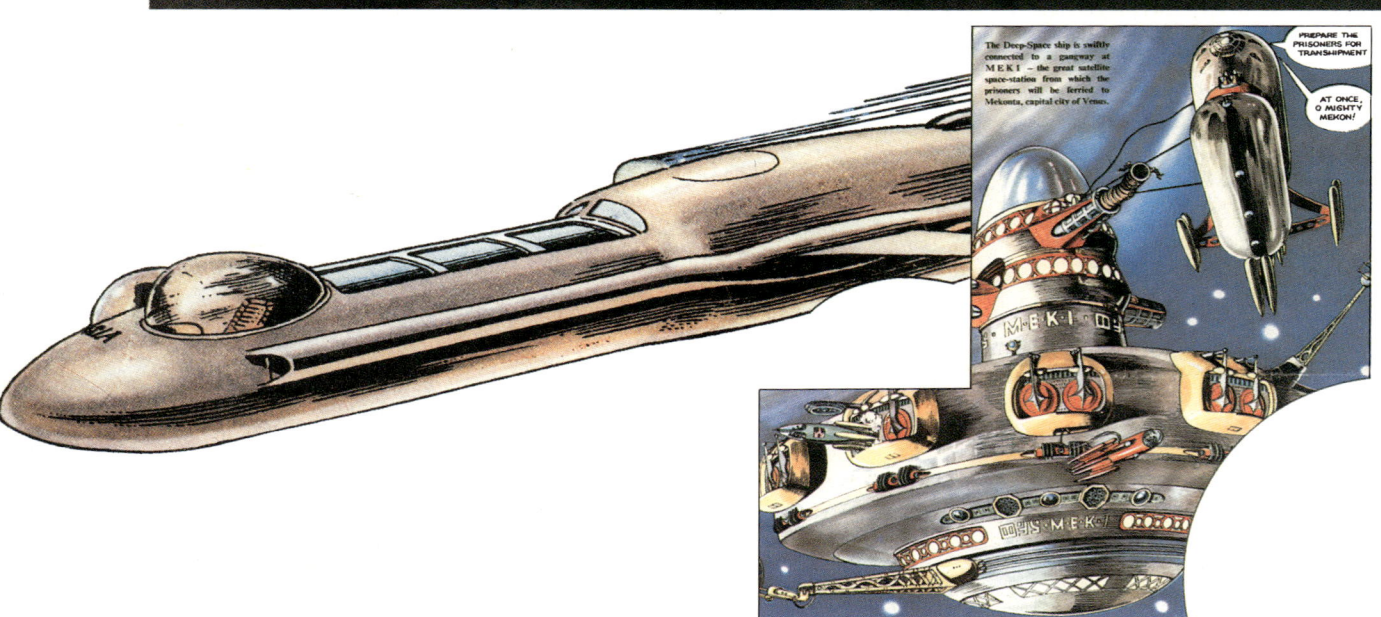

The WonderWorld Communications Centre

Above *Concept painting of the Communication station at dusk, together with two key pieces of hardware from the Dan Dare strip by Frank Hampson that helped influence its design, the Anastasia and MEK 1, a Treen space-station.*

Right *An artist's impression of the Dan Dare restaurant and two of Hampson's designs used in the painting. One is part of the interior of a Crypt spaceship and the other an example of Treen decoration.*

'HOUSE OF SILENCE'.

Left *One of the murals completed by Frank Hampson for the Science Museum 1977*

Below *Key drawing for the other Science Museum panel*

"I DON'T THINK I'M GOING TO LIKE THIS PLANET— IT'S MESSY"

lawsuit when someone introduced Superboy) and found themselves out of work. A true story tells of how, when a New York impresario decided to launch a Broadway show called 'Superman', the two comic men were so poor that they stood outside the theatre begging for enough money to buy them each a ticket. However, for those two Americans things look decidedly better for there is now – after much hassle – an agreement with DC Comics (publishers of the superhero books and a subsidiary of Warner Communications who distribute the films) that the creators get a credit at the top of every new strip drawn, although they are both too old to do any of the work themselves. They also get their names on the film titles and each gets paid $20,000 a year for life. Their descendants will get $10,000. Further, there is a law in the States today that says, thirty-five years after you sign a contract you can apply to get the copyright back. Not that this law did either of them any good when they applied, but at least it's there. There is no legislation of this kind in the UK – albeit there is a groundswell among strip artists to press for something like it – but perhaps one day Frank will get his name at the top of the new Dan Dare strip and on any film or television series that appears, for all to see. I don't need to spell out how much he got as nostalgic Dads took their sons to collect new Eagle number one from the newsagents.

The cover date of the first new Eagle was 27th March 1982. A year and two weeks later, while on a day trip with his wife to Bournemouth, Frank was felled by a massive stroke and it was around the same time that I began to seek out people who had worked with him in the fifties to get them to tell his story. Harold Johns, who met Frank when he began to study art and joined him freelancing at Southport, and who was subsequently fired from Eagle after four years, remained working in Epsom until the mid-sixties. He then decided to go home to Southport and at first – since he was unmarried – chose to live with his sister, continuing his freelance work and his watercolour painting. A Southport Art Gallery took all Harold's paintings of World War II; the more recent work he sold through a dealer who rated him as 'a significant national artist whose pictures will be collected long after many artists, like Lowry and Helen Bradley, whose names are famous now, have gone out of fashion'. Well, we shall see. Later Harold moved into a flat on his own and began to slow down and spend more time in the North Western Fell country where he concentrated on landscapes. 'When these included figures', writes the *Southport Visiter*, 'they were superlatively natural and realistic.' The artist was sketching in Ince Woods, not far from his home, when he died quite suddenly and unexpectedly in June 1980. He was sixty-two.

Jo Thomas, first of the young women artists to join Frank, is alive and well and living back in the Isle of Man. After she left Frank's studio to marry, she and her new husband left immediately for India, where they spent the next three years. She returned to the South of England to raise her family (one son, one daughter) and occasionally popped into the Bayford Lodge studio to see how Frank was getting on. Jo Thomas (now Jo Pattinson) softens when she remembers how the artists would sometimes pair off to go to the pictures or on rambles over Epsom Downs in summer. But overriding everything are the memories of the tensions and intolerable hours, the friction that grew up through all of them working so closely and the inevitable clash of personalities, especially between Frank and Bruce Cornwell.

The pressure of work which was, quite literally, disturbing, is the indelible impression carried by Greta Tomlinson too. She came back from the Middle East after over a decade of working in and touring the area. She admired the culture but could never reconcile herself to the corruption. When she called on Frank for old time's sake, he told her, 'Greta, I owe you thousands'. 'And so he does,' she says, 'but neither he nor I saw much of the money our work made.' Today Greta Edwards (as she became) has little to show for her time in the Dan Dare

Greta Tomlinson 'acting' the role of Professor Joceylyn Peabody.

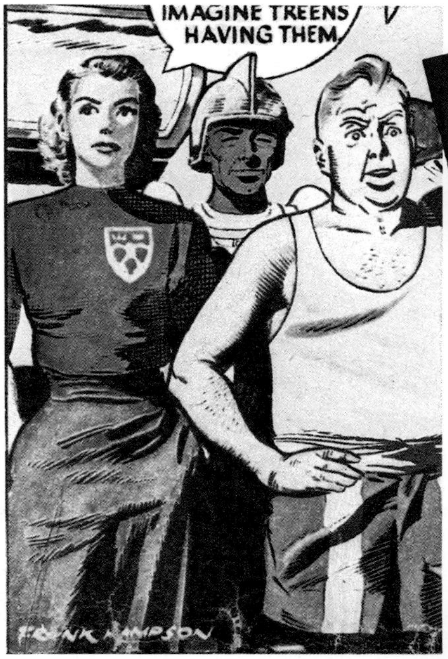
IMAGINE TREENS HAVING THEM.

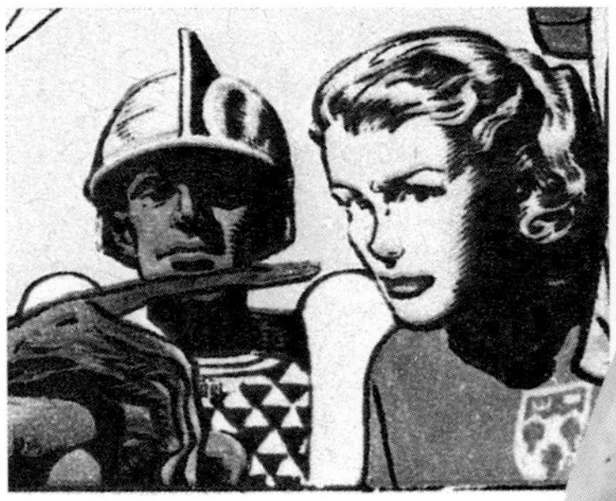

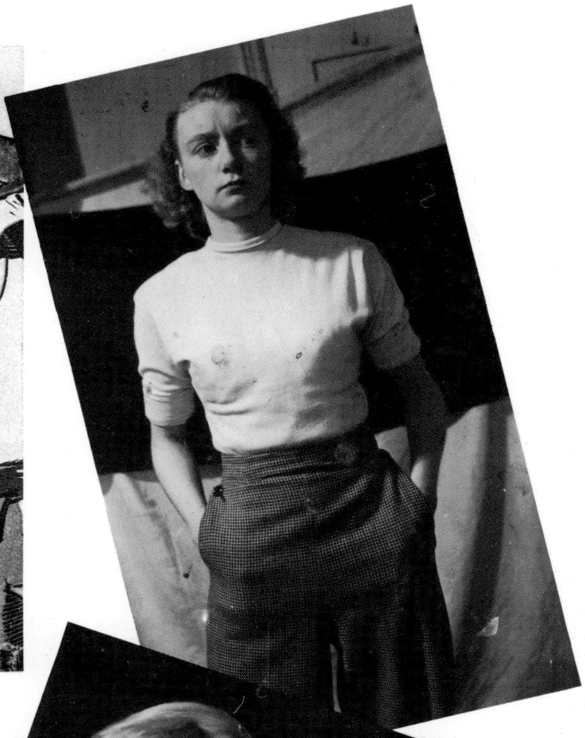

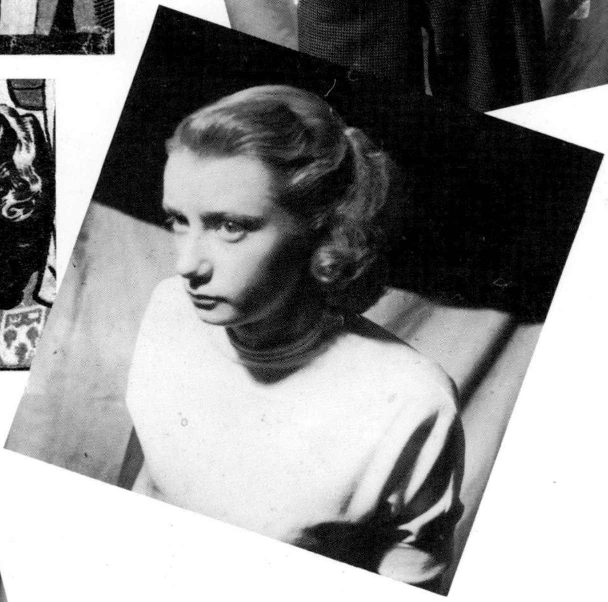

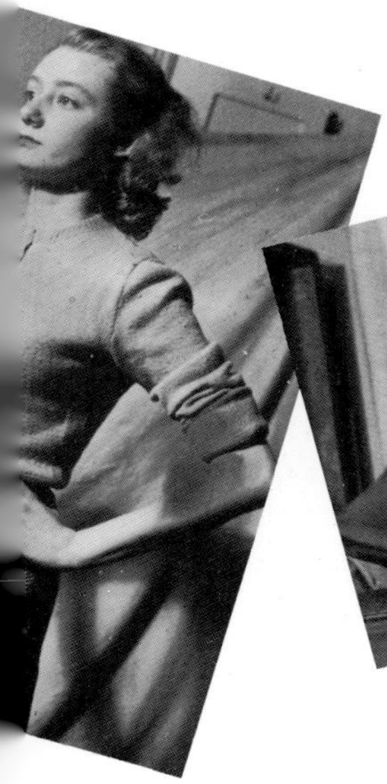

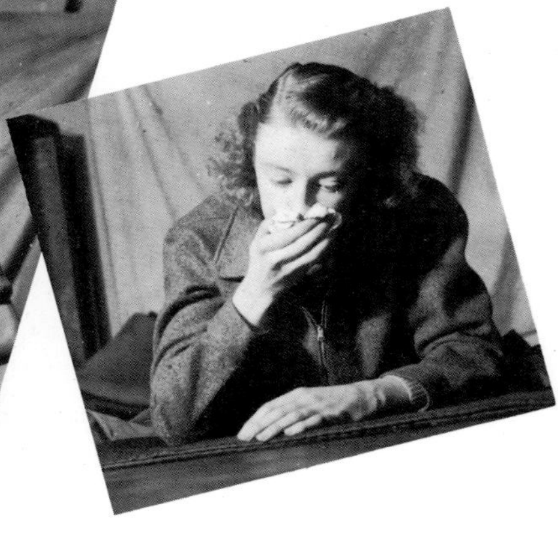

studio. The one piece of original artwork she owns she bought from a dealer who advertised it in the *Daily Telegraph*. He asked for £55.00 (more than the price Frank was paid for doing it) but when she explained she was the original Professor Peabody, who modelled for and drew the strip, he knocked the fee down by a fiver. Greta Edwards still earns a living from her art. She spends most of her time now in a delightful home with a large courtyard, well off the main roads in a secluded part of Surrey. The last time she spoke to Frank was at the convention to mark Eagle's thirtieth birthday, held in 1980.

Bruce Cornwell, the extrovert Canadian who arrived in the Bakery via Art School in Paris and freelance work in London, carried on drawing Dan Dare long after Frank had left the strip. He took on the job, despite the fact that he had left Frank's studio twice before, once in protest at the workload and once because Frank fired him (he was on holiday at the time and came home to find the letter of dismissal on his doormat). There is a long-time antipathy between them, the trans-Atlantic informality and ebullience Cornwell brought to work with him and his undeniable good looks, were both causes for tension and the Lancastrian Frank bristled when he was addressed as 'Bub'. The Canadian is still in his Ruislip home and if Frank should ever telephone him, there is no fear he would get a dusty answer. Cornwell is ex-directory.

Don Harley – 'the second best Dan Dare artist in the world' – has managed to keep objective about his days with Frank. In his view Frank ran the studio of seven or eight people in a manner inexplicable. 'Frank could have done the job by himself, easily, if only he hadn't insisted on all the posing, photography and re-drawing. His original roughs of the strip, with just a little cleaning up, were better than anything running in Eagle or anywhere else.' But, I asked, would this work have *sold* Eagle the way the finished artwork did? 'Definitely. The style was different but it was still very distinctive. I actually believe it was better, more relaxed, fresher and freer, even more original; but it wasn't what Frank saw in his mind.' Did no-one every say as much to Frank? 'No. They often thought it but I don't think anyone ever said it to him.' Why not? 'I think they were afraid.' Afraid of what? 'We were young. We didn't want to cross Frank; we didn't want to lose our jobs.' But the pay was low and the hours were impossible. 'Yes, but we were inexperienced artists, in our first jobs, glad to have them. We saw our work being printed every week, we were "famous", we didn't want to lose that. Although when I think about it now, I should have left him long ago. And seven or eight people to produce two pages of artwork; tell that to anyone who runs a comic today and they'll think you're mad.'

In 1982, Eric Eden, who had joined Frank's studio twice, retired from his job at the British Museum and moved onto a farm in Shropshire. It was early retirement, at the age of fifty-eight, for Eden was not well and nor was his wife Betty. After a series of illnesses both died tragically in 1983. In one of his letters to me Eden wrote: 'The problem for Frank was he could never chart his way through treacherous Fleet Street. His work was formidable but his name was apt to draw long silences from the people able to commission him. After Dare he wanted always to work with an assistant and I don't know anyone in Fleet Street who'd wear that.'

True, there were artists aplenty content to shut themselves in a closet and fill sheets of paper with any kind of pictures they were told to, just so they could get more sheets shoved under the door. One said 'I like it; if the time comes I need more cash to support the family, I'll pack it up and drive a bus. But right now it's the most fun I can have with my clothes on'.

Keith Watson, darling of the purists, the artist who tried – and many will say, succeeded – to restore Dan Dare to his former glory under the Mirror regime, thinks Frank's story is a tragedy. 'There was all this talent, all this energy, all this imagination and

Max Dunlop as the Lone Ranger in a costume originally tailored for Keith Watson.

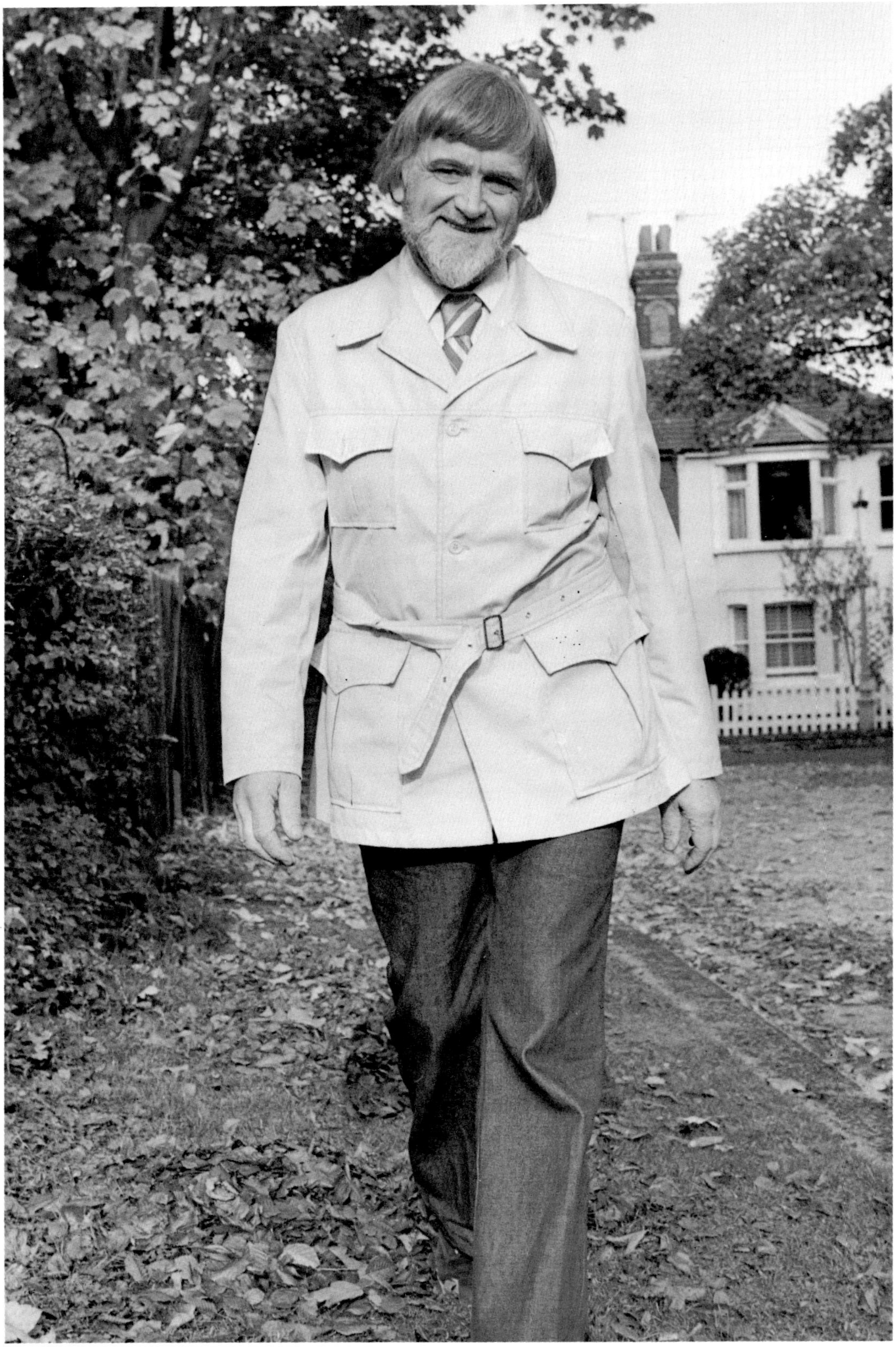

application. If only someone had used him.' Watson joined Frank in 1958 and says openly and with pride that he would rather have worked with Frank Hampson in his heyday than with Walt Disney. 'Have you heard,' Keith asked me, 'about the Lone Ranger thing for Quaker Oats? Frank got hold of me, turned my face to the light and said to Dorothy, "Doesn't he look like him?" "Who?" "The Lone Ranger." And so I was booked for riding lessons on Epsom Downs and a day or so later I was hanging onto the horse's neck as it cantered away, with Frank in the distance with his camera and sketch book. We even had a cowboy suit tailored for me by a merchant tailor in the City. I think this was the first, and possibly the only, branching out into a new line of drawing that Frank did. Around that time he had an agent and he got the job to draw the back of six packets of Quaker Oats. They were to carry the cowboy story and each episode was a mystery which the Lone Ranger solved. Not only did Frank have to get the horses and clothes right, we had to do a lot of research on the correct scenery. Anyway, all the strips were drawn and the reader had to see if he could solve the mystery too. The right answer was given on a separate piece of paper which was slipped into the pack and was discovered when you got to the bottom of the oats. This piece of paper had some secret writing on it. It was impregnated with a chemical and the answer to the mystery became clear when you rubbed the paper with a pencil. And then, disaster! We discovered that the chemical was lethal and must never come anywhere near food. There was no way you could leave it in a packet of unprotected oats. We couldn't find a way round it and the whole thing was scrapped. But the artwork was marvellous.

'When Frank decided to give up Dan Dare, I think we were fed to the wolves. Marcus came round the studio like some kind of predatory beast, looking for ways to save money. When Frank suggested Bellamy take over, the management expected him to do it on his own. Frank, of course, had a completely unrealistic view of what was going on outside. Clifford Makins couldn't wait to see the back of him. They'd made millions out of the Dan Dare studio and Frank's genius. When they got Bellamy in they were absolutely delighted and it wasn't until the readership began to fall off that they wondered whether perhaps it was a dreadful thing that they had done.'

Marcus has now retired from the post of Deputy Chairman of the National Magazine Company, whose offices are a stone's throw from London's Carnaby Street. He presided over some of the most successful women's magazines published today, including *Cosmopolitan*, *Company* and *She*. His office, on the fourth floor of the building, may originally have had windows, but while Marcus worked there they were curtained off and the room lit with dimmed concealed lights. Marcus tells his version of the Eagle story with a forthright precision. His words can be used verbatim off the tape machine into the typewriter. He admits that he may have been at a disadvantage approaching Hulton as he did without the protection of a lawyer. The signing away of the copyright of Dan Dare has been Frank's cross ever since. You may think that at one stage Marcus could have done to the Hulton management what he did to Chad Varah when they were discussing the script for the life of St Paul. Picking up the Acts of the Apostles, he threw it at Varah saying, 'Have you read that?'.

Robert Hampson with 'egg' on his face, posing for Digby

SUMMER LIGHTNING

During the preparation of this book I picked up a nicely researched piece in a fanzine called *Adastra*, a brave little effort, well printed and sold through newsagents. The piece compared Dan Dare – unfavourably – with Captain Condor, a spaceman who appeared for a time in *Lion*, the comic which eventually gobbled up Eagle. Captain Condor was written (but not drawn) by Frank S. Pepper, a veteran contributor to boy's papers. In an attempt to get the views of a second creator of space adventures (and a contemporary one at that), I wrote to Mr Pepper, who replied in the most charming and informative vein. His tale is worth recounting for it lights up a most violent contrast between Frank Pepper's way of working and Frank Hampson's. Mr Pepper writes:

'I was rung up by Reg Eves, Editor of Amalgamated Press Juveniles, to say that he was about to launch a new weekly – *Lion* – in a great hurry. All he could tell me was that it was to be an adventure story paper, and that the front and back covers were to carry a science fiction picture story of some sort. "I can't give you any help because I know absolutely nothing about science fiction," he said "you're on your own with a free hand. Do what you think best."' (*Is that, I wonder a measure of how most boy's papers are created?*)

'To make matters worse, none of us knew anything about the craft of telling a story in pictures. Anyway, there I was with this commission, and about three weeks to get it off the ground. I decided to play safe. I took one of the perennially sure-fire themes, the falsely accused hero, immured in some seemingly impregnable prison, determined to escape and prove his innocence but, instead of putting him in Alcatraz or on Devil's Island, I shifted him out to a futuristic penal settlement on Titan.

'The Condor job was half a day's work once a week, during which I was writing other things for *Lion*, three 5,000-word stories for *Champion* and weekly short stories for *Children's Newspaper* and *Knockout*. When I pulled one of these off the typewriter and stuffed it in an envelope, that was it finished as far as I was concerned. I thought no more about it but went on to the next job.'

Filled with admiration for the talent, energy and speed at which Frank Pepper worked I tried to sound him out about how he remained so objective towards his job. To be able to crank out successful adventure stories for boys and, when they left the typewriter, 'to think no more about them', is achievement indeed. If Frank Hampson had been able to think no more about Dan Dare a week after the spaceman appeared in print, this story would be quite different. Mr Pepper's answer is enlightening.

'We lived in an old rectory in South Devon which stood on top of a hill. I used its four attic rooms as a working flat and from the windows I looked down across my paddock to the village. From the village the lane went straight up a hill on the other side. I timed my daily stint so that I was taking the last sheet out of the typewriter when the post van appeared at the top of the opposite hill to begin its descent to the village postbox. I had just enough time to run down two flights of stairs and across the paddock to reach the box as the postman emptied it.

'As I always saw it, and still do, I was producing something purely ephemeral. It was designed to amuse children and be forgotten when next week's instalment came out. It is disconcerting when grown-ups take it so seriously.'

I think the picture of Frank Pepper tapping away at his typewriter, an eye cocked for the post van and accelerating his fingers to light speed as he finishes his cliff-hanger 'curtain', then taking the stairs three at a time to pop the missive in the postie's sack, delightful to contemplate. Pepper's output was prolific and many thousands of *Champion* readers will confirm his skill as a storyteller. Yet he kept his typewriter by a window and his working day ended with the evening collection. Compare what Pepper writes with what Don Harley has to say about his day.

'Because my family lived near to Frank's studio, I was usually able to get away at five and pop home for tea. If my day had ended then it would have been terrific; the trouble was, Frank expected me to come back. Some evenings in winter, when it was dark and cold and there was snow on the ground, I would try and nip out the back way in the hope that Frank wouldn't notice. I rarely got away with it; he seemed to sense me leaving and a hand would drop on my shoulder as I got to the door and he'd say, "You will be back later, won't you Don, to help us out tonight?" And of course I always was, no matter how hard we'd been at it during the day. He couldn't give up. I think it was during the first week I ever went to work with him that I came in – I was the first there – and saw him at his desk. Not working – asleep. He'd been working all night. I was a bit nonplussed. I had to get Dorothy to ask her what to do and together we helped him upstairs to his bed. And there was a regular event we smiled about, though I don't suppose I'd think it was funny now. The voice that boomed through to our side of the offices when he'd run out of his indigestion tablets. "Rennies!" he'd shout, "Rennies!" and "Humph" would leap up, ruffle through the appropriate drawer and take him another pack.'

Frank lived, dreamed, ate, slept and breathed Dan Dare. He even acted Dan Dare. Once, when Keith Watson had finished an important frame, he wanted to take it in to Frank for his approval. But he paused, for it was sometimes difficult to judge what mood Frank was in. Only one way to find out, so he opened the door and stepped in quietly. There Frank was, working away, pipe in mouth, head down, eyes sharp on the point of his brush and smiling. 'Ah! I thought. He's happy. He's got a smile on his face.' But when Keith said something chirpy the smile vanished. 'And then I looked at the drawing board and Frank was smiling because the character he was drawing was smiling.'

The fact is, of course, that Dan Dare remains and Captain Condor is nowhere, because Frank's strip didn't just hint at a better world, *it showed it*, in full, amazing, deeply thought-out detail. In the past space strips had always contained reams of words describing the advances of a particular civilisation, and very good some of them sounded. But in Dan Dare you could see for yourself and the realism was based on examinations of the way architects were thinking (and they were thinking with great élan in the fifties), the way scientists were thinking and the way politicians were hoping. Frank scored more than one bullseye when predicting technological advances and, in some instances, the scientists even came to him.

What price that realism today? In fact there is a high price on it; witness a business consortium called Group Five Holdings, whose headquarters are in London but whose hopes lie just east of Corby in Northamptonshire. They are planning a huge leisure and adventure playground – themepark is their word for it – WonderWorld (the two capital Ws are compulsory in the copyright title). WonderWorld is an activity centre where people from all over the country and – the consortium hopes – from parts of Europe during the holiday season, will come to play, or as they put it 'participate'. Obviously WonderWorld owes most of its concept to Disneyland (as the creators freely admit) but they are a bit disparaging when it comes to Disney's 'Tomorrowland', the area which predicts what we'll all be doing in the 21st century. The brochure puts it succinctly: 'When planning the communications centre much thought was given to it not becoming dated. Even Disney's "Tomorrowland" today seems distinctly yesteryear. So the space city architecture of Frank Hampson was chosen. Conceived in the 1940s (sic) his work still has the same futuristic appeal, protected from the aging process by its special wrap of fantasy.'

But the brochure writers miss the mark. What they mean is that Frank got nearer to the likely truth about tomorrow (Armageddon aside) than any other artist they could find. Here is support for Wolf Mankovitz's view that Frank created something bigger than himself. I wondered if Wolf had anything to add to that and tracked him down at the University of New Mexico where he is a professor in the Department of Theatre Arts. Yes, Wolf has got more to say; 'Frank is, without doubt, the creator of a new 21st century mythology and a great artist in his extraordinary powerful medium'.

I have to admit that I was mightily impressed by this tribute, although confused about what it meant. I thought maybe Frank Pepper would be able to help, so I tried it out on him. Mr. Pepper couldn't agree. As far as he could see the science fiction mythology began a long time before Dan Dare who, surely, for all his qualities, was merely an Anglicised version of people like Buck Rogers and Flash Gordon?

Whether Dan will be a myth in the year 2000 or not, he'll probably still be going strong; his furture is assured for longer, I very much regret to say, than the future of his creator. Who can doubt that the character is phenomenal? He has made fortunes for toy-makers, authors, vintage magazine shops, clothes makers and all sellers of nostalgia, has helped to promote Horlicks, and is shortly to make more money for the WonderWorld consortium who plan to have a Dan Dare restaurant in their themepark, serving Mekonburgers and Anastasia cocktails (whatever they may turn out to be).

How deeply sad, therefore, that Frank himself has not achieved equal success. He gave happiness to a generation of schoolboys. He became the greatest strip cartoon artist of all time. Fifteen years after he had done the job, he was recognised, at Lucca, for doing it. He has attracted a following which, to this day, has never deserted him. I believe, despite these achievements, he has never found a lasting, or even a longish term, of happiness and part of the reason for that is his belief that he has been denied both the rewards – by which I mean really worthwhile rewards – and also much of the credit for the work he has done.

Frank Hampson destroyed his own health. He worked under an impossible strain and with such ferocity that, after 1961, he was never able to create at the same level again. After his stroke in 1982, which deprived him of the use of his hands and lower limbs and made it difficult to read, I asked him if he could find joy in other spheres of life. Did he get great pleasure from music? 'Alas, no.' Did he follow a favourite sport, or have any hobbies? 'No, not really.' What about writing? He can put a mean sentence together, would he like to practise that, on a typewriter which he could probably master? 'Hmm, I might think about it.' What did he see ahead? 'More work with the Open University probably; it would be nice to get an MA to go with the BA.'

Frank's life pivots on art; studying it and, before the paralysis, practising it, with a spell in an art college where he was frustrated by the system which only allows contributions from those with letters after their names. For most of his time now he is confined to his home and his tight-hugging armchair.

Frank Pepper shut his office door at five o'clock and played with his family. Keith Watson plays the piano and with a small but impressive telescope he built and uses (with his son) to follow the stars. Frank only left his desk when his body and his doctor made him.

In a little-known work called, 'The Nature of Society', Leon Maclaren writes: 'To conceive

Dorothy and Frank Hampson 1975.

an idea, which is the sowing of the seed; to work it out and overcome all the difficulties, which is the cultivation of it; and to see it formulated to practical achievement, which is the harvesting of it; is the perfect type of human action.' Frank Hampson carried out this perfect type of human action on a scale beyond the dreams of most of us. All of us are endowed with faculties – and some of us with talents – in order that we might live. We may choose whether we will use those faculties, or whether we will not, and those which we do not use die. It seems to me that Frank used his one great faculty to the virtual exclusion of all others and used it not wisely, but too well. He took delight in art. He lived for his creation and it destroyed him. Art, and the summer lightning of individual human happiness are all the goods he has.

On Monday 8th July 1985, when the text for this book had been set and was already going to production, Frank Hampson died from cancer and heart disease in Epsom Cottage Hospital, Surrey. He was 66.

Alastair Crompton

The Man Who Drew Tomorrow is Alastair Crompton's third book. The other two are about the advertising business, in which he earns his daily bread. Born in Esher in 1935, Crompton was educated first in Scotland (where he was evacuated during the war) and then at Kingston Grammar School in Surrey. From there he went to Westminster Technical College to study hotel management, and when this course was finished, was called up for National Service. The army posted him to the SHAPE HEADQUARTERS in Paris and he was able to enjoy eighteen months in comparative luxury. He learned that in Paris you could find everything except sea, sand and sunshine, and that the hotel business was not for him.

On demobilisation he was offered a place in a small advertising agency where he learned the craft of copywriting. Thirty years in the business, writing for some of the giant advertising agents, has earned him a considerable reputation in this field. His campaigns include 'The Inch War', 'Central Heating for Kids' and some amusing commercials for Heinz Salad Creams and Sponge Puddings.

He began research on *The Man Who Drew Tomorrow* in March 1982, and the preparatory work took the best part of eighteen months. During this time he discovered literally hundreds of men who remembered the work Frank Hampson did for Eagle, and who still marvelled at the skill and ingenuity with which he created his drawings. A major stroke of luck was to find that Frank Hampson lived only a fifteen-minute drive away, in Epsom in rural Surrey. During the research Crompton has been helped on all sides, by journalists, artists, comic-buffs, professional comic archivists and art-school teachers and would like to say 'thankyou' to them all. In a work of this kind, nobody does it on his own.

Once Crompton was asked: 'What can a thoughtful schoolboy hope of mankind on Earth, given the experience of the last million years'. He was on the point of answering 'nothing' when he remembered Frank Hampson.

Alan Vince

Alan Vince worked with Alastair Crompton from the very beginning of the Frank Hampson book project. Born in Chatham, Kent in July 1943 Alan was first introduced to comics when his family moved to Bermuda where exposure to Batman and Roy Rogers awakened his interest in the strip cartoon and art in general. Arrival back in England coincided with the 1950 launch of Eagle and he soon found his ultimate space hero in Dan Dare – Pilot of the Future.

His school years were spent collecting, studying and writing to Eagle and visiting the offices in Fleet Street 'to view some of the original artwork'. In 1956 he met, briefly, Donald Harley at one of Hulton's successful Boys and Girls Exhibitions at Olympia and this led to correspondence with the Dan Dare studio in Epsom. But it was to be some eighteen years before he finally met 'the Master' and a close friendship was struck up with Frank Hampson following their first meeting in 1974.

Alan has written about and lectured on Frank, his creations and artwork, including a number of TV appearances, sometimes sharing the platform with the artist himself. He has also acted as consultant on a series of reprint editions of Frank's work for Dragons Dream, helping to bring Frank's genius to a new generation.

As Alan says: 'Frank once told me that creating Dan Dare took a lot of time, trouble and hard work. This book has been the same for Alastair and myself – but, like Dan Dare, we think it has been worth it.'

The Publishers wish to express their gratitude to IPC Magazines for their co-operation in the production of this book and would also like to give special thanks to the following:

Dorothy Hampson, Don Harley, Mike Walker, Margaret Walker, Richard Hegearty, Roger and Martyn Dean, Joan Porter, Richard Marschall, and Gerry Baptist.

The Publishers would also like to thank the following publishers who have kindly allowed us to use their material:

Michael Joseph Ltd. and Ebury Press for permission to quote a passage from 'The Best of Eagle' Edited by Marcus Morris.

Michael Joseph Ltd. for permission to use an extract from 'Boys will be Boys" by E.S. Turner.

Hutchinson Ltd. for permission to use an extract from 'Of this our Times' by Sir Tom Hopkinson.

Picture Credits:

Photographs:
Pages 14, 171, 206 and 212 Associated Newspaper Group p.l.c. Pages 161 and 167 Ric Gemmel, Pages 62–63 G.H. Loker, and Page 95 Paul Williams.

Illustrations:
Page 146 Express Newspapers p.l.c. Page 168 Radio Times, Pages 176/177 Marvel Comics Group, Page 198 (Top) Group Five holdings Ltd. Painting by Tom Simpson Page 199 (Top) Group Five Holdings Ltd. Painting by Peter Holt.

The Publishers would be pleased to hear from anyone who owns or knows of the whereabouts of any Hampson original artwork with a view to keeping an archival record and possible future publication. All information received will be kept confidential.